The Pursuit
of Innovation

The Pursuit of Innovation

Managing the People and Processes That Turn New Ideas into Profits

George Freedman

American Management Association

This book is available at a special
discount when ordered in bulk quantities.
For information, contact Special Sales Department,
AMACOM, a division of American Management Association,
135 West 50th Street, New York, NY 10020.

Library of Congress Cataloging-in-Publication Data

Freedman, George.
    The pursuit of innovation.

    Includes index.
    1. Technological innovations—Management.
I. Title.
HD45.F723   1988   658.5'14   87-47840
ISBN 0-8144-5923-4

Printing number

10 9 8 7 6 5 4 3 2 1

In the beginning, God created the heaven and the earth.

Gen. 1:1

—The first new products.

Dedication

Dedicated to the memory of Palmer Derby, Vice President for New Business Analysis at the Raytheon Company, and for many years my friend and my boss. Without his sponsorship there would never have been a New Products Center and my career would have been a much less interesting one.

He loved innovation.

Preface

Innovation is the process of implementing new ideas, of turning creative concepts into realities. For our purposes, there is a more meaningful concept, that of "effective innovation," which can benefit business. *Effective innovation* is "the timely and efficient implementation of new ideas that results in significantly increased revenues and profits."

It is with the elements of that definition that this book deals. It discusses how to make the innovation process more swift, more direct, less expensive, less subject to failure, and more of a contributor to the health of the enterprise that sponsors it.

Like all other business actions, success in innovation is most likely when it is not left to chance and is, instead, tailored to specific needs that are purposefully organized for and correctly managed. Thus, the book is directed to all those in a company who engage in innovation in a management or decision-making role. A person who "engages in innovation" is anyone who can influence the course of innovation; that includes, in addition to those who participate in it in a hands-on sense, those who manage or support them. The spectrum of people engaged in innovation extends from engineers and scientists or equivalent specialists, through manufacturing department managers, product planners, marketers, line managers, staff executives, personnel specialists, and finally to the executive office itself.

This book is based in large part on my personal experiences as a member of new venture and new product development organizations. I have spent virtually my entire career as a practitioner of the innovation process. Most of this was in a single company, a very large one, composed of a wide diversity of businesses—many of which I worked with. They addressed a wide range of marketplaces, from consumer and commercial products to capital equipment for industry and large systems for government, and

ix

were based on very different technologies, from the almost trivially simple to the elegantly high-tech. While the businesses differed greatly from each other, those who led them shared two characteristics: (1) They were in it for the money and (2) they always tried to make the businesses grow. (Growth occurred more or less in proportion to how innovative the management and key staff were.)

I once participated in the American dream, to the extent that I left the company and started my own business (with the aid of a venture capital firm). It featured—what else?—a line of innovative products. Thus, for a moment in my life I was a CEO, albeit of a very small business. And I discovered that being the chief executive meant that for the first time in my life I could find no one to blame but myself. . . . The business failed, the dream turned to nightmare, and I went back to work for my original employer (all was forgiven). That experience rendered me poor rather than rich (the exact opposite of my original intention), but I don't regret it because it enriched my level of knowledge in the field of new ventures and is thus good background for this book.

On the other hand, I was a team member or leader of several similar ventures for my employer that achieved better success. In fact, they resulted in the creation of five new ventures. Four of them survived and are now so mature that no one younger than I remembers they were once "new." They are now (in company jargon) a division, two cost centers, and a successful divestment (the one that didn't make it was an overseas subsidiary).

I was also a team member or leader of programs that resulted in more than 70 new products that fitted into existing businesses, thus expanding their product lines. Many are still in production and still in the marketplace, but in such refined and updated forms that even though they continue to incorporate the original basic concepts, they often bear little resemblance to the first models.

I am proud to have been part of those endeavors, but it wasn't easy. And nothing happened overnight. In fact, it took over 40 years.

Although my experience has been broad, it has gaps. I have never worked in a service industry, for example. Nor have I ever been associated with anything but "hardware." But, from what I have seen of the remainder of the world, much of my experience can be extrapolated to it.

I never did anything alone. I was always a member of a group—a team. Thus every action had to be organized and managed. It was clear to me that that was where the challenge of new ventures and new product development lay. We performed better or worse as a function of how well we were organized and managed. Creation and invention were always necessary, but they were easy. How well the team was run and how well it interrelated with the rest of the company and the marketplace were crucial.

But I have more to relate than my own experiences. I have been privileged over the years to interact with people from several dozen American companies whose roles are similar to my own. They have shared many of their joys and frustrations with me. (Innovation provides both generously.) In compiling material for this book. I conducted on-site interviews with managers and staff members at the 18 innovative companies listed below:

Allen-Bradley (subsidiary of Rockwell International)	Milwaukee, Wisc.
Ameritech Publishing Inc.	Troy, Mich.
Contex Graphics Systems, Inc. (subsidiary of Continental Can Company and Scitex, Inc.	Burlington, Mass.
Corning Glass Works	Corning, N.Y.
Eastman Kodak Company	Rochester, N.Y.
Emhart Corporation	Hartford, Conn.
General Motors Corporation	Detroit, Mich.
Hoechst Celanese Research Company	Summit, N.J.
Michigan Bell	Detroit, Mich.
MIT Technology and Licensing Office	Cambridge, Mass.
New York Telephone	New York, N.Y.
Ohio Bell	Cleveland, Ohio
Owens/Corning Fiberglas	Toledo, Ohio
Raytheon Company	Lexington, Mass.
Repligen Corporation	Cambridge, Mass.
Signode Corporation (subsidiary of Illinois Tool Works)	Chicago, Ill.
Venture Economics, Inc.	Wellesley, Mass.
Xerox Corporation	Rochester, N.Y.

Their individual contributions are noted in the Acknowledgments and will be apparent throughout the text, particularly in Part 4.

Are you interested in using innovation as a means to improve the health of your company—its size, its breadth, its competitive position, its profitability? Congratulations! I applaud your courageous and wise stand. And it is courageous, because innovation programs can be among the most gluttonous expenders of resources. What will you get in return? No one ever knows in advance. That which is new is only truly understood in retrospect and only accurately judged with hindsight—when the newness has worn off and when it may be too late to change your mind.

No one should commit to innovation without full awareness of the risks. But once you're aware of what's involved, go for it. As Shakespeare pointed out in a saying already old in his time, "Faint heart ne'er won fair lady." At the same time, it helps to do it right. If there are risks, why not minimize them? Enough people have won their fair ladies—and lost them too—to make studying and profiting from their experiences a fruitful endeavor. This book will document a diversity of experiences that I think have broad implications.

In a way, a company has no alternative. It is not a matter of guts or no guts—every enterprise has to engage in innovation because we live in a world of change. The Greek philosopher Heraclitus said it 2,500 years ago: "Nothing endures but change." Still, why complain? If Heraclitus had been wrong, the world would be a dull place. Let's enjoy change. In fact, let's be good at it. And if we are not good at it, let's improve ourselves until we are.

Changes—including the ones that will happen tomorrow that we don't know about yet—are profoundly important to business, because the new ways that people live determine what and how much they buy. If business is to react to change, indeed, if business is to swing with change and beat the competition with it—more than that, if business is to be a factor aggressively making it happen instead of passively waiting for it—then business must do so by imaginatively *participating* in the changing environment. Change is inevitable. Don't fight it, join it.

There is one way to do this. Be innovative.

Acknowledgments

Whatever good ideas this book contains on innovation are in large part the good ideas of Wes Teich and Bob Bowen, my successors as directors of the Raytheon New Products Center; Ross Giuliano, its business manager; Bev Shaw, its manager of materials engineering; and Will Hapgood, its star inventor during the center's early years. Our close to 20 years together as members of innovation teams were always exciting and usually productive, and each program provided a separate learning experience. And how exhilarating it was when what we created ended up in production.

I wish also to pay tribute to the executive officers, engineers, and market specialists in Raytheon's subsidiaries and divisions (Amana Refrigeration, Inc.; Caloric Corporation; Speed Queen Company; the Machlett Laboratories; Raytheon Medical Electronics; Microwave and Power Tube Division; Cedarapids, Inc., Laser Center) who were clients of innovation from the New Products Center and who coped well with the human problems associated with accepting and implementing new ideas from "the outside." Much of what I learned from those relationships is presented here—as recommended practice.

Individuals who manage innovation in 30 different companies graciously shared their experiences with me and, in most cases, allowed me to tour their facilities and observe their work. I consider their contributions to be the most valuable element in this book and I thank them and their companies for allowing me the privilege of meeting with them. Most notable of these are: Jan Gottfredsen of Allen-Bradley; George Seifert of Ameritech Publishing; Dan McConnell, Warren Wake, and Alan Green of Contex Graphics Systems; Thomas MacAvoy and Marie McKee of Corning Glass Works; Bob Bacon, Bob Tuite, and Bob Rosenfeld of Eastman Kodak; John Rydz of Emhart Corporation; Dave Steadman of GCA Corp.; Albert Sobey of General Motors; Greg Nelson, Richard

Daniel, and Alan Buckley of Hoechst Celanese Research Company; Tom Ossman of Michigan Bell; Kent Bowen of MIT's Ceramics Processing Research Laboratory; Ron Scharlack of MIT Technology and Licensing Office; Miriam Cohen of New York Telephone; Cyndi McCabe and Christine Miller of Ohio Bell; Jophn Zaloudek of Owens/Corning Fiberglas; Dave Dwelley, Don Mahoney, Clyde Rettig of Raytheon Company; Tom Fraser of Repligen Corporation; Jack Campbell of Signode Corporation; Mark Radtke of Venture Economics, Inc.; and Ken Stahl and Bill Volkers of Xerox Corporation.

Anyone undertaking a project such as this book can always use some professorial guidance. I got mine from Karl Vesper of the Graduate School of Business Administration at the University of Washington; he is the rare academic who understands the relationship between business venturing and innovation.

My wife, Ruth, graciously tolerated the upset the act of writing a book causes to any family and contributed more than mere toleration as she polished the text by applying her considerable language skills.

Finally, my editor, Adrienne Hickey, who gave the book much of its organization and whatever lucidity it possesses, deserves my most heartfelt gratitude. There can be no substitute for her wise influence, gently but firmly applied.

Contents

Part 1

Organizing for Innovation

1

The Pursuit of Innovation: Goals and Options

The goal of business is, simply, to flourish. A flourishing business prospers, it fares well—in short, it succeeds. The underlying premise of this book is that a company cannot flourish if it stands still. Thus, it follows that growth must be one of its major goals. To flourish, a business must construct a strategy for growth. Then it must build on that strategy by planning, organizing, and investing in growth. One way to grow is to innovate.

Commitment to innovation poses two challenges: (1) choosing the right thing to innovate (new products, new technologies, new approaches to marketing—anything in business and industry that appears as the result of implementation of a new idea) and (2) performing the very act of innovation. While this book discusses ways to choose innovation programs from the point of view of where existing products and technologies may be in their life cycles, it leaves the formulation of company strategy, which is different for each firm and for each industry, to those best fitted to formulate it. This book does not presume to influence strategists, other than to recommend that they include inputs from R&D staffs as part of their basis for strategizing. The book's main emphasis is on attempting to define the best ways to pursue the second of these challenges, innovation itself.

The Investment in Innovation

When a company decides to innovate, it makes an investment. It commits funds and resources. If the investment comes from existing businesses within the parent organization, it will show up on the respective balance sheets of each enterprise. If the corporate office decides to invest in a new innovation group (an action that will

3

Table 1-1.
The goals of innovation.

1. For Existing Product Lines
    a. Improved technologies and facilities
    b. New products
    c. Licensing from others and/or to others
    d. Minority positions in innovative companies
2. For New Product Lines and New Businesses
    a. Minority positions in innovative companies
    b. Licensing from others and/or to others
    c. Joint ventures
    d. New ventures
    e. Diversified new venture sectors

lead to new processes, new products, new systems, or new ventures), its commitment will often resemble that of a venture capital firm; this time the commitment will show up on the balance sheet of the corporation. In either case, an investment is being made and there is no reason why the investor should not impose his or her terms on those who will consume the moneys and resources that make up that investment. This brings us to several new issues: Which path should the innovation take? Who should the innovators be? How should they carry out their tasks?

Ways to Grow by Innovation

Growth based on innovation can take place in a variety of ways, depending on what the desired goals are. Table 1–1 presents two groups of goals: those concerned with improving existing business and those concerned with the creation of new business. Goals are listed in each category in order of increasing extent of departure from routine patterns of turning out products in most companies.

That is not to say that they are necessarily arranged in order of increasing dependence on creativity. The most exciting new inventions can be applied to the most mundane mature product lines, while a potential blockbuster of a new venture can be based on mere ingenuity.

Table 1–1 is not a complete list; there are other ways to apply innovation to business, but I haven't come across them in my own experience or acquaintance. (Of course, there are also ways to grow without innovation—for example, by simply running your business better.) Even here, a little creative thinking has its place, but I will not presume in this book to tell you how to do that. Nor will I attempt to supply guidance on which of these goals to select in terms of best company strategy. Your strategy is up to you.

Setting Up the Innovators

Once we know which of the goals listed in Table 1–1 we will invest in, we must take steps to achieve it by organizing it and managing it—just as we would for any activity in our company. "It"—innovation—requires ingenuity, imagination, creativity. Can actions based on such "unconcrete" thinking be planned, channeled, budgeted, scheduled—in short, managed, let alone organized? Of course. Unsure though the creative course may be, it is no more mysterious than many others with which businesses must deal.

Thus, as with any other practice in a company, effective management of innovation requires generation of a plan, organizing and allocating resources best fitted to carry out the plan, providing executive support both tangible and intangible, and ensuring that the plan is pursued with determination to a successful conclusion.

Planning the Innovation Process

Innovation is a process. It proceeds step by step. And it has variety. Each innovation differs from all others depending on the set of circumstances. Yet all cases have much in common—or they should have, if those in charge make a conscious attempt to endow the process with orderliness. The common elements of the process are simple and obvious (how strange, then, that innovation programs often don't include them, give them short shrift, or turn to them well after having embarked on the sea of innovation with the shore already far out of sight).

For example, the process of innovation—no matter where it takes place or under what circumstances—should include a step called "definition of the market to be addressed" and another called "definition of process or product to be developed." And there should be a projection of resulting incremental sales and profits with time.

Now we have an idea of what we will do and whether, if technically successful, the effort will prove worthwhile in a business sense. Then, knowing what we are aiming to achieve and why, a program plan, in phases, must be developed, with benchmark target dates and cost estimates established for each phase. Only when we have this plan can we justify proceeding to implement the process of innovation.

And all this should be preceded by a directive from the executive office (formal or not, but in any case understood by all) that states, "Yes, this is what we want; this is our policy in general and our instruction specifically." It can be argued that a policy statement is not strictly a process step, but I maintain it is the first process step upon which all following ones are to be based. Admittedly, it doesn't always happen this way. Innovators will initiate programs from below before the boss learns of them. But that can't go on for too long without blessings from above. Without such approval, prospects for success (as measured by entrance into the marketplace resulting in increased revenues and profits) are dim, and they get dimmer with every passing day.

As described above, planning for innovation is like planning any kind of program in business: All require a disciplined regimen of thinking. But we must not overlook that there are differences unique to the creative process and that there are different kinds of innovation, each to some extent requiring different plans for different sequences of events.

The Implementers of the Innovation Process

As in any business program, innovative or not, if there are complex and protracted activities to be carried out, such as planned innovation, assignments must be given to organized groups of individuals that have the capabilities and empowering charters to do them. I call such groups "implementation means" and categorize them into the following eight different modes of innovation function:

1. Technology centers.
2. Research centers.
3. Captive R&D programs.
4. New products centers (including skunk works).
5. External teams.
6. External ventures centers (including skunk works).
7. Internal ventures centers.
8. Licensing arrangements.

Each organization for each mode differs from those for the others and is characterized by different ingredients, qualities, styles, and procedures. These are derived from the nature of each respective mission and they in turn determine the unique path each must pursue to attain a desired goal selected from Table 1–1. If we examine this array of possible organizations, we arrive at the questions that are at the heart of this book:

- *Who will be recruited to carry out the steps of the innovation process for each type of goal within whatever innovation mode?*

- *How will they contrive to do it so that the process proceeds with a maximum of efficiency, swiftness, and effectiveness?*

Those who should be the innovators are easily described (but not so easily found and engaged): They are those who are best fitted for innovation tasks by reason of talent, training, inclination, and dedication. Those "best fitted" must be identified and ferreted out. They are probably already on the premises; but, if not, it becomes necessary to recruit from the outside. Then they must be injected into the groups set up expressly for these purposes, groups that will function effectively and efficiently to carry out the required tasks.

The Need for Autonomous Status

As implied above, I believe there is a best way to organize groups of innovators, and it is that way that I will advocate through the remainder of these pages; namely, that distinct organizational entities must be created whose entire reason for being is to perform innovation.

Note that this means that business will pursue innovation on purpose and not as an afterthought. (That is why there should be a formal investment in innovation. By their nature, investments are not afterthoughts.) Thus innovators will not be expected to produce their creations in their spare time, after performing their "real" tasks, like running production engineering or quality assurance or managing sales or modifying products so that they meet government codes. Some remarkable individuals,* ingeniously diverting funds and facilities in the process, will contrive to produce innovations under such circumstances, but they are few in number and so dedicated to their "avocation" that their bosses, who naively still expect them to perform their primary duties effectively, end up disliking them. Therefore, don't rely on them. Rather, form organizational entities that are *meant* to innovate, transfer such self-driven innovators in your company to them, and then support those innovators.

Such groups must possess a high level of autonomy. This means that they can then count on reasonable independence from funding worries of the sort that afflict operating organizations, such as ups and downs of production levels, spasmodic hirings and firings, reassignments, and so on—all functions of that quarter's financial performance. This immunity from short-term financial concerns is possible only because the (autonomous) innovation groups are the happy recipients of an investment commitment by management. That commitment is awarded on a periodic basis, usually yearly, by the corporate office or by a basic company business unit like a division or subsidiary, and makes up most, but not necessarily all, of the funds necessary to operate. Thus, autonomy also means freedom from involvement in day-to-day factory or field problems, which

* Such people have been called *bootleggers*. It's a good name because the dictionary defines them as people who "produce goods illicitly for sale." I will not include them in this book as a formal "implementation means" or "mode" because, by definition, management has no formal role in organizing or managing bootleggers (although there are instances of "sanctioned" bootlegging). That doesn't mean I don't admire them; no one makes better use of time or money than bootleggers, even if, in this case, both are stolen. Bootleg programs are often the best-managed ones.

may harass the operating organizations by shifting their priorities.

Autonomous groups can become effective for negative reasons, e.g., they can be shielded from diversions with such defenses as "independence from . . .," "immunity from . . .," and "freedom from. . . ." But let us not disregard the positive aspects of autonomy: "freedom to . . ." and "clout for. . . ." The point is, any organization in a company that has its own status, that is not just an ad hoc appendage to another, larger organization that "really" matters, has a kind of power in that company that it otherwise would not have.

An organization in a company that has its own separate identity independent of other company organizations—which is, after all, the definition of autonomy—has the power, for example, to "overlook" certain bureaucratic practices that may be inhibiting to the creative process. But more important, it can (innovatively) transcend organizational barriers and use—even exploit—the resources, talents, and facilities that exist elsewhere in the company. For large companies, these are often astonishing in their richness—their breadth and their depth. They are usually supported and maintained for the benefit of a single operation of that company. In asking for access to those resources, it helps for the asker to have an autonomous title, like "Director of . . ."

This all sounds like a grand arrangement for those fortunate enough to work under such conditions, and it is. It is so good that it seems unreal. That's why innovators appreciate autonomy. In fact, over a beer, you can easily get them to admit that it is heaven. It provides the best environment for them to produce what they are supposed to produce: innovation. If it's set up right, an autonomous innovation operation is what it should be—a good investment on the part of management.

Fitting into the Organization Chart

Company organization charts don't always show innovation groups, even autonomous ones. That is because such groups are often too small to warrant the honor. And in preparing a chart, only so many words can be arrayed on a single page. After all, the company's small Applied Research Lab takes up as many square inches on a page as the $200 million XXX Division. Yet the Applied

Research Lab may turn out in the end to be just as important to the company as XXX Division.

It is instructive to add missing innovation groups to your company's organization chart. Draw them in where they would have been had the executive chartist seen fit to include them. This useful exercise helps put everything into context.

In placing the actors of our drama into a visual schematic representation, be sure to provide a name for each one. Does a group's title influence its ultimate attitudes and traits, its style? You bet. And it will significantly influence how it performs as well.

"What's in a name?" asked Shakespeare, implying, "nothing much." I disagree. What you call something often shapes what it becomes. It is a kind of prophecy, a self-fulfilling one. Elspeth's performance in life is sure to be different from Sarah's, and a business entity with "International" or "Consolidated" in its name will behave accordingly. How about "Center"?

Centers

It is convenient to designate as centers innovation groups that have the mission of sustaining or expanding a number of existing businesses, and not just a single business. In most large companies, it is common to have a technology center and a research center and, if it is not included in one of the other two, a new products center. Depending on the goal or goals and how one contracts with them, external innovative teams, which the company has chosen to employ rather than building internal teams with the same capabilities, may also perform as centers. The directorate of licensing should be included here as well. It doesn't have "center" in its name, but its aim, much of the time, also is to sustain or expand existing businesses—and "directorate" has enough "central" implications to qualify it.

Then there are groups whose aim is to create new businesses. A reason to call them centers, or to think of them as such, is that, like the others, they report to a corporate executive rather than to the manager of a segment of the company that has its own profit-and-loss (P&L) status. These are the external and internal venture groups. They differ from the technology, research, and new products centers in that they tend to see their goals as going down their own paths and not as providing aid and succor to existing businesses in the company. They are venturers, and had they more guts (and perhaps less sense) they would leave the company altogether and found their own businesses.

None of these classifications is cast in concrete. Every kind of exception is possible. For example, an R&D group or a skunk works may be created by a separate business segment and thus have nothing to do with other business segments or with the corporate office. But then it won't be called a center; it is owned by that business segment and is captive to it.

Captives

The opposite of "center" is "captive." A captive group operates for the benefit and under the direction of a particular business entity within a corporation. It reports to a line executive within that business segment, while a center reports to corporate executives who perform staff functions. Captive innovation groups can be every bit as innovative and productive as noncaptive groups. But, by their nature, their range is more limited; they work on one product or one line of products rather than on many, as do the centers.

It is always dangerous to generalize; some companies are so enormous that a single business segment within that company may have several billions of dollars of sales a year and be based on a wide diversity of technologies and products. The innovative groups for such company segments are, in reality, centers.

The essential fact to keep in mind about captive innovative groups, in addition to their narrower focus, is that they tend to be more vulnerable to the short-term ups and downs of the business entities they serve than are corporate-supported centers. Although they are autonomous, they are less autonomous than true centers. I can count on the fingers of many hands how many times I have seen competent and productive captive innovation organizations that belong to a single division or operation destroyed by a crisis, which, like most crises, has appeared suddenly, if not explosively.

For example, the word goes out, "Field failures have gone from an acceptable .4 percent a year to 11 percent—and all within warranty." The cost of field repairs is staggering. All profits are wiped out and replaced by overwhelming losses. "Fix it!" commands the boss of that division. "Who knows how to fix it?" "Why Al, sir," is the response. "And where is Al?" "Oh, he's joined the skunk works we set up last year in that condemned warehouse we couldn't get rid of in the rotten part of town, sir." "Why is he wasting his time there when we're running 11 percent field returns?" is the next question. "Get his ass out of that stupid lab and onto that problem today!" The boss may phrase his command a bit more delicately; but guess what happens to the experiment Al had planned for that day—or for that year. . . .

A similar dramatic dialogue will occur if profits or market share decline below expectations for two quarters in a row and the CEO hints to the division manager that it would be advisable to reverse those declines by "the next time we meet . . . or else!"

What all this tells us is that in innovation organizations, if there is a choice between noncaptive and captive setups, noncaptive is better. Of course, central organizations can be demolished by external events. But all things being equal, they have by far the better chance to continue normal function.

This brings us to the next issue related to showing innovation groups on organization charts: permanency, or lack thereof.

Permanency

Centers tend to last, and they become involved with the budgeting process every year, automatically—unless they screw up. Captive groups, while more vulnerable than centers, also last, especially if they're lodged in prosperous business segments. But one-shot deals, the ad hoc groups with inelegant names like "skunk works," carry the seeds of their own demise in how we label them.

Construct the organization chart again next year. Certain innovation groups may be missing. But that is not necessarily bad. Some activities, because of the nature of their mission, should be carried through just once (successfully) and then disbanded. And some should go on year after year. Determine which fits your needs.

Support Functions

Innovation groups require bosses (or at least "godfathers") of a special sort. People who provide support are variously called sponsors, champions, encouragers/facilitators, and counselors. They may reside in the executive staff, the human resources department, in venture teams, or in ad hoc teams, but they all have a not inconsiderable importance in the firm. (You can't be an effective supporter, even if you have all the other desired good qualities, if you can't get the ear of the big boss when you want to.)

Support organizations or individuals provide, or ease the path to, tangible necessities, like funds and facilities; but they also give intangible sustenance, such as moral and philosophical support, including "sensitizing" of selected big shots. They pick up and carry forward that part of company culture that favors growth by innovation. If that cultural feature is not already entrenched in the mind of the CEO, the best support people contrive to implant it there over time, and to nurture its growth.

An innovation-responsive culture should not consist merely of a favorable attitude toward encouraging creative people. It should evolve into a philosophy (philosophies underlie cultures) that specifically aims at building the company by one or another means, such as acquisition, joint ventures, streamlining, enriching facilities, internal innovation, contracted external innovation, licensing (in or out), or any selection or combination of these.

Remember, support from the executive office is the most essential process step; without it a good case can be made for abandoning the idea of innovation altogether. Support from the front office is empowering, and no person and no group within a company achieves anything without some power.

Goal-Direction and Efficiency in the Pursuit of Innovation

If an innovation program plans to attain a certain growth goal and sponsorship and executive approval have been won, and if a formally organized group has been given the assignment to carry out the program plan, one might conclude that much of the randomness normally associated with innovation has been eliminated. We are now ready to proceed, right? Not quite. It is not enough to define goal-direction. The challenges to management are now to maintain the program on that course and at the same time to perform all the steps in the program with a high level of efficiency.

It is strange how easy it is for the innovators themselves to go astray in these two matters. They must be constantly reminded that there can be only one criterion for successful innovation: It must contribute to the health and growth of the enterprise that sponsors it. The primary challenge to be met by innovators (and they must always keep it in mind) is that each innovation exists only to provide a basis for new business, and that new business can be justified only if it results in increased revenues and profits for the company. Consistent with this criterion is the second challenge: Innovations should be created with a minimum expenditure of money and time; that is, efficiently. This implies minimum risk, which is also worth aiming for. On the other hand, there must always be some risk. If you want no risk, don't engage in innovation. This must be clear to—and accepted by—top management.

Management's Credo

Managers would put it this way: "We want the work of innovators to whom we provide funds and facilities to be goal-directed—our goals, not theirs—and the process by which innovations are produced to be managed cost-effectively and thus with minimum risk." Good innovators will respect these desires and strive to satisfy them.

The Management/Innovator Interface

Innovators will not slavishly adhere to cost-effective goals as defined by top management. If they think the goals are incorrectly conceived, they will not hesitate to put forth sincere arguments that point that out. And managers had better listen, because innovators can innovate effectively only if they "believe." This statement is not a contradiction of the preceding one. It just means that all aspects of the program have been examined beforehand. Good innovators, after they have had their say, will then strive to satisfy mangement's desires. But if the innovators remain unbelievers, they should ask for and receive reassignment to some other project.

We should recognize that all organizations, innovative or not, have personalities. They are all unique, but those of autonomous innovative groups are perhaps "uniquer." Good management prac-

Figure 1-1. Major factors in the flow of the innovation process.

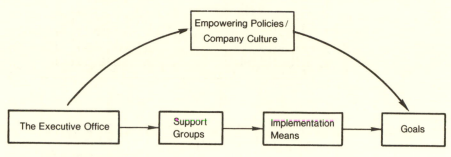

tice will simultaneously accommodate and benefit from the special personalities of innovators, while meeting the challenges of goal-direction and efficiency.

Innovation as a Flow Process

Figure 1–1 shows how all these ingredients of innovation are linked, the implementers and their backers with the executive office and its goals for growth. It also indicates how that linkage, if successful, will incorporate a kind of movement, a flow of the innovation process (and that is in fact what processes are—flows). But that flow had better be going in the right direction with a minimum of diversion from the path that leads to one of the goals of Table 1–1.

Thus far we have sketched out the major issues in the innovative process: planning for innovation, obtaining sponsorship and support for it, organizing for and managing it while maintaining goal-direction and maximizing efficiency. Before proceeding into more detailed treatment of each of these matters, it is useful to represent them in a chart that shows how the major elements of innovation, in all their variations, depend on each other. I call it, perhaps presumptuously, the "master chart of innovation," and it is shown in Figure 1–2.

The Master Chart of Innovation

The chart includes the eight "means" and the five "supports" that are discussed in this book. It shows how these organizational entities,

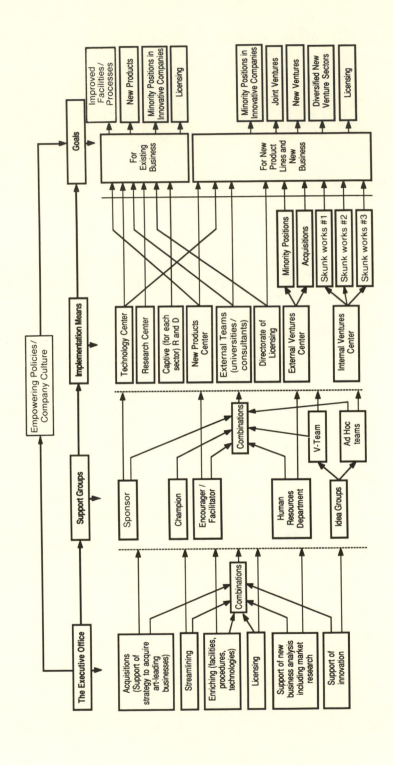

Figure 1-2. The master chart of innovation—the many paths to growth in business and industry.

empowered by top management, participate in the flow of the innovation process, moving with mutual dependency from sponsor through implementation means to goals. The chart is a graphic summary of innovation practices I have observed in this country. Everything I have absorbed by visiting different companies, by talking to innovators, by reading the literature, and by examining my own experience fits into it. For example:

- A recent model of General Electric's dishwasher, which utilizes new materials and new fabrication practices, is not so much a new product as it is an old product exemplifying the advances in reliability and lowered cost that can be achieved by new technologies. It was developed at a GE technical center, represented in Figure 1–2, and attained the goal, also on the chart, of "improved facilities/processes."
- Eastman Kodak could appear in at least five places. It has a set of offices of encouragers/facilitators that spawn internal ventures through a number of skunk works organized into an internal ventures center that will spin off new ventures. It also invests externally in small high-tech firms, taking minority positions.
- Ameritech Publishing has a similar well-functioning encourager/facilitator setup.
- Signode puts together venture teams (V-teams), which lead to skunk works, which lead to new ventures.
- At Motorola, the human resources department runs workshops for executives to sensitize them to the fact that they could do their company a service by becoming innovation sponsors.
- Hoechst Celanese Corporation develops state-of-the-art organic chemical materials that are the basis for new products. This is achieved through basic and applied research programs at its central research facility, which is its subsidiary, Hoechst Celanese Research Company.
- Contex Graphics Systems, a small high-tech firm that is a joint venture of Continental Can and Scitex, Inc., is producing an art-leading product for the graphics industry. The original conception and model of this product were the accomplishment of an external team, the services of which

were contracted from faculty members at Carnegie-Mellon University.

- In my own company, Raytheon, the new products center and the research center (sponsored, respectively, by the vice president for strategic planning and the vice president for research and engineering and empowered by the CEO) develop models of new products and evolve new understanding of fundamental scientific principles for more than a dozen company businesses.
- Raytheon also has an external ventures center that takes minority positions in innovative companies. It is run by a company officer, who is thus his center's own sponsor, and who also has the empowering support of the executive office.

The next time you read an article or are given a description about how some company has organized its growth patterns by utilizing innovation, it is likely that those patterns are reflected in this master chart. Take a close look and see.

Where Does Your Company Fit?

If your company fits someplace, it generally follows that it doesn't fit everyplace. That leads to a cautionary statement about the chart: It attempts to include every possible kind of organization and every possible support participant as well as every possible variation of goals and company philosophies, but some possibilities have no doubt been unintentionally overlooked. The chart attempts to describe "everything," which is too much. Even the biggest companies don't commit to all these choices.

Nevertheless, there are enough options presented so that your company probably nestles in one or another track of innovation flow that can be traced in the diagram. Your organization very likely is pursuing a mission that can be identified as one of the empowering policies in the company culture part of the diagram and is carrying on that pursuit with one or another of the modes, which in turn is given identity and viability by one of the support functions—all this in order to attain one of the goals.

One more caveat: The number of different courses of action and of organization possible necessarily diminishes as company size decreases. A small or even medium-size company simply can't afford all the departments and all the labs a large one can. Yet, I use the word "diminishes" rather than "disappears." The functions can still be there, albeit in a less formal, less elegant, almost invisible form. They may be combined with other functions, but are still active and still useful.

For example, only large companies have human motivation specialists within their personnel organizations (also known as human resources departments). And not even all large companies employ such specialists. But sensitivity to the issues that motivate all the actors in the innovation drama need not be lacking, no matter how small the company. Can a management that has no staff with degrees in motivational psychology or industrial sociology still operate effectively when attempting to lead complex people in complex tasks? Certainly, if it puts its mind to it. Like Molière's character who was astounded to discover that he had been talking prose all his life, we've been practicing psychology and sociology for all of ours. (Of course, some are better at it than others, and a little professional help in certain cases can do a lot of good.) Anyway, any company—large or small—can still do much to improve support and motivation of creative people, even without such specialists.

Also, sponsors, champions, encouragers, and facilitators can be present regardless of company size. The only difference is that in a small company, such people have to perform these functions part-time and still carry out other tasks. But such multi-faceted performances are acts of will. Those who really wish to will do them, and do them well.

Centers and the other organizational arrangements so much more easily set up in multi-billion-dollar corporations than in mere multi-million-dollar ones may be absent in the "smaller" organizations. Yet, central functions may still be performed by groups not known as centers. The facts of life usually dictate that all R&D in a small company takes place in a single group, and a captive one at that, rather than in centers. And the innovation group may double up on roles; for example, it might combine investigations into advances in technology and research into basic principles with new product development. Thus, such a group will not be parochial.

There is nothing to stop it from having broad visions, as a corporate center might. At the same time, it should not compromise its autonomy any more than it must. That may be more of a battle in a small company than in a large one, but it is one worth engaging in.

The conclusion is, whether a company is small or large, possessed of sophisticated specialty groups or not, the master chart of innovation pertains to it. Even though every business will tailor its organizations to whatever its real-world constraints are, if innovation proceeds to successful outcomes, then those constraints will not rule out the options shown. Not every option will be used, but the course taken will be defined by a (crooked) line proceeding from left to right through the chart.

A Functional Organization Chart

Now that we have our master chart, let us redraw it to show more than mere flow of the innovation process. This time we'll refine it to indicate not only where the different innovation organizations fit, but what their functional relationships with the other organizational entities in the company are—entities that do not have innovation as a primary interest but that will benefit from the breakthroughs developed by dedicated innovation groups. And while we are at it, we will schematically incorporate some features of a conventional organization chart, giving a rough idea of who reports to whom. The chart is shown in Figure 1–3.

As you can see, there is a block for each kind of innovation group, and these are connected by lines indicating respective reporting, service, and support relationships. As noted, the cross-hatched block at the bottom of the chart is not "organizational" at all. It represents a clumping together of many scattered elements that make up the enormous reservoir of talent and knowledge residing within the many different organizational entities in most companies. It poses a fascinating challenge in that it contains the solutions to many innovation problems. The heavy arrows emanating from it show how aid in the form of technical or other professional expertise may be rendered across organizational boundaries, a subject discussed in Chapter 2.

Figure 1-3. Organizational and functional relationships of innovation groups within a large company.

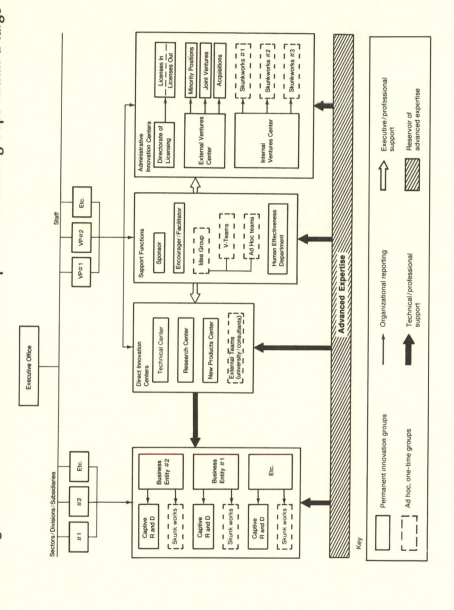

Figures 1–2 and 1–3 serve as a framework for this book. The remainder of Part 1 describes how to set up the eight autonomous innovation organizations so that they will function effectively. It treats the qualities and quantities of the elements they all share: staffs, facilities, and funds, as well as supplemental talent drawn from elsewhere in the company.

Part 1 may be placed within the context of the national scene by reference to Chapter 11, which defines the different kinds of research and development that make up innovation and provides data and rules of thumb on levels of commitment to these ingredients of the innovation process in the United States.

Part 2 deals with implementing techniques: how these groups incorporate maximum efficiency, speed, and effectiveness into the development of new products, systems, and processes.

Empowering policies and company culture are the subjects of Part 3. It addresses the subject of innovator motivation and its link to the five types of management support. These are described with recommendations on how to make best use of them. Company policies and company culture are shown to be the fundamental bases of such support. The point is made that with front-office backup, innovation happens; without it, it doesn't.

Part 4 gives a set of "examples" that show how these principles of organizing for innovation work. It describes the eight autonomous innovation groups—the "implementation means" of the master chart—their respective missions, and the unique qualities of each. Every organizational type is illustrated by one or more "real-life" cases drawn from a wide spectrum of American companies.

2

Staffing

The titles of employees who work in innovation organizations do not differ dramatically from those of employees who work elsewhere in the company carrying out duties that have nothing to do with innovation. But what is required of innovation employees does differ, and this chapter calls attention to the differences. It describes the special abilities and traits that work best in each category. In effect, with a few illustrative anecdotes thrown in, it amounts to a set of job descriptions. (Specific guidelines on hiring and other personnel issues are offered in Chapter 9.)

The staffs of autonomous innovation groups are made up of administrators, managers/leaders, implementers (generalists, technical specialists, and product/process transfer specialists), and nonprofessionals. Let's look at each in turn.

Administrators

For an organization to run, it must *be* run, by a manager or department head and with the help of an administrator or business manager.

Qualifications

Administrators must have a talent for handling (allocating, recording, monitoring) moneys and hours. Does this mean they have to be graduates of a business school? Not unless the organization is very large. But some knowledge of accounting, gained either by attending a single semester or by self-education, will help. And these days, that means an administrator must feel comfortable with computer-generated spread sheets.

They are set apart from their colleagues, the "real workers," because they fall into the "overhead" category: They do not charge their time to programs. But they are overhead in the best sense in that they recognize that they have a mission, which is to make sure that innovation programs *happen.* It means they have a certain style or mental outlook that is difficult to write into a job description. I call it "need to facilitate," and it is a qualification for this job.

It's been said that a good administrator can administer anything, but I don't think so. Administrators for innovation organizations have to be different. For one thing, they had better have a sense of humor, or they won't survive. In addition, they require a level of imagination compatible with the mission of the organization. That should include an ability to create the right rules—pragmatic ones for the benefit of occasionally unpragmatic people.

The Mission: Devising Operating Rules and Making Them Work

The rules or operating routines of any department will have a seminal influence on how well it functions. Policies and procedures, which make very dull reading if collected into a manual, nevertheless determine a large portion of the tone, atmosphere, style, and morale of any group, innovative or not. But more than that, they are instrumental in establishing the level of effectiveness and speed with which the group will produce. Rules and routines can exert a positive influence by becoming a way to grease the skids, to make every procedural course easier than it otherwise might have been—so that frustrations are minimized.

Unless rules are effective, the desired new innovation or marketing procedure might not emerge for an additional year—or never. Then the disgruntled would-be innovator could report that he or she had been frustrated in carrying out an assignment by an unwieldy company bureaucracy (which, by the way, is a wonderful whipping boy when something doesn't happen that should have).

The primary mission of the administrator is first to devise the rules and then to orchestrate and carry out the policies and procedures derived from those rules—all as ways to expedite action. If frustration still exists among workers, then administrators, those selfless folk, will absorb much of it, leaving little for the innovators to deal with. Admittedly it amounts to hand-holding, but it leaves the innovators free to innovate, which is what we desire, isn't it?

Policies and procedures are numbered in the dozens. They include rules for purchasing, receiving petty cash, making travel arrangements, taking courses, attending conferences and seminars, and gaining access to special work areas or equipments, technicians, overtime funds, or a secretary who can produce a document today and not tomorrow.

Working with the Establishment

Of course, a company will already have established policies and practices to handle these matters. The administrators of innovation groups will find a middle ground that will simultaneously conform to established practices and accelerate their normal uninspired and ponderous pace. How? By using imagination. Whoever said an administrator couldn't be innovative? (But resourceful might be a better word.)

The problem is that, in most companies, R&D needs appear small and unimportant compared with the main thrust of manufacturing vast quantities of product every day and creating each month's revenue and profit. Thus the various bureaucratic service departments relegate an innovation department to a low rung on the priority ladder. That is one reason the administrator is so important. A good one can work to improve his or her department's priority status.

I remember when the administrator of my innovation group presented a case for expediting action to the manager of the purchasing department. Our innovation organization didn't "belong" to the purchasing department's division—it was an autonomous tenant that paid rent as a monthly allocation. For this, the innovation group received not only a separate building and its utilities, but also, whether it wanted them or not, certain services. It used not only that division's purchasing department, but its receiving dock, its cafeteria, its personnel department, its accounting department, its security system, its infirmary, its janitors, landscapers, and snowplowers, its maintenance crew, and so on.

In his discussion with the head of purchasing, the administrator complained that a simple purchase order for a rather unusual, but available, coil of copper alloy wire that was desperately needed for a new product development program was unforgivably late in delivery. He described to the head of purchasing the crucial importance of that new product to our client company. Yet, four weeks had passed before the material finally arrived. "Four precious weeks lost!" he said, his voice cracking with emotion.

Imagine our administrator's surprise to discover that the head of purchasing wasn't all that thrilled with him or his group. We were a damned nuisance, "a pain in the rear end." "Do you think that all my buyers have to do," the head of purchasing asked, "is to turn handsprings over an order for ten pounds of your wire when they should be spending that time finding better vendors and prices for the tons of materials we need to produce what is going out the door?" The administrator couldn't restrain his first reaction, which was to agree. There was a certain logic to that attitude. But this led to dialogue—and to a solution.

It turned out that one of the buyers—in fact the brightest one—hated routine buying, longed for the challenge of buying exotic items. Tons or pounds, it made no difference to him. And it was difficult keeping him productive because he was bored with repetitive work. We were familiar with people like that—everyone in our group needed to be challenged. (In every department— even those of the most uninnovative sort—lurks at least one person who, whether or not he or she realizes it, yearns to work with innovation. Seek that person out and provide salvation.) That purchasing agent became our buyer. Keeping us happy took no more than 10 percent of his time, but that 10 percent made him happy too, and more effective in his routine job.

That kind of service, dredged out of a bureaucratic but nevertheless skilled and professional organization, is far superior to doing it yourself, with your own well-intentioned amateurs, under conditions of complete autonomy. And it never took four weeks again to receive something we desperately needed. In fact, if the administrator made certain requests at strategic intervals and for only what was *really* important to us, we were able to get crucial items *overnight*—even before the paperwork cleared.

This incident offers another message: Only administrators (and possibly their bosses) are attuned to how to perform the required interactions with the operational elements of the parent company. Whenever innovators themselves cross paths with company bureaucrats, the outcome tends to be traumatic and to lead to mutual animosity. What is needed is a bridge between these two kinds of people, and a good administrator provides that bridge.

Monitoring

There is another major responsibility for administrators: monitoring what has to be done by the "direct labor" innovators. Programs have been planned and time and money targets have been set (see Chapter 5). It is now up to the administrator to check these frequently and to point out when plans are not being conformed to or targets are in danger of not being met. This task of "calling attention to" is less elegantly denoted as "nagging." Good administrators are good naggers.

When such alerting fails to produce results, the challenge ceases to be the province of administrators. What is required next is action by the boss.

The Manager's Right Arm

So many of the administrator's duties are really the responsibilities of the department manager. If that manager can assign them with confidence to the administrator, his or her job becomes easier, since most of the mechanics of running the department are thus taken care of. It occurs when manager and administrator present a united front to their employees and to the rest of the company—when all involved know that they constitute a team. When that happens, the boss has more time available, and can function less as a manager and more as a leader—a very desirable state of affairs.

Managers/Leaders

Every innovation group needs a leader. Just one. Because most companies don't have many innovation groups—and many companies have none—leaders make up a rather exclusive brotherhood/sisterhood (there are probably less than 1,000 in the entire country). Good leaders of innovation organizations must possess some very special qualifications.

Qualifications

To be an effective leader of an innovation organization, a person must have the kind of authority that goes beyond "being in charge." It derives from having been an achiever in the field of innovation in his or her own right. This gives credibility to the leader's judgments and actions that can come no other way. That credibility works in all directions—up to the bosses, down to the "underlings," and sidewise to those who will someday take possession of the innovative achievements of the group.

There are exceptions, but they are rare. It is not unheard-of for the playboy heir to step into his father's shoes and run a billion-dollar company brilliantly, relying on nothing more than daddy's genes to fill in the gaps in his own experience and his lack of history of personal achievement. But it is better to turn to people who know—from personal experience—what they are doing. And more than that, they must be people who have, in the process, made their mark.

It may seem like asking too much that the leader also have management skills at the same time, but those skills had better be there too, and attested to by previous good performance. Should the leader's management attainments be "only average," how better to compensate for any deficiencies than by the presence of a good administrator? That is why I began this chapter with a discussion of the administrator, a good choice of whom can help ensure optimum leadership performance on the part of the leader. When we are faced with a choice, we want our boss to be a leader first and a manager second.

It is remarkable how easy it is for top managers to fall into the trap of assigning a "good manager" to lead an innovation organization, rather than assigning a good leader. I suppose it is because their instincts favor anyone who shows discipline and orderliness (not that those qualities are necessarily lacking in good leaders). But in steering the course for innovation, the preference should be for vision over fiscal matters, inspiration over discipline. Better to commit a management error than not to come up with an industry-leading innovation. That means it is better to recruit a good leader than a good manager. You can get all the good managers you need from the ranks of your enterprise or from the business schools. But a good innovation leader is a rarer bird and harder to find.

Another qualification is optimism. Leaders of innovation groups are almost always marked by an inveterate optimism that infects and permeates everyone and everything. Sometimes it seems so ridiculous that people call it "dumb optimism." That's all right. Better that than no optimism. You can't do without it, because both upbeat and downbeat thinking are self-fulfilling. If the leader *believes* something will work, it often does. If the leader doesn't believe in something, it's not likely to happen. If this smacks of faith and religion, so be it. You need faith if you are going to perform an act of creation.

Optimism is also the *sine qua non* of the champion. A champion of a program is by the same token a believer. All programs need champions, people who are driven to make the program succeed. They accomplish success not only by driving themselves and others with a sense of mission, but also by making their bosses into believers too. It is common, but not universal, for leaders and champions to be the same person. Further ramifications of championing are discussed in Chapter 8.

I would hate to cost anyone his job, but if the leader of any innovation group in your company is not optimistic, get rid of that person. As long as the leader of innovation has doubts about what is being innovated, you are wasting your money. On the other hand, don't confuse pessimism with skepticism. The optimism of good leaders is always circumscribed by their competence in their field. Optimism must always be constrained by an awareness of the limitations imposed by the laws of nature, and a good leader of innovation knows them.

A final qualification is the ability to deal effectively with people. Of course, that holds for any leaders, but those who lead innovators must have special sensitivity to unique personalities—the creative people described later in this chapter. Those leaders must be capable of doing more than "dealing with" innovators. They must be able, at times, to inspire them.

Actually, innovative leaders are well suited to this because they tend to have good imaginations. That is what it takes to get into the brains of others. And getting into those brains and reacting accordingly is a kind of definition of sensitivity. This leads us to the feature that is the ultimate in sensitivity—the creative boss must be receptive to the creative inputs of his or her subordinates as well.

It doesn't matter where creative spasms come from; a good leader will be as enthusiastic about others' concepts as his own. In fact, a leader who loves only his own ideas is a good candidate for reassignment. The key words for one who would lead innovation programs are *open-mindedness* and *flexibility*. Without these attributes, *any* leader is asking for trouble, but especially someone who heads up research and development.

Newness is never easy to take, especially for people who must put their money on the line if they commit to it. So leaders of innovation organizations must be good salespeople, and the best foundation for selling is that same sensitivity mentioned above—bolstered by the credibility based on an outstanding track record in the field of innovation. This leads us to the mission of leaders of innovation.

The Mission: Having a Vision, Selling It, and Turning It into Reality

Leaders must have vision. More than that—on occasion, when circumstances warrant—they must have visions. A vision means much more than just a great new idea combined with a great conception on how to implement it. It also entails perceiving the implications of the exploitation of a successful innovation—not only for the company that sponsors it but for the industry, the country, the world. It follows then that vision also implies emotional commitment. Indeed, it goes well with the title of this section: "Mission." People with vision are good salespeople, to the point of being evangelists. Not only can they gather believers, they can make things happen. Sometimes those things even seem like miracles.

I have purposely described the qualifications and mission of leaders of innovation in rather extravagant terms. No staff member is as important as the leader. If the leader is right, all the other requirements for people described in this chapter are secondary. Outstanding leaders have a way of prevailing, and if your innovation group is to succeed, pay attention to how you choose its leader.

The Implementers of Innovation

We come now to the workers, to direct labor as opposed to "burden." If innovation is defined as the implementation of a new idea, then these are the implementers. They apply ingenuity, inventiveness, and creativity to a new idea and, in the process, they turn the idea into reality. Any patents that result will be issued in their names; the implementers rightfully receive any other kind of credit for an accomplishment.

In centralized autonomous innovation organizations, the workers break down into two categories: generalists and specialists. There is another overlapping breakdown: professionals and nonprofessionals (who are also skilled practitioners at what they do). Nonprofessionals in innovation groups may also be divided into generalists or specialists.

In captive R&D organizations and in single-project organizations such as most skunk works, all the innovators tend to be specialists who are experts in the technology related to that one project only. It rarely occurs to anyone that there is anything to be "general" about.

Generalists

People who work in many fields simultaneously are called generalists. This term differentiates them from their (equally respectable) co-workers who perform within the limits of only one kind of expertise. Generalists are most commonly found in centers. It is in the nature of a group that works in several programs at the same time for several different parts of a company—and thus in different processes, products, and markets—to evolve their members into this generalist/specialist pattern.

Qualifications

To be a generalist, a person must have expertise in at least one field and must possess a fund of experience based on it.

Generalists don't start as generalists. They usually start out with the intent of specializing in something, and that is the way it should be. One can generalize effectively only from a strong base in specifics. So a qualification for being a good generalist is a good background of academic training and work in one definable field.

At Raytheon's New Products Center, for example, the generalists were trained as mechanical and electrical engineers, physicists, materials scientists, and so on. All of them worked in their specialty—with distinction—for more than a decade each. But now they leap across each others' boundaries with ease.

Generalists must be flexible—to the point of arrogance. Ask a generalist in an innovation center, "Can you work simultaneously in the fields of air conditioners, rock crushers, magnetic resonance for medical diagnosis, food processing, photography, and water purification? Can you develop products in those fields technically advanced from what is available in the world today?" Expect the answer to be accompanied with a sneer of contempt: "Of course. But not this week, I'm busy this week."

Another qualification is creativity. They have to have it. I am one who believes that everyone is creative to some extent and everyone gets to be more so when encouraged to take that path in creative environments like those described in this book. But to be a generalist in an innovation center is to be far beyond the average in this regard. Indeed, they get to be known by names like "guru." How will you know when such a person is in your midst? I have no formula for spotting one, and psychological testers don't either. All I can say is, if you are on the lookout you will recognize creative generalists when they appear on the doorstep.

Next, generalists must be a capable experimenters. Ability to generate concepts alone is never enough. Generalists should have the ability to carry their concepts into the realm of reality until feasibility is successfully demonstrated.

Finally, the generalist should be an able communicator. After he or she has done all we ask, the accomplishment still does not exist unless management can be convinced of its existence. No one can convince managers better than the person who had the basic conception and proved it feasible. There is another reason to look for communication capability: There are few better rewards for the innovator's ego than to be requested to educate his or her superiors. Such rewards are motivation for more good work in the future (see Chapter 9).

The Mission: Conception and Proof of Feasibility

The mission for generalists is to react to stimulation from other sources by producing something new that can eventually help the company flourish. The newness may take the form of an idea of their own or an idea from the outside. In both cases, generalists must go on to the next step: conceptualizing how to implement that idea. After that, they must engage in experiments that prove that both the idea and the conception have feasibility. These— idea, concept, proof of feasibility—are, in fact, the first three of the seven steps to efficient innovation (see Chapter 4).

Generalism as an Aid to Conception

What is unique about generalists is that they fall most easily into the role of conceivers. There is something about ranging wide that encourages conception. Eclecticism is stimulating; it is the opposite of a vacuum—one doesn't conceive in a vacuum. In my experience, it is the generalists, stimulated by a wide spectrum of often unrelated challenges, who provide us with our best new ideas and new concepts.

The fact is, the creative process does not happen automatically. It has to be stimulated. Like an author writing a novel, an inventor mills grist consisting of those phenomena that have been observed by him or her in the past. These are stimuli, and the more plentiful and diverse, the better. Can you imagine an author writing a significant work about life who hasn't, as we say, lived?

The same holds for innovators in business and industry. The more diverse experiences an innovator has, the more exciting things he or she will produce. Thus, we certainly want to recruit or develop such people in any central innovation organization.

Synergy

Not only does the exercise of generalism stimulate creativity, it stimulates expediency. A more elegant word is *synergy*.

Synergy for innovators, and for generalists in particular, becomes a vital force in a central innovation organization because technical solutions for one business sector are often quite unexpectedly applicable to another. Innovation is thus significantly speeded up. And speed is what innovation is all about. Creation, invention—those are relatively easy; doing them in a timely fashion and with minimum numbers of sallies into blind alleys—that's the challenge.

An interesting example of synergy occurred in Raytheon's New Products Center several years ago. A circuit board for controlling an Amana microwave oven was wired in as the hardware for controlling an x-ray system made by Machlett Laboratories for use by radiological technicians. (Amana and Machlett are Raytheon subsidiaries, and both are clients of the New Products Center.) The generalists perceived that the complexity and variety of controlling functions were approximately the same in both cases. Thus, the same circuit board could be used for both. (The best way to innovate is to find a way not to have to do it.) In fact, Amana's

vendor was used by Machlett, with the advantage of volume pricing.
All that was needed was a new software set.

How Many?
It takes very few generalists to keep everyone else in an innovation
organization busy. Once they get momentum, generalists become
running rivers of newness. One generalist for every dozen professionals is a ratio that I have found to be productive.

The Advantages of Central Organizations
These arguments make a case that central innovation organizations,
working simultaneously in many areas (with generalists), have advantages over similar organizations confined to a single area. It is
easier for them to be creative and to turn their ideas into products.
This is a fact that should be taken into account when management
contemplates whether to create a central innovation organization
or a non-central one.

Technical Specialists

Specialists are people so enamored of their field of expertise
that they cannot be stirred out of it, even though in an environment
devoted to innovation for many clients, they could be as capable
as the generalists in making creative use of multiple stimulations
and synergy. But don't ask them to leave the field in which they
feel competent and comfortable.

You should feel comfortable with them, too. When teamed
correctly with generalists, each doing what is right for each—and
there are roles for both in most innovation programs—significant
results can be expected. The results are better and happen sooner
than with any other arrangement.

Such teamwork is demonstrated in the previously mentioned
synergy example, in which a microwave oven circuit board was
used as a control for a radiologist's x-ray equipment. The generalists
needed a new software set, so they turned to a group of specialists,
the software mavens, who could address that unique kind of problem as only professionals dedicated to a single discipline can. The
generalists had no choice, for none of them were software specialists.
Why? Because software bored them. Strange, the specialists weren't

bored at all; they were "turned on." It takes all kinds, even in an innovation organization.

Qualifications

There are three for specialists: (1) They should be experts, which means being really good at their trade. (2) They must be creative. (3) They must be capable experimenters. Thus, most of the requirements for creative generalists pertain here as well.

In any particular company, the specialist groups evolve in a form tailored to that company's needs. They assume their special identities over time. In Raytheon's New Products Center, we had two sets of specialists: a computer/electronics group (because every product we worked on had to have a control circuit) and a materials group (because every product consisted of materials: metals, plastics, paper, glass, or ceramics).

The Mission: Provide Required Specialized Expertise as a Member of an Innovation Team

The title says it all.

How Many? The Issue of Critical Mass

There is always a danger when assembling a staff of specialists of falling into the trap of making it too thin. One specialist in any field is often not enough, if only because a lively approach to keeping up with latest developments requires another person with a similar specialty and interests with whom to discuss the nature and significance of new developments. Productivity may suffer if someone has no one else of the same expertise to interact with. One person working alone is about as effective as a half a person, but two working together can have the effectiveness of three people.

When the workload in a particular specialty is projected to be sufficient to keep only one person busy, consider contracting for the services of an outsider on an as-needed basis. This recommendation extends to providing support staff and equipment. Specialists, no less than any other innovators, require nonprofessionals to perform specialty work as technicians, data collectors, and so on, and there are special kinds of equipment that these people utilize as tools of their trade.

An expression from the nuclear industry describes what we have been discussing: *critical mass.* No nuclear power station can "deliver" until there is enough fissionable material to sustain a chain reaction. "Enough" means a certain crucial amount and no less, although more than enough will, by implication, not interfere with operation. By the same token, specialists don't contribute to and sustain the innovation chain reaction unless they are an entity in their own right—no smaller than the required critical mass in numbers and facilities.

The Danger of Class Distinctions

Two cautions about specialists. First, they are frequently and undeservedly treated as second-class citizens. One reason is that specialists rarely lead a project. They are called in for a single special task and then not used again. Such a pattern diminishes status. Project leaders always have more clout than the "occasional" workers. This happens in all kinds of business activities, innovative or not, and it can work to impede progress. We must guard against that second-class status by consciously making an effort to respect what specialists can contribute.

Second (a related matter): The simple pig-headedness of those who *should* employ specialists—but do not—is evidence of a distressing behavior pattern that I have observed over and over again. Bosses and program managers always attempt to duplicate themselves in those they hire. They often select a costly answer to a problem from their expertise, instead of finding the inexpensive solution from another specialty. Such single-mindedness leads to inefficient innovation.

Product/Process Transfer Specialists

One other group of specialists is needed to round out the professionals in an innovation organization. It consists of people who, by their nature as well as because of their experience, can act as bridges or conduits for the transfer of innovations to those within the company who will in the end own them, produce them, exploit them, profit from them. They are unique because they are simultaneously specialists and generalists. Like the new-concept generalists, they care not which product, which technology, or which market they work on. They work on all of them. For lack of a better name, we can call them the transfer group.

The transfer group understands what it means to produce a product repeatedly—so many an hour—while not compromising the product's attractiveness, profitability, reliability, and safety. Transfer specialists may, in their previous jobs, have been production managers. If the new product is to be manufactured in a factory, they understand tooling, assembly, and costs much better than other innovators do. If the innovation is to be a process, they have worked with such processes themselves—in a processing plant. If the innovation is to be a new publication or new way to communicate with customers, they have had "production" roles in these fields themselves—as a way to make a living. In comparison, most of their fellow workers in the innovation organization look like ivory-tower people (although they would never admit it).

Qualifications

To be an effective transfer specialist, one should have engaged professionally and effectively in non-innovation activities in a product or process field close to that of the organization that will receive the innovation.

Additionally, transfer people are innovative. They may even have the ability to create new concepts themselves. In the course of transferring innovations, they always leave their own creative mark. Indeed, that may be why they left their earlier affiliations, because the environment that surrounds managing routine production tends to be inimical to creative changes of the sort they enjoy making. But having resided in such an environment qualifies these people to function well in a bridging capacity, which is what transfer requires.

Added to these qualifications is an important personality requirement. Smooth transfer requires a smooth personality, the ability to deal with very different kinds of people, and the ability to foster productive interaction among people.

The Mission: Effectuate Innovation Transfer

The mission of the transfer group is to achieve transfer of the innovation, which comes down to three tasks:

1. Remake the innovation from feasibility models to a form close to prototype in appearance and function.

2. Generate an information package incorporating drawings and suggestions for tooling and manufacture based on low-cost designs.
3. Stay with the product, often on the premises of the client, until transition is completed.

The transfer group has a fourth task, which, like Task 3, qualifies as hand-holding. Its members must mollify the primary innovators who now see their darling new products taken away from them. ("Cheer up," they say. "The fact that you are losing this creation means you have succeeded.")

Do We Really Need Them?

Yes, we do. It is in the transfer process that many innovation organizations flounder. They may create brilliant functioning models based on outstandingly creative concepts, but they can't speak fluently the language of their clients' line-people, who must pick up the creations and make market-appealing competitive products out of them. This failing commonly occurs in consulting companies or university groups, referred to as external teams. Their excuse is that they are external and thus can't be expected to possess every kind of production expertise needed by their wide range of clients. But what is the excuse of in-house innovation groups who, over a period of years, confront a steady, unvarying set of businesses in one company?

Every innovation organization does need a transfer group. Because, to generalize (and of course there are exceptions), innovators tend to be lousy at the tasks transfer people excel at. They tend to be bored by such matters as aesthetic appearance and tooling design and costs and all those other necessary details that members of the transfer group love.

There is another mode in which the transferers function: as interpreters of what has been achieved. All the creators need is a rudimentary model to prove the wisdom of what they have invented. But that proof is satisfactory and convincing only to them. They expect that what they perceive so easily must also be obvious to everyone else. But ordinary folk have a hard time extrapolating mentally from a chaotic pile of noisy, dirty, ugly mechanisms to the slick and handsome devices that they will one day produce and that will eventually go out the door.

Here is where the transfer group steps in. They have had to receive new products themselves in their past lives, and thus are considered by the receivers of the new creation as compatriots and not aliens. The transfer group will present the model in a form that can be understood in all its implications. That means that their contribution will thus be appreciated and more likely be rendered successful by those who count most at this point in the life cycle of the innovation, the receivers. As for hand-holding, yes, the conceivers can do some of that, and often do it well. But the product transfer group can do it better because they relate better.

Nonprofessionals

Except for administrators and managers/leaders, all the people described thus far have been direct labor, the doers. Now for the directest of all: the nonprofessionals. (Perhaps a better name would be semi-professionals.) They may break down to subgroups, like technicians, lab assistants, test specialists, or model-makers. If they work for computer specialists they may be programmers; if they work for metallurgists they may be metallographers; if their task is nontechnical, they will have other analogous designations, different in every industry and in every specialty.

Qualifications
Nonprofessionals usually have schooling beyond high school, often an associate's degree or other trade or specialty training. They require the equivalent of this level of background, whether they have been awarded the certificate or not. This level of training puts them ahead of most bench workers, the hourly employees, who, while they may possess great manual skills, usually have no perception of the principles, scientific or otherwise, that underlie and determine the nature of the product, process, or system on which they work.

Thus, they can perform certain professional tasks, such as some calculations and tabulations; also, they can draw conclusions from experimental results, often very wise ones, because if they've been around for a while they have accumulated much experience and thus a fund of wisdom. But they can't do this as well as the professionals, if only because they don't have the technical education required to delve deeper.

At the same time, they must be able to perform bench work at least as well as routine bench workers. The routine and repetitiveness will get to them, and ultimately bore them. Fortunately, repetitiveness is not generally required in R&D work, and what they do at the bench is often elegant, because many of them are craftsmen. You can usually tell when something was produced by the hands of the technician and when it was made by the hands of the innovator (the boss). The technician's tends to be neater and slicker, and to work better. The smart innovator, except for the rare case when he or she is also a master craftsman, will always let the technician do whatever fabrication and assembly is required.

The Mission: Creative Assistantship

The good nonprofessionals are assistants, in the best sense. That means they are accredited team members.

To be good at this job, technicians must embrace the idea that being an assistant is honorable and desirable. While always faithfully assisting, they must never do it slavishly; they must challenge their superiors when they perceive that a challenge is called for.

They are to their bosses what Sancho Panza was to Don Quixote, and often bring a somewhat ridiculous experiment down to earth. They are also the "good sergeant," without whom the callow lieutenant might look like an idiot to his colonel.

How Many?

In innovation groups, a good rule of thumb is to have as many semi-professionals as professionals, which is to say, one for each. (Data from the National Science foundation says .85 is common practice in the United States.) It is a good idea to set up "pools" of nonprofessionals so as to maximize flexibility. But some combinations work out so well that in those cases a permanent assignment of a particular helper to a particular innovator makes the best sense.

Blurring the Caste Boundaries

Nonprofessional help often begins to resemble the professionals with whom they spend their working days. If they work for generalists, they become generalists. If they work for specialists, they become specialists. But most important, if they work for creative people, their creativity blossoms.

That is where they pose an interesting challenge. Nonprofessionals can be inventors too. Indeed, they can be so good at it, they may become a far greater resource than one would predict from their job descriptions. What should you do about this situation? Exploit it, of course—and enjoy it. If a technician's name appears as the author of a patent and he or she gets a patent bonus and other rewards, all the better for the innovation group, because it can chalk up one more innovation.

Sometimes nonprofessionals show so much potential, it's good to encourage them to "improve themselves." It helps if your company has a procedure to pay night-school college tuitions. When a technician becomes an engineer, you should feel fortunate to have him or her on your staff. Such a person can be the greatest of producers.

Critical Mass for the Entire Innovation Organization

How many people should an innovation organization employ? The answer is, "It depends. Neither too many nor too few."

Excessive size of an innovation organization usually means that someone is building an empire. That is undesirable because empires are easy to lop off in years of poor financial performance. But modestly sized groups often survive unscathed. In smallness there is strength, but it is possible to be too small.

How small is too small? Less than enough to form effective teams of innovators with all the skills needed. That's another way of saying that such teams should never be smaller than critical mass. And the critical mass for the whole organization will be the size resulting from adding up all its critically sized effective teams. The same kind of critical-mass thinking should be employed when setting up facilities—labs, shops, and so on (discussed in Chapter 3).

Let us consider what I mean by "an effective team." What I have found, both from my own experience and from observing innovation organizations such as research centers, new products groups, and skunk works in other companies in a wide range of industries around the country, is that such teams most frequently are made up of as few as two professionals and two technicians. Such a collection of people, together with an occasional infusion of talent from the outside (which can be purchased in small amounts as required) is often enough to provide the generalists, specialists, and nonprofessionals to achieve an innovation goal. It is a "basic innovation team," and it is very frequently encountered.

In a year, this basic team can proceed through the steps of concept and proof of feasibility well enough to achieve most of the meaningful task targets as set up in a good program plan (see Chapter 5). The team will occupy about 4,000 square feet. At going rates, as I write this, it will cost in the Northeast, with fringes and purchases, in the order of $350,000. The total size of the innovation organization is determined by adding up the numbers of people that its innovation teams consist of.

Utilizing Resources Outside the Innovation Organization

One might think, having provided all these generalists and specialists, we need have no more concern with professional staffing. Not so. No matter how talented their crews, innovation organizations never have enough people. Frequently, the actual number of people on the premises may be quite small. Or those present may not be the right ones for a particular job. That means that certain experts required at certain times will just not be there when they are needed. Thus, supplemental talent, such as might reside elsewhere in the company, can look quite attractive.

That is especially true for central innovation groups that, though autonomous, actually serve many masters. They must work in many diverse businesses based on many diverse technologies and procedures.

"Liberating" Required Resources

Now is a time to refer once again to Figure 1–3 (see Chapter 1), where the company's technical expertise is represented schematically as a large block underlying the whole organization. It is drawn large on purpose, because in most companies the extent of that expertise is often very impressive, even in smaller companies. Make a list of your company's experts, of the people recognized as such not only by their co-workers but also by your competitors. You might be surprised—even awed and humbled—and you might wonder why everyone doesn't make more use of them.

The fact that most companies are blessed with wide-ranging talent and expertise means that they already possess the resources required to meet most innovation challenges. Indeed, those may be so abundant that they are not merely just enough, they may be overwhelmingly too much. Countering that intriguing advantage, indeed, usually effectively wiping it out, is a distressing dilemma: In spite of the availability of resources, most are rarely utilized for more than a small fraction of their innovation capabilities.

That's because those resources, made up of talented, often well-recognized folk, and the manifold and elaborate facilities, substructures, and supporting personnel that serve them, were assembled with some other purpose. And that purpose did not include the job that the innovation group happens to be pursuing at just this moment. So, when it is suggested that these experts "give help," such a suggestion is perceived by their bosses as a diversion—and good management has no tolerance for diversions.

Yet, there is always some talent to spare. There has to be. And even a little bit can go a long way. But who will force the issue? Well, how about the CEO? Only someone of the CEO's stature combines a grand overview of company priorities with clout enough to borrow people from Division A for the benefit of Division B, knowing that the destructive impact on A will not be fatal. Alas, we can't depend on our CEOs to exert this leadership on a regular basis. Perhaps occasionally, but not often enough. Even if tempted, the chief executive will resist, because making a business entity behave helpfully to another is seen as being disruptive to the (reluctant) giver.

Also, don't hold your breath waiting for the division manager of Division A to offer to help the division manager of Division B. Nor will Division B's manager request such aid. For division managers are too gentlemanly and ladylike to ask for favors. If they have anything, they have their pride. This subject is dealt with in depth in Rosabeth Kanter's *The Change Masters.* She points out, on the basis of investigations in nearly 200 companies, that for a business to flourish it must foster change; those who act to make change happen are the changemasters. Kanter contends that a changemaster's greatest challenge is to overcome those organizational barriers that effectively hamper utilizing crucial company resources. People who succeed in doing this win, and so do their companies (as Kanter shows with numerous case examples).[1]

There is no reason why a leader of an autonomous innovation group in a large company can't try his or her hand at being a changemaster. It's amazing how available those "unavailable" experts actually are, if one just asks the right way.

To maximize its effectiveness, any innovation organization, but especially a small one, should extend itself so that it becomes larger than its official body count. One way to do this is to obtain the services of experts who do not formally work for the group, many of whom work for the same company, often in close proximity. Don't be thwarted by the dilemma. Resolve it.

Know Who They Are

In most large companies, there are hundreds, even thousands, of engineers and scientists of every discipline. There are also other kinds of experts, nontechnical ones, who know procedures, markets, the rules of every game. What a rich bonanza! I used to feel that if only I could tap that resource, if only all those experts belonged to me, I would think I had died and gone to heaven. There is only one way to know who's out there: become a student of the company. Learn about all of the firm's operations—what each does and who works for them and where.

How do you do it? Just by making the effort. Those you want to learn about are only people. So if you like people and are interested in them, you've already breached the first barrier and made a powerful beginning. If you pay attention, you can't help but become aware of many of them through normal company activities. Nearly every firm publishes a company newsletter. Read it. Many individuals, some of them experts, are mentioned in terms of function and recent praiseworthy accomplishment. As you read, you will inevitably come across someone who is skilled in something that exactly fits a problem currently giving you trouble. That newspaper item triggers a reaction, and you'll say, "Aha!"

Without consciously meaning to, most companies throw different people together who would otherwise never have met. I was fortunate enough to have been selected to attend my company's advanced management course. It met for two full days and some evenings every month for a year. There were attendees from dozens of different divisions and businesses of the company, many of whom had to fly in from afar for the occasion.

I don't recall much about what I learned of management, advanced or otherwise, but I can remember virtually every one of my classmates. Through them I had a contact in almost every important segment of the company. I only needed to pick up the phone. . . . In addition, it is likely that many of the innovation group staff are long-term employees who once worked in other capacities in subsidiaries and divisions of the company. They have connections.

Finally, the process replenishes itself. Once you have worked with one person in a particular location, and that work was a pleasant and productive episode, then that person becomes an automatic conduit to his or her colleagues. This is "networking" in the best sense of the word.

Pay for Their Services

A cardinal rule is: Expect nothing free. The first meeting, when the relationship is in the process of being set up, may actually yield some valuable nuggets of expertise without money changing hands; but count on no more than that. From then on, set up a formal way to charge time and materials. Most companies have established procedures, with names like IWR (internal work request), which administrators know exactly how to handle. He or she is careful to couch the IWR in businesslike terms; for example, "funding not to exceed. . . ." and "delivery of Phase I Report by. . . ." When such procedures are followed, a contractual relationship exists. The expert—and his or her boss—have agreed to deliver something and to be paid for their efforts. Now the autonomous innovation organization is a customer, not a beggar. It can even "demand" good performance. That's not a bad position to be in.

Where will the money come from? That's easy. Budget for it. If your organization is funded for 15 professionals, hire 14. The IWR people will together constitute number 15.

Going Outside the Company for Experts

It makes little difference where technical expertise comes from. An expert is an expert. Some, by their nature, will never be found in the company, and all that means is that you should look for them on the outside.

It has been my experience that money for the correct consultant, whether that person be a company employee or an outsider, is well spent—but only if it's done with the correct selection of assignments and the correct constraints of scope.

Use Them Properly

They Are Consultants, Not Innovators

Experts are best used as experts, which means that they reveal knowledge not otherwise known; don't ask them to be innovators, even if they have creative talent (and most do). Because they are not in an autonomous innovation group, they usually find that their own business culture is not friendly to their innovation efforts. That other culture will tend to influence them to emphasize the wrong problem, set up the wrong priorities, cost too much, and take too long. If you limit their work to very carefully selected consulting tasks that match their exact expertise with your exact needs, then you will get your money's worth.

Use Them as Teachers

One of the best ways to use consultants is to have them teach what they know. They can be very valuable in broadcasting their expertise, so invite them to give a tutorial.

We once had a two-lecture course from the company's expert in vibration. He worked in the company's Missile System Division and had devoted himself to designing missile structures so that they would not vibrate destructively at speeds three times the speed of sound. But the compressor in a refrigerator vibrates too. So does the rotating anode in an x-ray tube used in a hospital, and we did work on those products for our company's clients in the home appliance and medical businesses. The same principles of mechanics and physics pertain in all three cases. The conference room was full both days, and we all learned much that was useful in designing quieter new refrigerators and x-ray tubes.

It's a good idea to start all of your work relationships with experts with a day or two of tutorial. Then you can get down to business, which means requesting that they address the specific problem at hand.

Generate a Stable

Time passes. The list of consulting experts, both internal and external, grows. Some people and some relationships shine through as extraordinarily productive and useful, others don't. Some experts are needed only once; the problem may never come up again. Others are on constant call. What evolves is a reservoir—a stable— of expertise that can always be drawn on.

Let's return to Figure 1–3 in Chapter 1, with which we began this section. Draw your own version for your own company. In the "Advanced Expertise" block, write down the names of experts in your company and their respective skills. Pay no attention to which departments they work for. Take the attitude that if they work for the company, they work for you. (In fact, many of those horses are just itching to get into your stable, if only for a little while, because their present assignments keep them cantering on a slow and narrow track.) Write up some internal work requests and divert talent along those heavy black lines with the arrows pointing in the right directions.

The Special Case of Government Business

Government-sponsored industrial R&D can be stunning in size and scope. Our largest contractors bring together literally thousands of engineers and scientists in single locations. Indeed, government innovation proceeds by marshalling forces—not in squads but in regiments and divisions. Does the program need 200 mechanical engineers to create a new mechanical device? No problem. Here are the funds. Will a task require 400 programmers? Just put an ad for programmers in the Sunday paper and go to it.

I do not presume to challenge the wisdom of this massive mobilization of technical talent. I only take the occasion to point out that our competitors in the rest of the free world employ most of their innovation resources not to create innovative military products but rather to create ever more innovative industrial, commercial, and domestic products. That's all the more reason for us to improve our own commercial and domestic innovation capabilities.

Reference

1. R. Kanter, *The Change Masters* (New York: Simon & Schuster, 1983).

3

Providing Facilities and Funds

Having recruited a staff, you must now provide two things: the physical environment in which they may engage in the innovation process and the funding to finance that activity. These are challenges, with special requirements that are unique to the business of implementing new ideas. The first three sections of this chapter describe these requirements as they pertain to facilities, their location and their size. The remaining two treat techniques for obtaining funding that does more than simply provide resources to meet a budget. If funding is done right, the levels of motivation and involvement are improved for "funders" and "fundees" alike.

Physical Resources

Ideally, an autonomous innovation group should be located in an autonomous building. That helps to establish its separate identity. A number of such plants around the country are illustrated for establishments that work in different innovation modes (see Figures 3–1 through 3–5).

But ideal conditions are not always available, and it is not unlikely that, in most cases, a group of innovators will merely be allocated space in someone else's facility, at least during its formative years, before it earns the right to be separate. Should that occur, it will bring with it some obvious advantages and disadvantages. Most notable of the advantages is that as a renter, the innovation group can piggyback on existing equipment and services. It is thus off to a flying start since it need not establish these from scratch. By the same token, as a guest at the landlord's table, the group may be there on sufferance and may experience the disadvantage of always being served last—and with leftovers. The way to look

Figure 3-1. Raytheon's New Products Center.

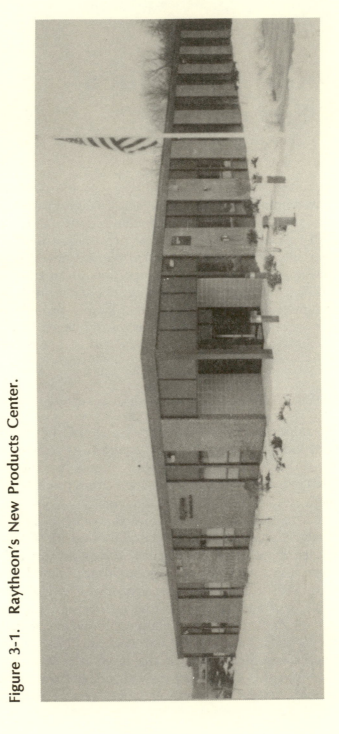

Figure 3-2. Corning's Sullivan Park Technical Center.

Photo courtesy of Corning Glass Works

at this is to accept the bad with the good. It is a way to get started, and often the best way, since new innovation organizations are usually small, especially in small or mid-size companies, and the idea of setting up in a separate building is impractical.

But the goal of achieving a distinctive look is just as valid for a facility located in rental quarters in someone else's territory as it is for one in a separate building. Most autonomous innovation groups must introduce skeptical folk to unfamiliar things, which means they must always be in a selling mode. And the best way to sell is to be credible, which is attainable, in part, by presenting a good image.

Credibility

Image is an important ingredient of credibility. A respectable building (or wing, floor, even former cafeteria) with tasteful fittings and decor gives the message that management has seen fit to

Figure 3-3. The Xerox skunk works: East Rochester Operations (ERO).

Photo courtesy of Xerox Corporation

Figure 3-4. Robert L. Mitchell Technical Center of the Hoechst Celanese Research Company.

Photo courtesy of Hoechst Celanese Corporation

Figure 3-5.   Eastman Kodak's six-story building for New Opportunity Development (right, foreground) and world headquarters (tower in background).

Reprinted courtesy of Eastman Kodak Company

commit the moneys required to set up and maintain that unique environment. Plaques and displays in the lobby that testify to previous accomplishments are desirable. That's what a good law firm has in its lobby. It too tries to sell itself to potential clients.

We know that relationships in a manufacturing company differ from those in a law firm. When you visit a lawyer, you are automatically ready to put yourself in the hands of a professional.

But the potential company client who just might be interested in innovation usually thinks of creative people as oddballs, and is not so predisposed to accept the innovators. Try to make your innovation staff look like solid citizens (with only a hint of oddness). A respectable, even impressive, setting helps.

Not only will a professional-looking facility proclaim credibility to insiders like company clients, it will do the same for outsiders. A well-set-up autonomous innovation facility is a great place to bring potential customers. "Here is where we first conceived and developed that new model 34-ALV that we are offering you," says the client's vice president for sales, "and there's a lot more coming from these people. . . ." And when the local newspaper needs a feature article, what better place to go than the high-tech R&D lab?

It is true that skunk works (one important kind of autonomous innovation organization) seem not to conform to the principles stated here. They usually flaunt their scruffiness—that's their image. I must admit it can be successful, for the same reasons that respectability is. It has sales appeal and credibility value in that it reinforces the popular concept that the blockbuster innovation can only be derived from creatures who are more akin to extraterrestrials than to mere earthlings. The "soul of the new machine" presided over by Mr. West as described in Tracy Kidder's book was housed in just such an unpretentious setting.[1] Like many lifestyles, "skunking" contains some elements of posing. However, it can work, so leave it alone.

For the most part, though, innovators benefit from projecting an image of being respectable, company-oriented team members. An attractive facility with a look of permanence has a self-fulfilling impact. Its denizens tend to become permanent too, which in no way means that they will stop being innovative.

Types of "Rooms"

Let us describe what the major "rooms" should be in a facility that houses an innovation organization. In some regards, they are not different from what one would find in a plant housing any business organization, so this discussion is confined to features that are special for people engaged in R&D. They are: conference rooms, laboratories, shops, pilot production lines (sometimes), provision for documentation and display, and offices.

Conference Rooms

Innovation starts with communication. Innovators need to discuss specifications, drawings, models, and performance and cost data with one another, and also need to brainstorm. That happens most effectively around a conference table in a large room that has a blackboard at one end.

The staff of the innovation group needs a place that conveys a feeling of isolation from everyday tasks where people can sit together on occasion and bounce ideas off each other. Those generalists, specialists, and leaders described in Chapter 2 become ever so much more creative when they are in a quiet room with each other than when they're left to sit in their own niches. Many innovative people, left to their own ways of doing things, would be inclined to stay away from their co-workers for days on end. An important function of the boss is to call meetings to counteract this tendency. "We will meet in the central conference room tomorrow at 9 A.M.," reads the announcement, "to brainstorm Fred's idea on how to switch the operation of his compressor from the oscillating to the continuous mode. . . ." Used in this way, a conference room becomes as important as a laboratory.

Discussions with visiting company clients are equally important. Before an innovation created by an R&D group is accepted for manufacture by the client, a lot of information must be exchanged. The conference room provides the perfect environment for intense, frequent, often protracted meetings between innovator and client.

As with any good conference rooms, those of an autonomous innovation group should have provision for good visual aids: slides, overhead projectors, video systems, tables for demonstration models (if the models lend themselves to conference-room presentation), and a convenient setup for serving coffee and sandwiches (it's better to stay put than to go out to lunch). The conference room should also be comfortable and attractive.

Ideally, there should be more than one conference room. By their nature, centers will have links to many company clients, who somehow seem always to visit on the same day. The way to handle this situation is to run simultaneous meetings in the different conference rooms, with the innovators leaping adroitly from room to room at just the crucial moments. (They get to be rather good at it—like baby doctors confronting a row of booths, each containing an expectant mother.) If different clients from the same company meet each other when it comes time to eat their brown-bag sandwiches, how wonderful!

Laboratories and Shops

Just as labor can be categorized as either indirect or direct, so too can physical resources. What we have discussed thus far, the facilities in general with their lobbies and conference rooms, are indirect facilities. Direct facilities are the actual workplaces in which the first steps in the process of implementing new ideas take place. If the work is technical in nature, these workplaces are laboratories and shops. If the work is nontechnical, they may go by other names, but they always will serve laboratory-like and shop-like functions. All contain equipment used to aid the innovation process.

Innovation laboratories should provide a setting in which operating models can be developed and tested in their many evolutionary stages. Because useful innovation requires timeliness and efficiency, the laboratory should be organized so that it aids in providing these. Thus, a good laboratory will offer flexible and easily usable workbenches on which the innovators and their technicians may perform experiments.

An innovation facility should be outfitted with a variety of fabrication and test equipments organized and located separately in shops. Large shops should be staffed with specialists in the craft to which the shop is devoted.

If models require that parts be welded together, it is desirable that the innovation center have a set of welding machines and a technician who is skilled in their use—a welding shop. If models require plastic shaping, vacuum-forming equipment is desirable. If computerized test equipments are frequently required to evaluate certain test parameters, they should be available in test labs.

In setting up innovation facilities, you will confront the classic make-or-buy decision: Would it be better to buy parts or services from another part of the company or from an outside vendor, or should you create them from scratch in your own area? If outside fabricators or testers can deliver fast enough, then by all means use them and save the capital investment in tools and equipment as well as the floor space they would consume. But if waiting for them to deliver will render viscous an otherwise fluid process, then take action to become self-sufficient. Keep in mind that it little profits any innovation endeavor to have to wait two weeks for a routine operation or test to be conducted off-site when the same process could have been done in the next room in a day or two. Delays work against creativity and the juices of ingenuity lose their freshness.

An innovation center usually needs some type of special system, a sophisticated tool, often complex in concept and often not inexpensive, the use of which is required in many company locations, but only occasionally in each. It might be an elegant thermal scanner that feeds temperature distributions measured by infrared scanning on the surface of a product into a computer system for analysis. Every client can find occasion to use it because virtually every product experiences temperature excursions in operation. Or, it might be a state-of-the-art electromagnetic spectrum analyzer needed from time to time by any business making communications products, radar systems, or microwave cooking products. Such special equipment should be centrally located. What better place than in a center—an innovation center?

Pilot Production Lines

A pilot line may be considered a kind of laboratory. It is a small-scale production facility that attempts to simulate a future production process. The "pilot run" is the final step of the innovation process prior to complete transfer to production, and is actually an ingredient of transfer itself. The nature of the innovation determines whether such a line is to be part of the innovation facility or not. If the innovation is a product, it is best piloted in the client's facility; if it is a process, it may benefit from an off-site trial run before transfer.

Which course to take is a major decision for an innovation organization and for those who provide its capital funds; pilot lines cost orders of magnitude more money than the average innovation lab. In addition to small-scale production machinery, they must include every kind of instrumentation and safety provision to be found in a manufacturing plant. Also, such lines may look small to the company's production managers, but often appear massive when installed in an innovation facility. Indeed, it may make it necessary for the facility to be many times the size of what it would have been had a pilot line not been included. Hoechst Celanese Research Company considers its pilot lines to be part of R&D but it locates them in Corpus Christi, 1,000 miles from the central research facility in New Jersey that maintains authority over those lines.

When innovators undertake piloting, they are often tempted to become entrepreneurs. I have seen pilot lines that continue "piloting" year after year, and the innovators end up selling the product to the public in competition with the client. That's when the client, who is no longer getting innovation out of the innovation group, will respond by starting up a captive R&D operation.

Documentation and Display

A new product or process born in an autonomous innovation organization has to consist of more than merely an operating model. It must include essential information about that model, the concept on which it is based, and the implications of that concept. In fact, most of what innovators produce is paperwork—reports and specification books—and other non-hardware items, such as visual models. The facility must be set up to provide these items, with drafters, designers, secretaries, and the equipment they require.

In the end, however, the best way to show something new is to demonstrate a working model right in the lab. Videotaping it is almost as good—maybe better, because it is guaranteed that the new product will perform perfectly. Videocassettes offer a very convenient and effective medium for presenting new products, and an innovation organization should have a room set up as a studio.

In the past, drafters always needed drafting boards and blueprint machines. But as we move toward the final decade of this millennium, drafting boards are becoming obsolete. CAD, computer-aided design, is what will replace them. Who will sit before a CAD keyboard—the drafter or the innovator? Both, so it will be wise to leave a room for a CAD setup.

Offices

Offices are to innovators what they are to everyone else: expressions of status. Aside from the issue of ego-massage, however, an innovator does require two things: a quiet, private place to work and dream up new ideas and a place for his or her computer. (A computer is the only work tool that should be allowed; I always remind innovators, "Don't turn your office into a lab or your lab into an office.")

Technicians may not need offices, but they do need desks in order to keep up with their considerable paperwork.

Location of Facilities

Central Innovation Organizations

Central innovation organizations usually do best when they are not too far from corporate headquarters. This proximity helps when innovators want to display an innovation to company officers who otherwise might not find it "convenient" to visit for that purpose. Such visits mean that innovation in general, and your own innovations in particular, can extend their influence.

Once innovators trap top managers in their lairs, they almost always make a favorable impression. What CEO can resist a remarkable new thing as he or she watches it gyrating and sputtering and giving off sparks? In fact, at that moment a CEO usually takes credit for virtually having invented the device—because he or she didn't kill the project. Other company executives will "drop in" on their way to or from the executive office, and this, too, is all to the good.

More important, lower-level client personnel to whom innovations will one day be transferred often accompany their bosses on these excursions. Such visits can have an important effect on how easily the process proceeds through its steps of transfer and implementation.

Administrative innovation groups such as those who engage in external and internal venturing and licensing are also central in nature. In fact, their offices are usually located right in the headquarters building itself, and that helps them.

Captive R&D Organizations

Captive R&D groups are best located close to their masters. For them, as for any innovators, isolation is good. But closeness is also desirable. How about a building on the other side of the parking lot?

Skunk Works

Skunk works and havens for assemblages of spinoff ventures fall somewhere in between centers and captive R&D groups. They are often captive, but even when they are not, they are usually "related" to an existing company entity. Yet they work best when they're out of sight. "Off-campus" is a convenient euphemism. The Xerox and Eastman Kodak facilities provide good examples; they seem to end up five to 15 miles away, a distance that experience tells us is just right.

A Place of One's Own

What should not be countenanced, however, is for the activity to be located in someone else's department. "Oh, by the way," says the big boss. "Jennifer and Harold are going to be our inventors. Hey, Sam," he yells out, "find them a bench in your place, will you?" Oh, how that makes me grit my teeth. If you don't mean it, Mr. Boss, don't do it.

Size

How big is best? Not too big, but not too small either. That applies not only to the staff but also to the facility it will occupy. The "critical mass" concept applies here too, and it precludes allowing leaders of innovation to be empire builders rather than innovation builders.

Let's get specific. How big *should* the physical innovation structure (and by that token, its staff) be? It's hard to know in advance, but once you understand how large a team of participants are required to innovate in your industry and particular company, then you can determine how large the quarters should be.

A Rule of Thumb

As discussed in Chapter 2, a small team of innovators consisting of generalists, specialists, and their technicians are usually what it takes to launch an innovation program. Four people—half of them professionals, half technicians—is a common size for such a team. How much space—benches, shops, offices, conference rooms, drafting rooms—will they occupy in our facility? In my experience, 4,000 square feet will be all they need, which leads to a nice rule of thumb: about 1,000 square feet per person. Later on, depending on the complexity and size of the new product, the group may need more than this, and pilot lines will require a lot more room.

Using our rule of thumb, the size of an innovation facility and its running cost can be gauged. Will there be ten innovation programs going simultaneously? Then 40 people and 40,000 square feet will probably be needed.

Of course, while 1,000 square feet per innovator has worked for me, it may not pertain to your company or industry. And the four-person team may be wrong too. So change the numbers accordingly.

The Best Size

Remember to keep in mind your ultimate goal. Maybe you don't need ten programs. Most client enterprises find it hard to absorb more than one innovation every two or three years. Perhaps two successful new developments are all your company can handle. Still, the batting average is never 1.000, so it may take three programs for every one that makes it. In that case, space for six programs is what needs to be provided.

The best size for an innovation organization is what is best for achieving success in each individual company. Just consider all the arguments given above, and back them by your long-term strategy, before deciding what that size should be for yours.

Funding Practices

Being provided with a satisfactory facility is only half the challenge that confronts the staff of an innovation organization. It must at the same time obtain financing consistent with the levels of effort demanded by the programs it will undertake. Possibly the most important factors in determining its success, as well as its style and morale, are those determined by the money it will live on. Putting aside the issue of how much money, the primary questions are: Under what conditions is the money provided? Who is the money from? Who has provided assent or approval?

The act of getting funds should be a once-a-year exercise set up in a formal procedure. It should involve all who will make use of the potential innovations in a way that ensures, even if they do not provide the actual moneys, that the process has received their serious attention. Thus the answers to these questions take on additional importance as factors in determining the posture toward innovation that will be taken by those providers and assenters.

Those who manage innovation organizations, like managers of other kinds of organizations in a company, must end every fiscal year by generating a budget for the coming one. (Budgeting is considered in this book to be an element of implementing the innovation process, the subject of Part 2, and is treated in detail in Chapter 5.) Next they must present the budget to their higher-ups and win the budget. Then they spend the year doing the job that has been budgeted for.

However, things don't always work this way. Instead, the manager of the innovation organization often has to sally out, hat in hand, proposing projects and then begging for funds for each individual project from many different executives in many different business entities within the company. The ramifications of such actions—few of them good—are discussed in the following text. First the "good" way, one-time allocation, is presented as a desirable standard; then the "less good" way ("bad" may be too strong), project-by-project, follows, along with a recommendation of a desirable variation and combination of these two approaches, which includes mandated allocations.

One-Time Allocation from the Executive Office

A well-established practice should be in place to ensure that the manager of *any* kind of innovation group periodically has an audience with top management for the purpose of presenting a budget with the goal of winning it. This should occur once a year.

How long should the presentation last? One hour should be enough for most innovation organizations. (This should be good news for most CEOs, who always have "more important" things to do.) Of course, if a company has a major commitment to innovation and gives a significant percentage of its sales dollars to it, a more elaborate and time-consuming exercise is warranted. But the same rule still should hold: Innovation leaders must have a formal periodic review with top management for yearly allocation of funds.

A consequence of adopting this funding-approval practice is that the top corporate executive gets a firsthand introduction to what that innovation organization consists of, what its goals and motivations are, and what it means to the company—and achieving that state of understanding can only be good.

Admittedly, one can suggest a countervailing argument. This procedure deprives the company's individual businesses of some control, because when an innovation center's leader makes a pitch to the top company officer, decentralization suffers. True, but one can carry decentralization too far. This is such an instance. Innovation centers *should* be centralized and should get their funds from a central source.

But the argument is not limited to centers. Everything that has been said pertains to every mode of innovation, even the captive ones, and to organizations in small companies as well as those in large ones. No innovation manager should have to dissipate energy in exasperating, multiple, never-ending sales pitches—one per project—in order to obtain operating moneys.

The underlying message is: Innovation proceeds best when the organization that does it has stability and continuity. Those qualities are the primary consequences of yearly funding commitments by management.

Funding on a Project-by-Project Basis

When innovation organizations constantly have to money-grub for each funding segment, there is no stability and no assurance of continuity. I know the department head in the manufacturing technology center of a large company who has maintained a staff of about ten engineers and 20 supporting nonprofessionals for more than a decade. He is esteemed by his company and can point to a number of innovations developed by his group that have made major positive impact on the ways the products of that company are processed and fabricated. But consider how he spends his days.

The majority of his working hours are consumed in the offices and conference rooms of executives of a half-dozen separate businesses in his company—his clients—in order to negotiate the level of funds he requires to carry out each task of technology innovation. His personal output for any year consists mostly of carefully wrought presentations that outline program steps and associated costs, and these are made up of dozens of elegant transparencies or slides to be flashed on a screen. He does this throughout the year, his pursuit of funds is unrelenting. If he slackens the pace and loses funds, he must lay off people.

His employees know that this is how he consumes his energies, and they perform their work at a level of low morale compatible with such a circumstance. What good spirits they do have result from their boss's constant pep talks and hand-holding (his other major task and skill). My friend finds this as draining, both physically and emotionally, as his huckstering efforts.

This resourceful leader has evolved an innovative way of operating under these circumstances. It is a way that mitigates trauma without eliminating it. He maintains a core of his best people and supplements them with contract labor at peak times. He tells me he is the best customer of the local body shop, where he is held in reverence even though he brutally slashes the contract labor at low times. But this is only a make-do arrangement. If he is lucky, some of the contracted help are repeats, but the first two weeks of any hurry-up month are usually spent training new people.

Under such conditions, how can he consider any long-term innovation? How can he summon up, let alone implement, a creative vision? He can't, for he is too busy fund raising. Even if he had some free time to address a marvel of an idea, the best engineer for the job has either just been transferred out or laid off, or has resigned in disgust.

What is astonishing when one looks over his records for the entire time his department has existed is that his funding level, the total dollars he has won, comes out about the same every year. So what is all this fuss about? What value has accrued to this multi-billion-dollar company as a result of using up the energies and emotions of a valuable employee whose time should have been spent as an innovation leader rather than as a money grubber? Very little benefit. But much damage.

I know of another innovation manager in another company who concocted a novel approach to avoid laying off employees under similar circumstances. He used his sales skills to "sell" his employees—as contract workers—to another company (not a competitor) that needed to perform work similar to what he was supposed to do for his own company. This is always easy to do if you try, because you always look better to strangers than to relatives. Thus he was able to tide his group over lean times.

The survival actions taken in these examples are abominations. Yes, they are clever expedients that work, and I've even resorted to them myself; but they fly in the face of the intent of an innovation organization. It was not created to parlay hired help cleverly or to go into the outside consulting business. And those things would never have happened had adequate funds been allocated at the beginning of every year.

In fact, it is close to a miracle that the requester ever wins any money at all in project-by-project begging. If dollars are provided as a result of constant wheedling, money must then be subtracted from the profit column of the sponsoring business. During the process of signing the money over, a manager might ask, "Why give all this money to an 'outsider'? Why not allocate it to my own captive people, from whom it is easier to take it back if I fall short later on?"

An innovation leader becomes very good at wheeling and begging, not at innovating. Such leaders are like college presidents and directors of museums and cultural centers who may once have been eminent scholars or artists in their own right but whose highest priority now is fund raising. The "best" college presidents are the best fund raisers.

But we don't have to work this way; industry can set its own rules. So let us do it differently—and better. Business should not force its innovation talent to be diverted into the time-consuming, unnecessary, and often demeaning practice of winning fiscal support on a project-by-project basis. It should fund innovation with "inviolate" funds, and should do it once a year. If that means the money comes from the corporate office and some company businesses get these services "without charge," so be it.

Outside Funding

There are occasional circumstances when it may be wise to obtain funds from sources outside of the company. (I emphasize the word *occasional.*) Outsiders are, in fact, *outsiders.* In principle, they have no right to participate in your business. If they give you money, most of the time they do it for the wrong reasons (like buying your soul). Nevertheless, there are times when it is better to accept their money than not.

Certainly, companies engaged in developing a new art-leading torpedo or a new laser weapon have little choice but to get their money from the Pentagon. Do those companies fall into the once-a-year category or the item-by-item category? The answer, because of the grand scale of most of these programs, is the former.

In fact, some government-sponsored innovation programs tend to be so massive that their budgets will commonly cover periods of five years rather than one, and the only interruptions and changes of direction will occur with changes of administration in Washington—or if some country inadvertently declares peace. If you are looking for relative stability and continuity, this is a good way to attain them.

But accepting the U.S. government as a funding source brings its own kind of pain. There are all of the accountability requirements (supervised by the resident inspector), the mountains of reports that must be generated, and the fact that innovators, as ego-driven here as in commercial business, chafe under the restriction that much of what they create can never be publicized. On the other hand, the money is good. . . .

Then there are trade associations that have no motive other than what sounds like altruism. "Further the state of the art of your products," they say, "and we'll help you do it. With money." I don't use that altruism statement facetiously. The Gas Research Institute, which is sponsored by the country's gas producers, will fund R&D programs to aid in the more efficient use of gas, which means using less gas. Why do they do it? To improve the image of gas and make it more attractive to consumers than electricity or oil. The public benefits, but it pays too, for GRI is supported by a percentage taken from every consumer's gas bill. New products that otherwise would never have appeared on the marketplace are developed. For example, the Lennox Furnace Company's 95 percent efficient home heating system (Figure 3–6), based on the principle of pulse combustion, a highly unconventional and creative concept, was the result of an innovation program sponsored at that company by the Gas Research Institute. The product was good for Lennox commercially, and the American public benefitted, too.

How much of its birthright did Lennox have to give up in exchange for these outside funds? I do not know for sure, but I

Figure 3-6. Data sheet describing the Pulse combustion furnace, a product development that resulted from Lennox Industries' cooperation with the American Gas Association, Gas Research Institute.

ENGINEERING DATA

HEATING UNITS

GAS

Page 21

April 1986

Supersedes Nov. 1985

G14 SERIES PULSE™
UP-FLO GAS FURNACES
40,000 to 100,000 Btuh Input
Add-On Cooling 1-1/2 thru 5 Nominal Tons

Lennox Pulse Combustion Design
Provides Heating Efficiency Up to 97%

The Lennox G14 series pulse combustion up-flo gas furnaces provide efficiencies (AFUE) of up to 97%. Eight models (natural gas or LPG) are available with input capacities of 40,000, 60,000, 80,000 and 100,000 Btu. The units operate on the pulse combustion principle and do not require a pilot burner, main burners, conventional flue or chimney. Compact, standard size cabinet design, with side or bottom return air entry, permits installation in a basement, utility room or closet. Lennox add-on evaporator coils, electronic air cleaners and power humidifiers can easily be added to the furnace for Total Comfort all season installations. Additionally, replacement of most Lennox furnaces manufactured by Lennox in the last 20 years can be accomplished with only minor modifications to ductwork or add-on cooling coils.

The high efficiency of the G14 line of furnaces is achieved through a unique heat exchanger design which features a finned cast iron combustion chamber, temperature resistant steel tailpipe, aluminized steel exhaust decoupler section and a finned stainless steel tube condenser coil similar to an air conditioner coil. Moisture, in the products of combustion, is condensed in the coil thus wringing almost every usable Btu out of the gas. Since most of the combustion heat is utilized in the heat transfer from the coil, flue vent temperatures are as low as 100°F to 130°F allowing the use of 2 inch diameter PVC (polyvinyl chloride) pipe for venting. The furnace can be vented through a side wall, roof or to the top of an existing chimney with up to 35 ft. of PVC pipe and four 90 degree elbows. Condensate created in the coil may be disposed of in an indoor drain. The condensate (PH ranges from 4.0 to 6) is not harmful to standard household plumbing and can be drained into city sewers and septic tanks without damage.

The G14 furnace has no pilot light or burners. An automotive type spark plug is used for ignition on the initial cycle only, saving gas and electrical energy. Due to the pulse combustion principle the use of atmospheric gas burners is eliminated with the combustion process confined to the heat exchanger combustion chamber. The sealed combustion system virtually eliminates the loss of conditioned air due to combustion and stack dilution. Combustion air is piped to the furnace with same type PVC pipe as used for exhaust gases.

The furnace is equipped with a standard type redundant gas valve in series with a gas expansion tank, gas intake flapper valve and air intake flapper valve. Also factory installed are a purge blower, spark plug igniter and flame sensor with solid-state control circuit board.

Furnished with the G14 furnace as standard equipment are a fan and limit control, 30 VA transformer, blower cooling relay, flexible gas line connector, (4) isolation mounting pads, base insulation pad, condensate drip leg and cleanable air filter. Flue vent/air intake line roof or wall termination installation kits, LPG conversion kits and thermostat are available as accessories and must be ordered extra.

G14 units are shipped completely factory assembled with all controls installed and wired. In addition, the units are fire tested at the factory and require no field adjustments on start up.

Typical Applications

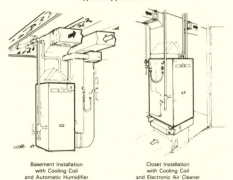

Basement Installation
with Cooling Coil
and Automatic Humidifier

Closet Installation
with Cooling Coil
and Electronic Air Cleaner

NOTE — Specifications, Ratings and Dimensions subject to change without notice.

Courtesy of Lennox Industries, Inc.

would imagine not enough to hurt. All parties, on balance, benefitted, including Lennox's innovation group, which had what all innovation groups want: a creative challenge that has a chance to result in significant impact on the marketplace.

Outside funding is in the category of "yearly one-time allocation" in terms of how one obtains it. It looks good when we get it, but it carries a negative aspect with it, in addition to the fact that a stranger has crept into the boss's bed. It will not always contribute to our goals of stability and continuity for the innovation organization, for it is a truism that outside funding never goes on forever. It always ends.

A final point: If the project does not accord with company plans, businesses should never accept outside sponsorship just because the money is needed. Company strategy should come first, not the goals of the outsider. Remember, the company is the client; the source of the money is not. The outsider's function is to be a champion and sponsor—and only on a temporary basis or guest status.

The Merits of Mandated Funding Allocations

The foregoing sections have argued that a one-time budget exercise has advantages over project-by-project pleas for funding spread over time. But there are variations on this theme. They all come down to techniques to achieve positive psychological and motivational influences on all the people involved in the innovation process—the donors and the receivers both, but primarily the receivers.

Flipping through the yellowed pages of my high school year book, I recently noted that fully one tenth of my classmates, when asked what they wanted to be, disdained answers like "financier" or "nurse." They said "successful." I always admired that answer and regretted that I did not use it too. Because that indeed has always been my goal—and that's what innovation in a company should be too. I make this point, which should be obvious, because so many companies behave in a manner that makes one think their goal is to make their businesses unsuccessful, at least insofar as innovation is concerned.

Reference to the disadvantages of project-by-project funding practices reinforces that argument. Indeed, sad to say, many managers of innovation organizations have told me, because of management's apparent hostility toward innovation, "The company is the enemy." By which they mean a one-way situation. For they, noble souls, remain steadfastly their clients' devoted allies. It is a case of unrequited love. But success cannot be founded on enmity, even if unidirectional.

The way to be successful is to make sure that innovation organizations are viewed by everyone in the company as part of the scheme of things, that their interactions with other organizations in the company are not adversarial in nature, and that everyone in this innovation act—and that includes the funders as well as those on whom they bestow their dollars—*wants* it to happen, the more passionately the better. And you'll want something a lot if you're footing the bill.

The yearly allocation of budget from the executive office is a good system, but is it the best? Does it maximize motivation of all parties, and thus their prospects for success? Desirable though it may be, it can be improved upon.

People who get things for free often don't appreciate what they are getting. Our work ethic imprints on us the principle that good things should be accompanied by proportionate pain. Thus, this section addresses how to make sure that those who will benefit from innovation programs experience feelings of involvement, pain if you will, to the extent that their interest in those programs is maximized.

The most efficient way to get client participation is to mandate it. And that is what I propose doing. This is a retreat from an ideal situation in which managers take the initiative for innovation. Unfortunately, put ten P&L managers into a room and only one or two will advocate long-term actions involving innovation. And those two will tend to retreat when they learn what the cost will be. Thus, with regret, I take the position that each P&L operation that uses innovation (and all of them should use it) be *required* to contribute a yearly sum to the innovation organizations that serve it. This allocation becomes part of that operation's direct cost overhead burden, similar in fiscal nature to yearly allocations for other corporate expenses.

The innovation organizations must still present their programs and associated required budgets once a year—and win them. But, now there is a difference from the practice of funding entirely derived from the corporate office (as advocated earlier in this chapter). Now the company client is footing some of the bill—but not all of it. How much? Enough to be noticeable on the P&L sheets, but less than the majority of the funds allocated. A formula of 25 percent from the client, 75 percent from the corporate office is about right.

Funding of innovation centers from the head office, with no contribution from company organizations served by those centers, is not uncommon—nor is funding to such centers from separate profit and loss entities, with no contribution by the executive office. It is the combination of both—the distribution of a portion of funds from each, with most coming from the head office—that I have almost never encountered. But I am led to believe that this practice of proportioning funding from the combination of both sources—even if one source is "forced" into making its contribution—is sound.

The reason I recommend resorting to this manipulative practice is that there is always a danger that, with innovation totally funded by others, clients will allow R&D organizations to expend effort that they will later disregard. I have even seen reverse manipulation, where clients direct "free" innovators down a course that will keep them busy for a year just to get them out of their hair. Then, when the innovation culminates in success in the form of good operating models (there is never a problem if the program is a failure), the client claims to have never really wanted that product or process in the first place.

The "apportioned" funding practice recommended here introduces a complication based on the fact that now we have the client's attention. In fact, the client is involved enough to want to influence the course of the innovation. What is bad about that? Mostly it is good. The only negative aspect that arises is that clients who are rewarded on the basis of short-term fiscal results tend to have short-term views. These will tempt them to exert negative pressures when investing in innovations with long-term or uncertain payback. Let the client express those views and succeed—but not all the time. With minority participation in funding, the client has only a minority vote. But it is a vote, and thus the interests of

the company are served. That client is involved—and interested—
even if some of the more "visionary" programs end up being
pursued anyway.

Reference

1. T. Kidder, *The Soul of a New Machine* (Boston/Toronto: Atlantic–Little, Brown, 1981).

Part 2

Implementing the Creative Process

4

The Seven Steps
to Innovation

Now that we have set up our innovation organization with its staff, its facility, and its funds we are ready to proceed down the road to innovation. Of course, in the real world, things don't happen as deliberately and logically as you might infer from Part 1. More likely, there have been years of evolution involving false starts, changes of personnel, and reversals of sponsorship and purpose. But, as discussed in this chapter, we do not create viable entities of any sort without creating an eventful history.

Thus, every innovation organization has had to go through its formative years. Having been formed, how shall it operate so that it may produce "useful innovation" and, while so doing, function speedily and efficiently? These are the subjects of Part 2.

The Innovation Sequence

I have found that to produce innovation, it is necessary to go, step by step, through "the innovation sequence."

R&D groups with which I have been associated have used this sequence almost automatically, often not even being aware they were conforming to it. When I explore how others in the same line of work in other companies go about innovation, I find that they too seem to do about the same things in about the same order. If there are differences, they are only in emphasis given to the different steps. Thus, we may conclude that the elements of this sequence are fundamental and universal. There are seven steps in the innovation sequence:

1. The idea.
2. The innovation concept report (ICR).

3. The feasibility model (FM).
4. The engineering, or functional, model (EM).
5. The visual model (VM), or mock-up.
6. The prototype (PT).
7. The pilot production unit (PPU).

Production and exploitation in the marketplace follow the seven steps. They are not covered in this book because by then innovation is over.

Theme and Variations

While this list of the seven steps is called a sequence and in fact looks like one, it should not be considered strictly linear. A VM, for example, could well precede an EM. And there is generally more than a single version of anything. In fact, it is in the nature of the development process to be iterative. Thus there may be a series of EMs, each more refined and sophisticated, and more effective in performing the required function, than the model that preceded it. In such a case, it is convenient to label each version as it appears: EM-1, EM-2, and so on.

This list is a framework on which to construct change. A musician might call it theme and variations. As product or process development advances, it may become apparent that the original concept was not quite right, that a partially or wholly new one must be constructed. Should that happen, the sequence must loop back on itself, back to the ICR step to start again; but it is rare, in that case, that the model development work has been wasted. With modest modifications (FM-2, FM-3 or EM-2, EM-3) the early versions will be generally useful in implementing the new modifications of the concept.

Another roadblock to linear progress is the (fascinating) likelihood that unexpected creative perceptions will pop up. These are fallouts. To continue our musical analogy, they might become more than mere variations on our original tune; they might cause us to sing another song altogether. But, one way or another, they must be dealt with; they cannot be ignored.

When fallout perceptions appear that address a need and a market that was not originally intended, a decision has to be made. Should a change of direction be implemented, or should a separate

parallel project—following its own separate innovation sequence—
be established? Should the new concept be put on the shelf to be
dealt with later? Or should it be forgotten altogether? These are
strategic decisions to be made by the executive office. Never disregard the fallout. If you can't use an unexpected creation right
now, maybe some day you can sell or license it to others.

All this does not change the fact that fallouts are diversions.
The way to proceed is to get back on the track, back to the original
innovation sequence for the original purpose. Let us now proceed
to detailed discussion of each of these steps in the innovation
process:

Step 1. The Idea

In the beginning there is the idea. Someone gets it. Anyone. It
may come from the field; it may come from management. It may
come from the press or the literature or even the competition. It
may come from the sales force or from the product planners. It
may occur to the engineering staff or to the manufacturing departments. Or it may have its genesis in the innovation department.
It may even come from the "suggestion box" (don't forget those).

There are always more ideas surfacing than we can use. The
challenge is to give each its deserved level of consideration and to
select those that have the best technical and market prognoses as
well as the best fit with company strategy. What about the other
ideas? We have no choice but to "file" them.

As if these ideas aren't enough, we can generate more by
forcing them into existence out of the innermost recesses of our
minds. There are techniques for doing this, usually promoted by
professionals with backgrounds in psychology. What they promul-
gate is generally sound and the techniques work. But it's hard to
be enthusiastic about ways to have new ideas. In most businesses,
ideas come easy—often too easy. Choosing among them and implementing them are what is hard.

Step 2. The Innovation Concept Report (ICR)

Once the idea—the product or process or system opportunity—is
identified, the research and development process (the remaining

six steps) can get under way. While much of the creativity of the process takes place in conception, there is a regimen, a discipline of conception, that includes attempting to foresee all its consequences, and it should be conformed to. The concept must be formalized in a written document, the "innovation concept report." For an example, see Appendix 1. Before proceeding to describe it, I wish to acknowledge that its form and content are the creation of Mr. Wes Teich, for many years the chief engineer of Raytheon's New Products Center, and my successor as its director. What follows is a distillation of many trial-and-error variations that he experimented with over the years. It works, as evidenced by dozens of new products now in the marketplace that started out as ICRs. The innovation concept report consists of discussions of the following:

1. The idea.
2. Constraints within which the idea must operate.
3. The concept.
4. Manufacturing procedures.
5. Market prospects.
6. Experimental program.

Each of these topics is treated in the following text along with a final comment about the ongoing revision process that renders this document an iterative one.

Statement of the Idea: The Introduction

The idea takes on the qualities of a wish and can usually be expressed in several short sentences. The idea has little meaning without context; there must be a statement defining the present state of affairs—which implementation of the idea will one day change. These two statements, what there is now and what the product's impact will be, constitute the introduction.

Constraints Within Which the Idea Must Operate

The list of limiting factors can be a long one indeed; it includes price, size, technique of manufacture, safety, reliability, appearance, and so on. Here we must address an interesting philosophical issue:

Does early identification of imposed limits to which an innovation must conform throttle creativity? Yes and no. In fact, innovators must be of two minds.

There is always a tradeoff. The more an innovator is confined and channeled, the less innovatively he or she performs. It is better for the innovator to start off in unfettered fashion, as though there were no constraints, and then allow the constraints to lead his or her thinking, step by step, back to reality. Yet, even at the beginning, one should always be aware of the limits within which the new product, process, or system should operate.

Limitations represented by imposed constraints are not always bad. Sometimes they even suggest an unexpected way to success. After a while, a constraint ceases to be an inhibition and becomes just one more creative challenge.

One more thing about constraints: They must never be slavishly and automatically accepted. Sometimes they are poorly founded. They may be imposed by unthinking authority figures who do not realize the massive consequences of each requirement to which the new product must conform. The danger is that a throwaway line by a boss to his disciple may take on the aura of Scripture. There is no better way to add a year to product development than by constraining too much.

The innovator assigned to the project should question the validity of dubious constraints. Challenging constraints is part of innovation, and the sponsor of the innovation, who may also be its godfather, should not resent such challenges. Rather, he or she should appreciate them because they mean that wrong and costly· actions may thereby be avoided. By the same token, accepting constraints that have withstood challenge is something that innovators must do. Such acceptance is also part of the innovating process. Consider the following real-life example of an unchallenged constraint.

I once lost a year in a new product development program because the product line manager for whom the work was being done said the product would never sell if it exceeded 38 inches in width. "It has to fit into a 39-inch slot," he said. What acrobatics, what inventiveness we had to provide to meet that requirement. And we succeeded. We had to "bend" and tilt the mechanism and make it work against gravity; indeed, we made an invention, a good one—just so it would fit into that restricted space. When we were done, we discovered that there was nothing sacred about that 38 inches! The customer would have been perfectly content with 40 inches, 50 inches! We had wasted a year and a few hundred thousand dollars, all because I had not challenged the validity of that constraint. It could have turned out that the original dimensional limitation was right. Then the work would have been justified. But the truth was not known because the constraint had not been challenged. My problem was that I did not challenge that 38-inch constraint—and I still feel guilty.

I can't tell you how much to allow yourself to be inhibited by the constraints. It is a decision based on experience and wisdom. (Yours, not mine.)

(One more comment about constraints deserves at least a single pair of parentheses: Not all of them can be conquered. Then they become more than inhibitions, they become prohibitions—and that might even kill the project. But let us not get too distressed. Even the greatest hitter does not bat 1.000.)

What appear in the ICR are the agreed-upon constraints that have survived the challenges. The constraints having been identified, one is ready to formulate the innovation concept.

The Concept

In conceiving an innovation, we formulate a *way* to convert the idea to reality. An explanation of that must appear in the innovation concept report. Indeed, it *is* the concept.

Accomplishing the transformation from idea to reality could involve mere ingenuity, the clever putting together of already available facts and parts, or might require creativity worthy of a Nobel Prize. Somewhere within that range is invention. For swift innovation leading to rapid new product introduction, it is desirable to avoid invention and to lean rather in the direction of ingenuity. If ingenious utilization of elements that are readily at hand will result in success, why venture into the unknown—glamorous though the unknown may seem? Why journey down a complex route when a direct and simple one will bring us to our destination? In addition, the concept should be compatible with the constraints.

All this—or at least much of it—becomes evident during the act of writing down the design concept.

Manufacturing Procedures

Similar issues are revealed in an analysis, even at this early stage, of how the new product will be produced in a factory or the new process installed in a production line.

How can an innovator, who doesn't know about manufacturing, produce an authoritative statement about production procedures? By trying. It is wrong to pigeonhole people and say this person can only be expected to know about A and not B. After all, what is being innovated partakes of both A and B. So the innovator must learn about manufacturing. There are people in his or her own department from whom to enlist aid, such as the transfer specialists described in Chapter 2. And there is nothing to prevent a visit to manufacturing departments in the company, including those that some day must accept this new product if the innovation process succeeds.

The act of describing proposed manufacturing procedures, tooling, and related costs may reveal otherwise unknown and unpleasant difficulties. These comprise just another category of constraints to be challenged or to be conquered by a creative act. Again, constraints are not to be viewed as prohibitions. They are challenges, and their existence in the production area is first recognized in the generation of the ICR.

Market Prospects

It is a common belief that innovators know and care nothing about the marketplace, or customers, or what will sell. While that may at times unfortunately be true, such ignorance and insensitivity is not tolerable or even acceptable. A good innovator must understand not only the technical aspects of a new product, but also how it will interact with those who will ultimately buy and use it. If no one buys or uses an innovation—even a brilliant one—it is a failure, a way to waste time and money. That is certainly not efficient.

The ICR includes a section on projected market prospects of the new product being conceived. In order to write intelligently about this subject, the innovator must proceed as he or she did when writing about manufacturing. The ICR writer must cultivate marketers, read the literature, go to trade shows, and venture into stores where similar products are sold so as to see public reactions. Does this mean getting the inventor out of the lab and into the cruel world of business? You bet it does. The resulting inventions will be the better for it.

Innovators are creative people. There are creative challenges in market thinking as well as in technical thinking. Perhaps some interesting new insights will surface during this exercise that a sales or marketing person will find useful, coming as they will from this fresh point of view. But even if no one uses the market-oriented conclusions the innovator comes up with, the investigation itself will add to the innovator's grasp of reality as it relates to the innovation goal. And an infusion of reality should be very welcome at this point, because the innovation doesn't exist yet, and has therefore no other reality at all. In the end, the innovator can propose a market niche for the new product and can speculate on a plan for channels to the marketplace. The speculation should go on to include unit price, sales volume growth with time, market share, competitors displaced, and margin projections.

Experimental Program

The time approaches to conduct experiments, to build models. On the basis of the exercise of generating the first five sections of this document, the program leader can now formulate the skeleton of a wise experimental sequence.

There is a single philosophical principle that should dominate the generation of a sequence of experimental actions: *Address the most uncertain element first.* People often fall into the trap of addressing sure things first and confirming what they already know, just because sure things are more likely to give predictable answers. It's also tempting to discuss pet topics, which are pleasant and corroborate favorite biases. Don't do those things first. Rather, analyze the innovation challenge and determine what is really unknown and open to question and that is, at the same time, going to be a key to success or failure. Then identify the next most unsure element and the next and the next. List them, and then proceed to do them (see Step 3) in that order, all the time building increasing levels of certainty. How better to achieve efficiency in carrying out the innovation process?

The name for the principle advocated here is "critical path." It sets all priorities and sequences. Chapter 5 describes the technique for presenting the critical path on a PERT chart, a useful mechanism for keeping on track.

Revising

The innovator is not finished with the report even months after the appearance of its first version, when the project has proceeded far into the next steps of the innovation sequence— even after operating engineering models or even prototypes have already been developed. Newly discovered knowledge may dictate new approaches. This may be the time to loop back and start some aspect of the project again. Indeed, that might be the most efficient thing to do. The first step in such a case is to rewrite at least a portion of the report (you may be up to ICR-7 by now).

The point is, the innovation concept and the report that describes it are, by their nature, dynamic. Because the innovator is walking where no one has trod before, it is inevitable that some features of the concept will change during the course of a new product or process development.

The Value of the Innovation Concept Report

The forced thinking necessary to generate an ICR is the report's greatest value. It means that random and poorly conceived false starts at the lab bench have been avoided. That's why we give so much attention to creating this document, because thinking before taking action always results in swifter and less expensive programs.

In addition to functioning as a foundation on which all the forthcoming steps of the innovation process are built, the report has another purpose: documentation. It is an exemplary mechanism for communication. When a copy is handed to a company client for whom the work will be done, it tells the client in detail what the innovation is. And it does this in writing, on the record. There is thus little chance for confusion and misunderstanding, as would be the case in verbal descriptions.

Furthermore, the ICR saves much future writing on the part of the innovators. Selected paragraphs, lifted through the magic of the word processor and cunningly pieced together, become the text of patent disclosures or of monthly or quarterly progress reports.

Step 3. The Feasibility Model (FM)

This is the most inexpensive and most exhilarating part of innovation. It is inexpensive because usually it takes very little effort to validate the correctness or incorrectness of the basic nugget of a concept. And that is the point: One must discipline oneself to address that nugget first.

Keep in mind that the "nugget" is not a single monolithic thing. Innovation is rarely that simple. It can usually be subdivided into a series of elements that, as pointed out in the preceding section, should be addressed in order of increasing certainty, with the most uncertain element first.

It is in the course of carrying out feasibility experiments that the popular image of the chewing gum and baling wire inventor are most frequently seen. Nevertheless, the feasibility of the approach may emerge with good credibility from crude experiments at this stage.

These experiments are exhilarating because they are usually successful. If the innovation concept has been well thought out and if the correct priorities of what is most uncertain have been identified, then the first or second experiment usually "works."

I consider feasibility experiments to be analogous to investing seed money. It doesn't cost much to plant a seed. It's growing a good crop that uses up money. Successful feasibility experiments could consume less than 5 percent of the innovation dollar investment—and produce 95 percent of the invention.

The steps that follow, the remaining four of this sequence, are far more elaborate in nature and will easily use up the bulk of the innovation program budget. Also, these next four steps are, by nature, grubbier and duller. Blessed are those who spend all their time conceiving and delivering first embodiments (performing the first three steps of our list of seven). These creative people are generally not asked to (and generally are not good at) the other four more dreary steps; so their lives are filled with pleasure and, occasionally, ecstasy (nice work if you can get it).

Step 4. The Engineering, or Functional, Model (EM)

The goal of Step 4 is to develop a pragmatic embodiment of the concept. Just as Step 3 demonstrated the feasibility of the concept, showing that it *could* work, this step will *make* it work. And that is how far it will go. It will not polish that embodiment beyond making it testify, by reason of showing how well it functions, that it is ready to serve as a basis for investing in the next steps of the development, often called by the all-encompassing term, "productizing" (for which please refer to Steps 5, 6, and 7 following).

The goal of Step 4 is limited, but that does not mean it is a small goal. In fact, it is in the development of engineering models that the largest amount of innovation (remember, the term means implementation of the idea) takes place.

This embodiment is what we call the EM, the engineering model. It is sometimes a misnomer, as when the term is used to designate a model achieved without recourse to engineering, or indeed to any technical action at all. It is more accurate to call it a functional model, but then it would have been an FM, and I have already used those letters for the feasibility model. So let us compromise on EM.

Functional models are rarely exactly what we encounter in our normal day-to-day activities. By the time we run across the product or process or system, it has ceased to be an innovation. It may be new, but it is already much permutated from the early lab version. As with an adult man, by the time we meet him his voice has deepened and his beard has sprouted; he little resembles the boy he was when his speech was soprano and his cheek was pink and smooth—when he was the early engineering model.

EM-1 Through EM-4 and Beyond . . .

In pursuing the innovation process, we normally go through a series of models, each advanced in features and refinement over the preceding one. I suppose it is possible for a single engineering model to be enough to serve as a basis for going on to the production phases of the innovation program. But I have never seen that happen. Unless you count Adam.

Adam was the only model—EM-1. There was never a need for an EM-2. But when man creates first models, Frankenstein is a better example. The monster truly conformed to what we encounter in early engineering models. In the first place, he was too big. Eight feet! And that stench would never do. What about those bolts sticking out of his temples? Talk about poor workmanship. Also, who would ever hire a person with "rolling bloodshot eyes and yellow features so distorted and loathsome that no one can look upon them for an instant without a scream of terror."

His innovator, Dr. Frankenstein, who headed a small skunk works team, primary among whom was his technician, Igor, was so unnerved that he died of exhaustion and remorse. But had he lived and persevered, he would have constructed his next and much improved model, EM-2, and then EM-3 through EM-8, by which time I am sure we would have found the monster acceptable, if not lovable.

And by then, there would have been good reason for Dr. Frankenstein to seek a venture capital firm to finance tooling up. In no time everyone would have become rich. But I am getting ahead of myself. Tooling won't be discussed until Step 6.

Before a satisfactory engineering model appears, it is common to have had to develop iteration after iteration of it—a half dozen or so is usual—each one an improvement over the one before it. Why so many? Because so many pragmatic criteria have to be satisfied that it is not easy to achieve the final practical version the first time around. We called them "goals" and "constraints" when we wrote the innovation concept report. They all have to be satisfied. And we haven't yet mentioned all the setbacks common in experimentation—they have to be resolved too.

Teamwork: The Model Developer

The act of embodying a concept as a series of EMs can be an emotional one for its conceiver. That is because he or she may have to be phased out of the program to some extent while people with other skills are phased in and, in many instances, take over.

That is why the innovation organization is organized as a multi-faceted group, because someone else might do certain tasks better.

Consider the popular notion of the lone inventor. He works by himself in his unheated garret, year after year, living on potato skins. His once-jet-black wavy hair goes gray, his once-erect body begins to stoop. Yet he goes doggedly on, surrounded by test tubes and gurgling distillation retorts. Then, one day, he comes to the last possible experiment—and it works! "Eureka!" he cries to his patient and adoring wife, "I have it! We're going to be rich!" They clinch. The End. No wonder it took so long. He had no one to turn to to take over the embodiment of his concept, and he happened to be a rotten embodier. Little did he know that the reason for all those years of work was that he had used inferior materials and an ineffective design for the valves connecting the tubes to the retorts. I don't call that efficiency in the pursuit of innovation.

The time has come for someone in the innovation group to take over who has skills in making models that closely resemble production versions. Remember Chapter 2, on staffing? In setting up a R&D unit, we purposely recruit engineers and technicians who are specialists in particular areas. Now we need a "transfer group" specialist.

Transfer specialists contribute more than just different skills from what new product conceivers and feasibility provers possess. They have different priorities. Early-stage innovators care most that their innovation works, that it shows performance beyond any achieved in the world to date. Those who will convey the invention to the factory floor also are enthralled by the fact that it performs as touted; but for them, performance ranks fifth in a list of priorities ordered as follows:

1. *Safety*—What good is creativity if it results in damage to people?
2. *Reliability*—What good is creativity if it results in failure in the field?
3. *Reasonable cost-to-produce goals.*
4. *Attractiveness in the marketplace.*
5. *Remarkable performance*—To a level well beyond the state of the art, so as to outstrip all competition.

Interestingly, these priorities match those of the clients. So who better to assume responsibility for the transfer process to clients than the transfer group? Sharing priorities facilitates the transfer process. To be efficient and effective, the transfer process must start very early, no later than the EM step. Each of our steps is part of the progression to transfer—at least transfer specialists see it that way. They hover over all the steps of the innovation activity, propelled by their own initiative, persistently and patiently asking mundane questions, like what material and assembly process to use. They also instruct the technicians, who will do the actual assembly. These instructions are not scrawls on the back of an envelope (which was the way it was done up to this point); rather, a drafter generates a drawing, complete with dimensions and dimensional tolerances. While it is far from the final production drawing, it is nevertheless the first formal one. Thus we proceed into formality, which will be needed later when product transfer occurs. Most conceivers (generalists and specialists both) would not have made a drawing at this point.

What has been achieved? The first pragmatic functioning embodiment, EM-1, has been made in professional fashion, which means that when it performs, that performance will be credible and the information it provides will be reproducible. The same holds for the EMs that follow. And if you thought that EM-1 was good, wait till you see EM-5. . . .

Efficient innovation is never a one-person job. It results from well-managed teamwork. But there is nothing unusual about that statement. Efficient anything results from well-managed teamwork. So innovation is like everything else we encounter in business. It is a management challenge.

A new participant has made an entrance, injecting both unique skills and a fresh point of view. And the impact on the project is more than adding one more body. It has been my experience that in such cases 1 + 1 always equals more than 2. The figure 2.7 is more likely.

When new people enter the act, they cannot function without instruction; and when such people are instructed, they have no choice but to "take notes." This means that the level of documentation goes up—and into the records, from where we can dredge it up a decade later in order to prevail in a patent suit.

Who is the instructor? The original conceiver, of course—functioning as a team member.

When the EM is completed and functioning, new people who have constructed it need data to determine whether it is working. The conceiver knows even before the "on" button is pressed that it is going to work. So, he reasons, why bother with taking data, which can be so boring to do? New people in the act are often best for data taking.

Is the conceiver now out of it, shoved aside, told that he or she has done the job and should turn all attention to the next conception? No way. The conceiver is still the ultimate authority and must remain an important member of the team, with continuing creative participation in the further growth of the creation.

The Client as a Team Member

Very soon after the establishment of the relationship between conceiver and model developer, along comes someone else who wants to get into the family too: the company client.

And we had better take him in. The sooner the better. It's nice if he wants to join. Sometimes he is reluctant at first and needs some persuading, but in the end that innovation will be the *client's*, no one else's. It will contribute to his profits and growth— or his losses and decline. Yes, the client had better get involved, to the point of using his staff to exert strong influence. Which staff people? Everybody who will eventually be involved with the innovation when it becomes the client's property. That includes:

The client's manufacturing engineers. They will examine EM-1 and point out that a different material or a different shape will make the new product easier to manufacture on existing equipment. Then EM-2 is designed to incorporate that suggestion.

The value engineers. They will have a similar input with regard to a purchased part. "Can you use this similar device?" they might ask. "It will cost one-third as much as the one you are designing in and it will perform about the same." The new part goes into EM-2.

The sales manager. He or she critiques the human interface of the new clothes dryer, for example, and points out that little ladies with big bosoms and short arms won't be able to reach in comfortably for that last sock, and they make up 11 percent of potential customers. Better redesign that door and shorten the chamber for EM-3.

The marketers. They tell of a new Japanese product (the news is hot out of the international rumor mill) that will do everything our new product will, but will make less noise and will operate at a faster rate. That means that a new invention is required. "Say, Joe," says the project leader, "will you please make that invention by this time next month, and show Harry how to get it into EM-4."

The manager of quality assurance. "Is it safe?" he asks. We all remember too well the crash of the Challenger. Our astronauts died because gasket material lost its flexibility at low temperatures. With sad hindsight we comment that an extra EM or two for that rocket innovation would have been desirable. Better make sure that the marginal feature we have tolerated through the first four models is designed out of EM-5.

The director of reliability. He or she wants to know if the product is *inherently* reliable. What we don't need is a product with an Achilles' heel. It takes only a few service calls within the warranty period to wipe out the profit margins.

Company counsel and directors of patents and licensing. They will have something to say about legal complications, and their pronouncements may require that the innovation go back to the drawing board rather than forward to the production floors.

The CEO. This important person has an opinion too. "Oh, no. Seven million dollars for tooling, you say? Forget it. I've got my tooling money all allocated for next year." This is the time to meet that challenge. Redesign EM-6 so that the resulting new product can be made on existing tooling.

Shoot the Engineer

The time comes when we have to do this. The conceiver and his new-found buddy, the iterative model developer from the transfer group, have ideas enough for 20 more EMs. But after a reasonable number of EMs, the end has to come. Either the product will be viable or it will not; we should know by now. Who makes the judgment? We (the managers), after careful consideration of all the facts, make it. That means we can go on to the next steps.

Step 5. The Visual Model (VM), or Mock-up

Implied by the completion of the engineering model step is the beginning of the process of transferring it to the client. More and more from here on the innovation assumes the ways and personality of the client.

The first thing clients want to know is, "What will it look like?" If they don't like the appearance, they may want to change their mind about accepting the innovation, but if they think it looks great, then they can't wait till it's theirs, all theirs. The best way to show a client—and the innovators too—what something new is going to look like is to build a visual model. And it costs far less to build something out of foamboard than to construct a functional EM.

Two Ways to Visualize a New Product: Appearance and Simulation of Function

Every innovation organization should have the capability to build attractive non-operating models. The function of such models is not only to show a client what the final product's visual impression might be, but also to sell him or her on it.

Figure 4-1 illustrates a visual model we made at Raytheon's New Products Center of a control panel for use by radiological technicians in a hospital x-ray department. We knew that it had to have an elegant, classy look, so we engaged the services of a design firm to help conceive its form, color, and so on. But the model was more than just a "good looker." When completed, the model simulated a technical advance in computer control, allowing for minimization of patient exposure to x-rays. The final product would make the technician's job easier because certain calculations would be automatically provided as a response to keyboarded information about a patient's size and the particular bone or organ to be diagnosed. But all the model did was to simulate function— without functioning.

The model so impressed our company client that it was shown at that year's RSNA (Radiological Society of North America) conference, an expression of faith by the client that it would be ready for sale later that year.

Figure 4-1.   Visual model of X-ray control panel.

Photo courtesy of Raytheon Company

Impact of a Visual Model on Innovators

Beyond providing insight into considerations of aesthetics and human engineering, the visual model also has a pragmatic value for the innovators themselves. Even the best of visualizers and imaginers are surprised when confronted with the real thing or a simulation of it. "I didn't know it was going to look like that," they always say. "It's bigger [or smaller] than I expected it to be." Or, "Look at how that edge projects over the handle. That will interfere with changing the focus setting. We have to change that." And so on. . . .

Visualizing the Intangible

It is easy to understand a visual model of a tangible new product, but what about an intangible one? How does one make a visual model of a product that has no concreteness? It is hard to do, because *visual* means perceptible to the eye. Such a class of product might include, for example, innovative procedures for a bank or an insurance company or a mailing service. The answer is that there is always something that can be handsomely mocked up, if only a sheaf of papers or a floppy-disk readout. It will simulate in some way a concept that has just undergone a series of similarly intangible EM embodiments. It can be done.

Visualizing Technology

The same holds for newly developed technology. A new assembly machine can be mocked up, as can a new form or structural subassembly. A new material can be presented in terms of simulating its resistance to simulated imposed stresses, both mechanical and chemical. How it interacts with the environment can be demonstrated even before it is completely developed.

The most tangible result of new technology development is the new processing line that may be placed within a newly constructed plant. Now things get easier. Enlist the architect, or at least his model-maker. Architects engaged in major programs know that formal drawings and even perspective sketches are never enough. They always top these off—triumphantly—with a scaled three-dimensional model that incorporates little scaled equipment run by little scaled people. Now the boss will understand what the company is buying.

Appearance as an Innovation Goal—It Qualifies

From what has been said, it would seem that investment in visual models is justified because they enhance the impact of an innovation by presenting a good appearance. That's nice, but compared with the other world-shaking creations, it seems rather trivial. Is the visual impact of an innovation trivial? Never. In some industries it is less important than in others. But where it counts, it deserves much attention, especially by the innovation group. Indeed, when one thinks about it, maybe experiments with appearance are what certain kinds of innovators can do better than anyone, even though they might then be called "designers."

I recall going to a home-builders convention at the Astrodome in Houston a few years ago. NAHB, the National Association of Home Builders, with more than 120,000 builder members, is one of the most prodigious of our country's trade associations. To indicate what a large show that was, the Astrodome itself could hold only about one-fourth of the exhibits, the remainder being housed in the large, adjacent livestock hall. "What's new?" I asked the instant I arrived, not even waiting to check into my room or to seek refreshment to calm my nerves after my long and harrowing flight from Boston. The answer came back in one word: "Almond!"

I expected innovation, by which I meant *innovation*. Why had I come, if not to see whether some rival company might have invented a new way to heat a home? Perhaps someone would show an advanced system to use solar energy, making it at last practical and cost-effective. Or possibly a new kind of insulation twice as good as glass wool and half its price was being announced (I had heard a rumor). No, none of that. What was considered new that year—the only thing—was that home appliances had taken on a new color. Something between the lightest of beige and the darkest of cream—a kind of dark white. If your refrigerators and gas ranges were not offered in almond, you could kiss your sales for the coming year good-bye.

That set me thinking. Was the change to almond an innovation? Was the anonymous instigator of that change at GE or Whirlpool or Magic Chef, wherever, a conceiver? Had my innovation group served our company client poorly because we had not proposed almond first? Had that new choice of color outsmarted the Japanese, who resolutely stuck by their deep orange? I noted to myself that whether the introduction of almond is an innovation or not, I would be proud to have any innovation of mine have that sort of impact, not only on the show that day, but on American culture and lifestyle.

The point is, a visual model will cause us to think about the appearance of our innovation and how it feels to handle and to touch and to carry and to operate. It deserves careful attention and, should the stakes be high enough, a company will employ a design group.

Interchangeability of Steps

The creation of a visual model usually occurs as Step 5 in the innovation process, but not always. Sometimes it is best to build a VM before the first EM is designed because confrontation with a visual model will significantly modify the course taken in the EM development process. Circumstances dictate. But, in any case, it is wrong not to have created a VM before going on to develop the prototype.

Step 6. The Prototype (PT)

The *American Heritage Dictionary* defines a prototype as "an original type, form, or instance that serves as a model on which later stages are based or judged." That is my definition too. But I would point out that it does not define the results of our steps 4 and 5. EMs and VMs do not qualify as prototypes; they are *precursors* to the prototype.

It is true that the final visual model will probably be close to what the prototype might look like, but not necessarily. What appears in catalogues, announcements, and advertisements will be a variation on, an extension of, that VM—and the prototype will certainly be a variation and extension of the final EM.

The prototype has to be the creation of the client (although with innovation organization involvement), just as those final EMs and VMs are the creation of the innovation department (with client involvement). This is another way of saying that by the time we get to the PT step, we are already deep into transition from the innovation organization to the client organization. This is a process with many ramifications, some of which we have already treated. It deserves a section for itself, with which this chapter concludes. When we get to Step 6, the client takes over. Either (1) a new product, process, or system will be imposed into an existing facility, production line, or procedure, or (2) the prototype will be so different from what is currently being made that it will require a new facility, production line, or procedure to accommodate it. In fact, it may be a new venture—and that certainly will demand a new and separate location. In either case, the innovation must be made to "accommodate" to its new home.

If clients are to adopt a newly spawned waif, don't expect the foundling to be left very long in the scruffy swaddlings and dowdy basket that was deposited on the doorstep. "He's one of us now," said the kind folk who took in Oliver Twist. "For God's sake, get him out those rags and make him presentable." Implied in that statement was the conviction that from here on Oliver would not only look upper-middle-class, he would also begin to speak more grammatically and to wash regularly. In short, he would become so acceptable in every way that he could be taken anywhere without embarrassment.

For a business confronted with committing to an innovation, the task is the same: Make it acceptable in every way. The first step toward achieving that (the sixth of our sequence) is for the new owner to build the model on which all later stages are to be based and judged, the prototype.

Developing the Prototype: An Act of Innovation

When clients undertake to build a prototype, they are performing a task the essential nature of which is innovation. Did you think the innovation phase was over when the innovation organization gave over the fruit of its loins? You were wrong. What is over is only the first burst of innovation, admittedly the most exciting part and certainly the least expensive part. Now we must enter the more gritty nuts-and-bolts stage of innovation. But it remains innovation. Good adjustment to the real world is not going to be easy. To do it right and to do it best still requires creation, invention, and ingenuity.

Here is another illustrative episode from my own experience. When we delivered our final EM (a ground-breaking combination microwave/self-cleaning electric range) so that the client, Caloric, could proceed with developing the prototype, the manager of manufacturing was obviously dismayed. "What's the matter, Bernie?" I asked.

"You built the door with a right-angle corner. We can't apply a porcelain coating to a right-angle corner," he explained. "Anyone who has ever porcelainized anything knows that it will flake off a right-angle bend." Then he took me on a tour of his plant to show that every door had rounded corners. "There's never been anything but rounded corners in this industry since the Civil War," he muttered.

What did this mean? It could have meant two years of product development down the drain, because without that right-angle, the product didn't work. But Bernie and his crew, the engineer in charge of the porcelain process, in particular, rose to the challenge. They invented a way, a most ingenious original way, to porcelainize that right-angle corner so that the coating would never chip off. It had never been achieved before. If they gave Nobel prizes for porcelainizing, our client would have won for that year.

Furthermore, no one in my innovation organization could have achieved this. It required a lifelong practitioner of the porcelainizing art. People like that do not inhabit innovation organizations devoted to new product development. They live in factories.

So the new way to porcelainize was first used on—guess what?—the prototype, along with a dozen other innovative structures or practices that had never been thought of "back in the lab." But they were necessary. Had they not been incorporated, the new product would have had the following failings:

- It would have cost too much.
- It would have looked ridiculous.
- It would have required an operator with a college degree in computer science.
- It would have required a service call after having been turned on just a half-dozen times.
- It would have failed to meet codes.

Phasing Out the Innovation Organization's Involvement

Although in the prototype step the innovation group that spawned the new creature is being phased out, it is still in the act. It has to be. In fact, the hours given by that group may exceed any time allotment given to date, as innovators often must make frequent trips to wherever the client has chosen to produce the new item (usually the other side of the country). What has changed is the name of the person in charge.

Ingredients of a Successful Prototype

If it is successful, a prototype consists of far more than the physical item itself. In fact, that's the smallest part. After it is operated and shown to function as required, and after data is taken to record its performance, a complete set of characterizing documents must be generated by the client. These will typically include:

- Drawings, if the product is of a sort as to be so specified, or their equivalent.
- Tooling specifications or their equivalent.
- Assembly process specifications.
- Statements of conformity to codes.
- Quality assurance specifications.
- Vendor list.
- Cost breakdown.

These will serve as the basis for proceeding to the next step, the pilot run, and they will ultimately evolve into the specification for going into production.

Step 7. The Pilot Production Unit (PPU)

The prototype is the model on which to build the next functional units, the pilot run; the pilot run is the final model on which to base production. Responsibility for it is the province of the business that has accepted the innovation, the client. The innovation organization watches from afar, with interest and with certain privileges of perusing the results, but as an outsider.

The product, called here a "pilot production unit," is meant to be a model for production, maybe even for mass production. By the time the pilot run is complete, most tools have been committed to—although the most expensive of them might be of a temporary nature, to have on hand "just in case." In case of what? In case a change has to be made at the last moment, of course.

By now, millions of dollars may have been spent. We are in deep, but if we have done it right, we're not in over our heads. Most of the spending has been by the client, not the innovation organization. Figure 4-2 shows schematically how the scale of spending changes and grows as the innovation moves through the seven steps of the innovation process and as it makes its transition from the laboratory of its birth to its final home in the factory or equivalent. Total spending rate increases with each step until we reach the VM. Then the innovation organization begins to phase out, and its spending rate drops drastically while that of the receiving organization zooms.

The number of units that will make up the run depends on the nature of the innovation. There must be enough units in the run to give the product credibility in an atmosphere of strangers—its customers. Indeed, it is at this juncture that products can be evaluated by focus groups and even sold to a test market. The pilot run provides grist for field tests, for safety tests, for reliability tests, for customer satisfaction tests, for everything we can think of.

Where is the pilot run run? It depends. As discussed in Chapter 3, some innovation organizations own their own piloting plant. Then the innovation organization holds off the client a bit longer and retains responsibility longer. But in most cases, especially where a product rather than a process has been developed, the client is the one that sets up the pilot line—alongside the regular production line.

The PPU is the last step in the innovative process. If it is OK, we know we have done it and we commit the innovation to production.

Some Final Reflections on Transfer

Transfer is an innocuous word, but it can have stark implications. It can mean much more than merely a new location for something. It can set intense personal feelings in motion, especially when the creator of the item remembers guiding it into being from nothing. Transfer means someone is going to be deprived of something with which he or she has become heavily identified; it means someone else—some interloper—will acquire that thing and take it away.

Just to complicate things, the receiver of this wonderful creation may not want it. He may have a secret creation all his own that he loves better; taking this new one may mean that his precious child will have to be abandoned. It helps for those with responsibility

Figure 4-2. Comparative spending rates for the seven steps of the innovation process.

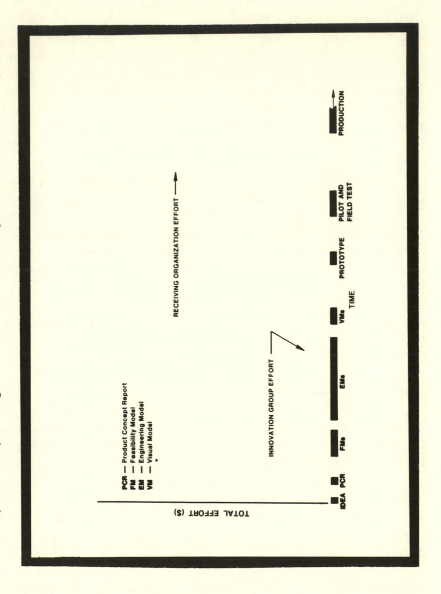

for the transfer process to make a conscious effort to be sensitive to all the personalities participating in the transfer process and their motivations. The transfer group must understand that the attitudes of both the givers and the receivers can subvert the transfer process so severely that the whole innovation program could die.

Let us examine what the act of transfer involves for both the givers-up and the receivers.

Transfer Within the Innovation Organization

The first task of transferring takes place well before transfer to the client and happens within the innovation organization itself. With Step 4, the engineering models, the role of the conceivers is diminished. At this point, the transfer specialists literally take over. It is they who will develop the later models of EMs, a process that can be fraught with difficulty.

There has to be teamwork, enforced if necessary, between transfer specialists and conceivers as ever more mature models of EMs are fabricated. The innovators who ran the project during Steps 1 through 3 remain the savants; there's no way to replace them in that function, but now they are observing, evaluating, interpreting, and suggesting rather than experimenting.

By the time EM-4 or EM-5 emerges, looking much slicker than the conceivers would ever have made it, the transfer group is inclined to say to those biological parents, "Thanks a lot, fellows; but this is my kid now. I'll be back to you if I have a problem. Otherwise, watch my smoke as I take it out of here and into its new home in our plant in Nebraska." This in itself can be a wrenching experience for the originators in the innovation center (which, by the way, is in New Hampshire).

The Receivers Enter the Act

When the internal transfer phase is completed, the transfer group must now undertake to educate the client in the history of the innovation, how it works and how it might be fabricated. After that, the group must physically convey the innovation to the client's premises, making sure first that it survives and then that it is launched into a state of viability.

The Historical Documents

The best way to initiate the transfer process is to ensure that every relevant document ever generated by the innovation organization, from the innovation concept report in its final version to all the fabrication and test data, finds its way into the hands of the client's innovation team and is *really* understood by them. If this is done well, the client will grasp the historical events that shaped the evolution of the innovation—what was tried, what worked well, what failed, what changes of direction were required.

Without a knowledge of previous history, it is inevitable that the new owners of the product would divert time and money to experiment on approaches that have already been investigated. (They're creative too, you see.) Not that they should be prohibited from such experiments, but they should know that the idea was tried at least once before.

The Physical Contacts: People/Thing and People/People

Once the documents have been digested, it is good for the baton receivers in this relay race to "experience" what they have absorbed intellectually from the documents. The ideal way to do this is for the client's new team to live at the innovation facility for as long as it takes. It need not be so long as to disrupt their lives. If they are well qualified, a week or so is generally sufficient, but a single day is never enough.

Give them hands-on experience: Let them press all the buttons and observe all the performance foibles for themselves. Let them collect data. Then let them engage in long conversations with the conceivers of the new product, and with everyone else who ever worked on it, including the nonprofessionals.

All these different kinds of people may even end up liking each other. But whether they do or not, if the product is worth exploiting, they have no choice but to respect each other and, if all information is given with nothing withheld, to trust each other. But most of all, what is thus achieved is the establishment of a basis of mutual understanding, in detail, of the innovation being transferred.

Sending the First Model to the Client

With understanding established, the time has come for actual shipment of the best physical embodiments, the final EM and VM, to their future owner, the client. This phase also includes setting it up on site and evaluating it.

Now clients test it on their premises and under their ground rules, and accept it. Or do they? Don't count those chickens just yet. . . .

The client's engineering staff (or its equivalent) and the newly assigned product manager and market specialist have to live with that engineering (or functional) model for a few weeks or months before all of them clasp it to their respective bosoms. (All the more reason to have involved them in the early planning and in the preceding "understanding" phase.) And even though the plan is for the innovation to go into production this year, it requires very few negative inputs at this point to cause those plans to change.

There is always a villain who pours cold water on a project, either because the innovation has a basic deficiency that is unexpectedly identified, or because the villain simply doesn't like other people's ideas. NIH is the acronym that describes his pathology, "not invented here."

Even without a villain, and even when the new product is really good, there is always the letdown after the euphoria. People in the transfer group understand this, so they don't let that model go alone. "If you take my model, you must take me too—at least for the first few weeks" is what it comes down to. The first rule of product transfer is to stay with it for as long as necessary until acceptance is complete.

Even with the best of goodwill, clients may draw superficial conclusions on seeing the earliest performance data or the preliminary materials list, or be turned off by erroneous first impressions. Then they say, "Maybe next year." That is why innovation organizations always have large travel budgets. Transfer is an art and it will not happen smoothly, or at all, without close personal attention by those who care. The transfer group cares. Because these people consider any transfer that aborts to be their failure.

Preliminary Manufacturing Specifications
Simultaneously with the shipment of the model to the receiving organization, the transfer group submits preliminary specifications for fabrication of the innovation to the client's manager of manufacture.

The emphasis is on the word *preliminary*. Of course, clients have their own way of making something; they're experts in "making." How can they accept the specifications of mere innovators? Accept is too strong a word, but wise clients will at least study the transfer group's preliminary specifications, if only to use them as points of departure to speed up the process. The point is, those specs are the best thing to start with; in fact, the only thing. And they help the client create preliminary specs, as described in this chapter in the section on Step 6, the prototype.

The transfer group submits a packet that includes its version of:

- Parts drawings.
- Assembly drawings.
- Assembly procedures.
- Aesthetic design drawings.
- Tool designs.
- Recommended vendor list.
- Projected cost estimates.

While the final manufacturing specifications may end up quite different from what has been submitted by the transfer group, frequently many of the preliminary projections are in the right ball park. Recommended tooling designs may actually be adopted, as well as recommended vendors and ways to assemble. And—most remarkable of all—product costs may come in as predicted. All of which simply means that transfer people, with time, can get to be rather good at their job.

Ongoing Liaison

It is natural, at the moment of declared commitment to the innovation, for the client to feel that the time has come for the innovators to fold their tents and disappear. To a certain extent they are right, but "disappear" is too strong an action. "Remain available and somewhat involved" is better. A good transfer group maintains an ongoing, if dwindling, liaison.

If transferrers have a single trait, it is that they are extroverts. They know that liaison is their next task and they must perform it actively, not passively. They become a bridge between individuals who would otherwise not talk to each other, or who, if left to their own ways of communicating, would inadvertently transmit the wrong information with the wrong emphasis. The transfer specialists efforts help minimize these bad practices.

Here is where the client must take some initiative. Unless some people on the client's staff are designated to carry out their side of the transfer process, accompanied by similar attitudes favoring ongoing liaison and with similar motives, the process will proceed poorly. There must be people with matching functions. Givers must have designated receivers—people to give to and to have a back-and-forth continuing liaison with.

The Scale of Effort as It Relates to Transfer

Let us not neglect the relative degrees of effort and resources expended by both sets of participants in the transfer process. As we go through prototype and pilot run and finally to facilitating and staffing for production, costs take on a new dimension, increasing by orders of magnitude over what they were in the innovation organization.

Now we can identify a company hero. It is neither the innovator nor the transferrer (both of whom are from the innovation organization that conceived and implemented the new product idea), exemplary though their contribution may be. The real hero is the bottom-line manager who has committed to the new product—who has accepted and expedited the transfer process into his or her realm of responsibility. Figure 4-2, presented earlier, illustrates the scale of that manager's considerable heroism.

This long chapter shows that the steps to successful innovation add up to a complex and drawn-out procedure. How extraordinary it is, therefore, to contemplate the fact that every product was once a new product, and that every business was once a new business. Did they all go through all these seven steps? And all the tortures of transfer? The ones that were efficiently conceived and executed did.

5

Program Planning, Budgeting, and Monitoring

Nowhere can there be so much waste, so many pitfalls and blind alleys, as in a creative process. Thomas Edison's famous "Edisonian Process," an orderly set of investigations of every possible variable, is a formula for waste. Edison tried 1,600 kinds of filaments before he settled on carbon for incandescent lights. If he had tried carbon first, he might have saved 1,599 experiments. I recognize that I am oversimplifying, but it is possible that he didn't think through his innovation concept well enough before beginning experimentation. Of course, it is presumptuous of me to criticize the great Edison. And, to let him off the hook, high-temperature filamentary materials weren't readily available or well understood in the late 19th century when he did his work. In fact, tungsten, which later replaced carbon, was a "rare metal" at the time, and hardly a practical candidate. Yet, Edison did succeed—spectacularly.

Edison changed our lifestyle patterns as much as any man in history—and got rich in the process. The electric light bulb is a classic "great" innovation. It established new profitable businesses, with enormous dollar volumes, by replacing (obsolescing) established products: the candle and the kerosene lamp.

Still, I can't help but think his project could have proceeded more speedily, that he could have lopped a year or so off certain target dates in his Gantt or PERT chart (had such ways of programming future events existed in his day) if he had given more attention to generating a plan for implementing his idea in a more disciplined fashion. Edison's plan would have entailed organizing the seven steps to innovation (even the legendary Edison must have gone through every one of them, more or less), which are the subject of the preceding chapter, in terms of allocation of time to each subtask and scale of commitment of resources for each step.

Timeliness

What we are discussing is efficiency: minimizing sallies down blind allies. When we achieve efficiency, we stop wasting time and money.

Not wasting time also has a strategic aspect. A useful innovation provides the right product or process or system for a particular industry and the specific business that will exploit it, and provides it in timely fashion—which means not too late.

Nowhere in business is time—perhaps a better term is timeliness—more important than in the case of innovation. In the United States (and in many other countries as well, but culturally and historically more in this country than in others), if you don't come up with the inevitable next innovation, your competitor will. He will have a new product before you will. As shown in the master chart of innovation (see Chapter 1, Figure 1-2), there are many ways to achieve innovation. Whichever one you choose, make sure you proceed "in a timely fashion."

Of course, it is possible to get new or replacement products in a timely fashion by other means than sponsoring in-house innovation. The master chart suggests several other modes to attain this end. Companies that have already produced the desired innovations can be acquired, or minority positions can be established in them, or joint ventures can be set up with them (all discussed in Chapter 18). Or a new product that has been painfully developed by the competition can be licensed (see Chapter 19) or otherwise copied. One of these will give results faster than the others.

It is interesting that to be timely, it is not necessary to be on the market first; being close to first will do just as well. Indeed, it is well known that being second when a new technology creates a new market is neither a disaster nor a disgrace, and, in fact, could be helpful in maximizing ultimate growth and profits. Neither Texas Instruments nor the Bell System was first in selling semiconductor products in America in the decade after the Bell Labs scientists Shockley, Bardeen, and Brattain won their Nobel prize by inventing the transistor in the late 1940s. Other companies, now forgotten, were. But TI was an early contender, and is now first (unless you include the Japanese, who weren't first either).

Being in business means being in a race, whether one wants to be or not. There is no substitute for innovating fast enough at least to stay among the leaders for the first lap or two, and then maybe to win at the end.

Our kind of race is not a passionate dash around a track. Rather, it is a planned enterprise consisting of deliberately advancing "steps" in a process often extending back many years. But can one plan an innovation process for maximum efficiency and timeliness? Can one schedule creativity to happen at a pace faster than might be "natural"? I think so. At least for modest inventions, innovators sheltered and nurtured in an autonomous innovation organization will respond by doing their work like any other well-treated employees. If you ask them to produce something—invent it, in fact—by a certain date and within a certain budget, they will consider that a reasonable request and will attempt to accommodate you.

For blockbuster creations, like a cure for AIDS or something else that would warrant a chapter in history books, it might be a different story. Few of us work on anything of those grand dimensions. Yet the pursuit of any goal, blockbuster or not, benefits from laying out time-designated milestones before starting, then monitoring and, if required, updating and taking corrective actions during the process.

There is always a temptation to allow innovators free rein, to let creative tasks run on in open-ended fashion, but no good manager will yield to such temptation. No program can be run effectively without defined limits and targets. The manager must see to it that these are conformed to and met. Happily, the mere practice of assigning target dates tends more often than not to be self-fulfilling.

We are talking about hurrying the creative process, and I am contending that it can be done. I often make requests like, "I need a new concept on this new product idea no later than three weeks from now, and a first proof of feasibility six weeks later." I usually find that around the time of the target date, give or take a week, I'll have what I've asked for. In will walk Sam or Mike or Florence, with a smug look on his or her face, saying, "If you happen to be down at my end of the building, stop in. I've got something to show you that might interest you. . . ."

If one doesn't request that something be completed by a certain date, one doesn't get it. So request. I am reminded of a saying of Yiddish origin: "Sleep fast. We need the pillows."

Chapter 1 states that the way to start an innovation program is by formulating a plan. The plan then provides the basis for generating funding requirements from which, in turn, a budget may be derived. When the individual tasks that make up the plan and the costs of carrying them out are reduced to diagram and table form, they provide a good mechanism for monitoring progress. This chapter discusses how to tailor these conventional management practices to the innovation process.

Diagramming Plans

An innovation program consists of sets of events that occur in interlocking, interrelated steps that extend over time. Such a program is best visualized with a diagram.

Blocking Out Time Segments

The simplest plan is simply to do the seven steps of innovation one by one in order. In that case, the program for a typical three-year innovation development would appear in diagram form as shown in Figure 5-1. It is a one-dimensional chart showing packets of events, the steps, on a horizontal time scale, with the typical time estimate required for each indicated by the length of that line segment. The horizontal line could as well have been in dollars rather than calendar months; it would then have been an expression of projected expenditures of money for each step.

Indeed, Figure 5-1 is simple to the point of being simplistic. It shows events occurring in linear, sequential fashion, with no task starting until the preceding one is finished. For it to have more than minimal value, it must be expanded and refined as required by the specific innovation program being planned. This can be done by deploying each line segment separately and in a vertical array, each vertical index describing a separate task or subtask.

Figure 5-1. A three-year "linear" innovation program.

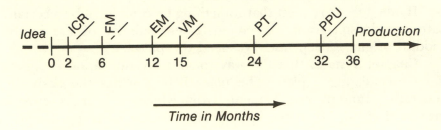

Key

ICR	Innovation concept report
FM	Feasibility model
EM	Engineering or functional model
VM	Visual model or mock-up
PT	Prototype
PPU	Pilot production unit

This becomes the well-known bar chart, invented by Mr. Gantt, of which Figure 5-2 is an example.

Bar Charts: A Way to Communicate with Management

The biggest difference between Figure 5-1 and Figure 5-2 is that the second chart has become two-dimensional and we now can represent ways in which the steps may overlap each other. In looking at Figure 5-2, it becomes evident that there is no reason why some feasibility experiments cannot begin even while the ICR (innovation concept report) is going through its various incarnations. Indeed, if such overlap occurs, the experiments will influence the nature of the evolving concept, and conception becomes part of a dynamically interactive system. Also, the different expected iterations of each step can now be enumerated and shown in their relation to each other.

Figure 5-2. Schematic bar chart.

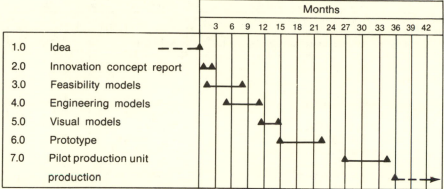

Project Title: A Three-Year Innovation Program (The Seven Steps)

Key

The chart becomes even more useful when it is extended so that it depicts every major task broken down into its elements, the subtasks, which are what the actual work consists of. So if we can represent them as sub-bars under each main task bar, we are really creating *the plan.*

Figure 5-3 is an example of such a bar chart. It represents a portion of a projected plan to carry out the development of metal glue described in the innovation concept report shown as Appendix 1.

It is convenient to designate bars with numerals such as 2.0 and 3.0 for main tasks and 2.1 and 3.1 for subtasks. Then it may help to describe each on an accompanying page or two with a simple one-sentence statement, if the readers require this.

It is also convenient to superimpose a graph showing planned cumulative program costs (dotted line) with one showing actual expenditures (solid line). The symbols that can be used for monitoring task performance are shown in the key at the bottom of the chart.

With the creation of a bar chart, we have outlined all the tasks to be done with predictions of how long they will take in

Figure 5-3.   Bar chart for a typical program, with subtasks.

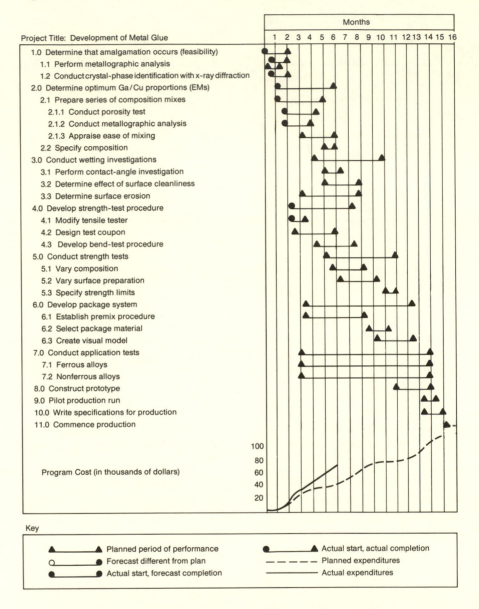

enough detail to give credibility to the program and to justify an allotment from the budget. Thus, we have produced a document that innovators can use to communicate with management in easily understood and succinct terms.

We still don't have a really useful *working* plan, which the innovators themselves will employ as an aid in meeting their objectives and those of their immediate supervisors. Now the time has come to detail, for the benefit of those who will really do the work, even at this early moment in the program, not only *what* substeps are expected to be involved in each step, but *how* it is predicted they will interact with each other. Then we must plot them, interactions and all, as a function of time. That leads us to Figure 5-4, a PERT chart.

Fine-Grained Planning: The PERT Chart

PERT (program evaluation review technique) was created by the U.S. Navy in the 1950s and has been much utilized in the planning of large implementation programs—sometimes based on new concepts, sometimes not—for military weaponry and surveillance systems. It defines the implementation actions as time-consuming activities leading to successful conclusions, called events, and diagrams them together in an easily comprehended visual representation that illustrates their interrelationships, possible options for changing course, and projected completion dates.

PERT in its most elegant applications may serve as a basis for mathematically determining likely times of completion and for framing these within a band, the boundaries of which are optimistic and pessimistic, should that much detail be desired. PERT also defines decision points (those moments when the program could change direction), making them easily perceptible, and shows where each change option may lead and what it may involve in terms of investment of effort. But most important, PERT clearly identifies the critical path, which is the route to completion of the entire project that guarantees that sufficient time will be available for the goal to be met. No other path from start to completion provides that guarantee.

The chart identifies this route and characterizes it in time units. The only way to have things happen sooner is to change the plan, and that can result when the chart is inspected and the plan's point of weakness becomes apparent. The eye focuses on the activity that will not give good return for the effort required. What the chart really shows is how one can go astray, how one can blunder and allow the critical path to get too long, by allowing

Figure 5-4. PERT chart for a typical innovation program.

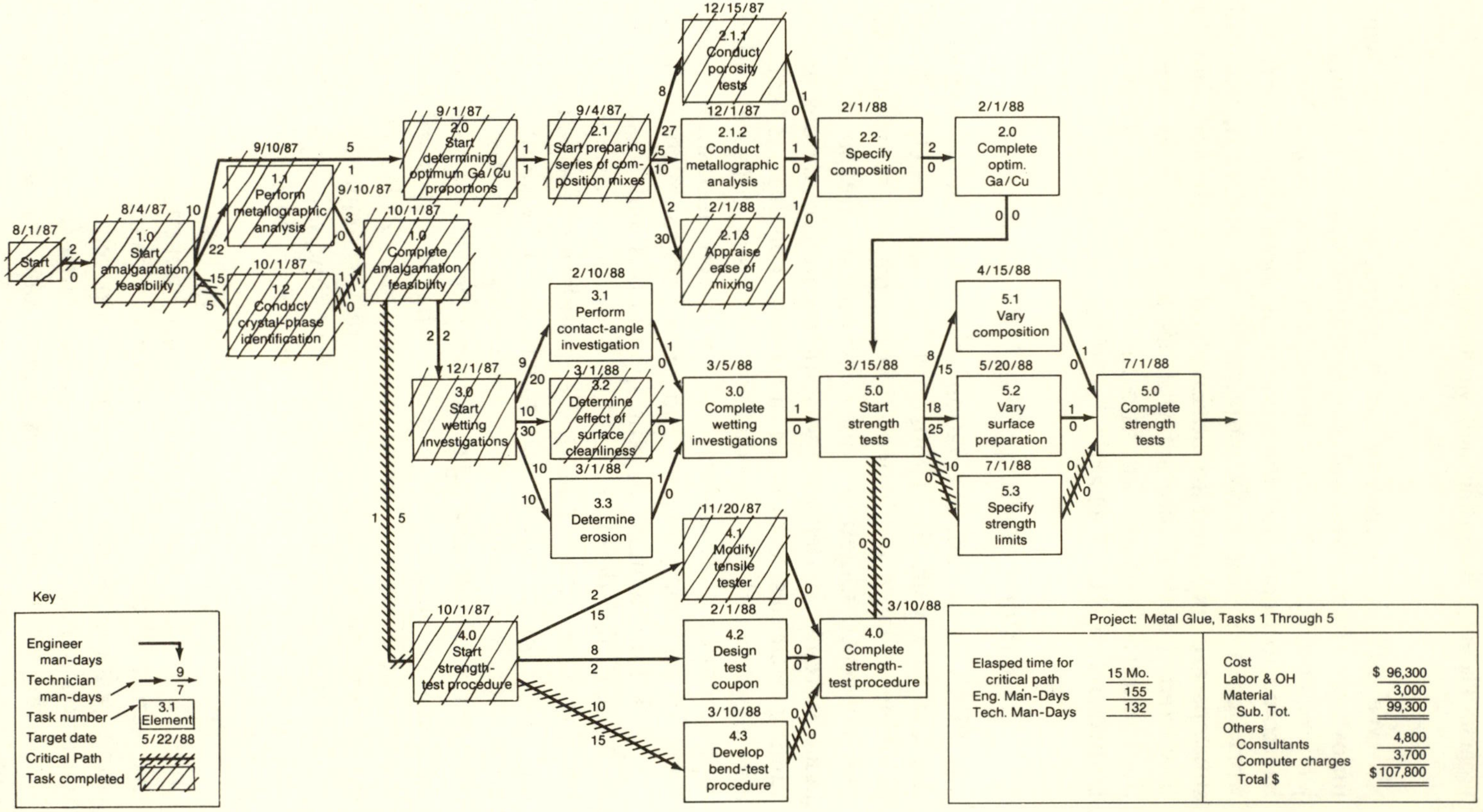

a particular task to stretch out too long in time and by investing too much effort going down noncritical byways.

In Figure 5-4, which proposes a plan for performing the first five innovation steps of the metal-glue program laid out in Appendix 1, perusal of the critical path reveals two weak points, one minor, one major. The minor one is Task 4.3. If that can be completed by March 5 instead of March 10, five days will be saved, because Task 3.0 will be done on that day, and Task 2.0 would have been completed a month earlier. This will allow you to start strength tests Task 5.0, on March 5. But Task 5.3 is more important. What justifies waiting until July 1 for its completion? Just asking that question might reveal that a June 1 target is reasonable. If so— Eureka!—the program now has a critical path of less than 14 months. We save 35 days before we even begin. This exercise is evidence that identifying one's critical path—and then optimizing it before proceeding down it—is a means to attain efficiency and timeliness.

Our analysis of Figure 5-4 demonstrates how useful this elaborate military planning tool, which carries with it all the ramifications of complexity and mammoth size we associate with government-sponsored programs, can be to innovators engaged in commercial innovation programs that are often small in numbers of people and amount of dollars invested, PERT's premises are sound, and I recommend using a bare-bones version of it.

Here is my scheme of simple PERT (SimPERT?). Professional practitioners of PERT (known as "pertniks") collapse with laughter when I describe it to them. For them, a typical program will have 5,000 to 10,000 events and the chart will cover acres of walls in PERT rooms. (In my mind, these rooms are located thousands of feet beneath a secret Rocky Mountain peak that appears on no map. I visualize some crisp admiral or general—Sterling Hayden on leave from *Dr. Strangelove* will do—walking by those charts, 100 yards along one wall and 100 yards back along the facing wall, contemplating all those little circles and lines while meditatively slapping his thigh with his swagger stick.) But a PERT chart that meets our needs and describes a single task set will fit on a couple of pages—like Figure 5-4 does—and two dozen events are usually enough to provide our planning message.

We need to define the two terms *event* and *activity*. An event is the completion of a subtask. It is represented by a closed figure, usually a circle or oval or rectangle, in which the name of the subtask is given or referenced. It also contains a designated number, so we can talk about it as Event 7, for example. For events best described in a phrase rather than a single word, the number alone may be used with a reference list tabulated below.

With the completion of each event, we go on to the next one. Events are connected by straight lines, the directions of which are shown by arrowheads; these lines are called activities. An *activity* represents the time it takes to complete a task, that achievement being designated by the event. Numbers may be written next to the lines to designate the effort and time estimated to achieve the completion of the subtask (that is, the event) they are aiming at.

Note that effort expended and calendar date are somewhat independent of each other. Something that will consume ten man-months of effort can presumably be completed by the work of one man or woman in ten months or by ten people in one month. The level of intensity that is adopted depends on the urgency of the program and the ability of the innovation group to muster forces. (See the section on the "sushi approach" later on in this chapter.) The calendar date will then be written above or next to the event. It becomes a "target date," and if a bar chart exists for the same project, that date will be the same for the same subtask on both documents.

It is not uncommon for three or four different activity lines to emanate from a single event. These might represent options or required parallel paths; investigating all of them could lead to choosing the best ones. So the PERT chart gives us a picture of our options. But they all must at some time reconverge on a future single event, which could simply be the end result of making a choice of which option or options to proceed with. Thus these are "loops." At once we see what this means: A loop that doesn't terminate at an event has been worked on to no purpose. We don't want any of those.

How do we define the critical path? Simple: It is the one that consumes the maximum time and, at least at the time the chart was prepared, appears unable to be shortened. Other paths may take the same number of days, but some of that time is consumed waiting around while the critical path is being pursued. Were it not for the need to wait, those noncritical paths would have consumed less time. Find the critical path and show it with a bold line. (A red one makes it stand out and carries with it the desirable connotations of criticality.)

The chart can also be used to indicate manpower commitments and costs. Figure 5-4 shows these for each activity using the procedure illustrated in the boxed legend.

As each event is completed, one can cross it out with the bold slashing strokes of a blunt pencil, broad-tipped yellow felt pen, or greasy orange crayon. This pleasurable act means that we have successfully followed the path we laid out for ourselves. Note the slashes through subtasks in Figure 5-4, which show that the innovation program is about one-third complete.

Do It Your Way—But Do It

There is nothing sacred about either bar charts or PERT charts. I have used both, selecting one or the other or both together, depending on the clientele. I find that most innovation organizations use bar charts. Fewer supplement them with PERT diagrams, and I think more should. But everyone who manages innovation should use some charting technique for planning and monitoring.

Program planning diagrams are usually idiosyncratic to a particular company; *idiosyncratic* is defined as "peculiar to an individual or group." Respect your peculiarities (at least they are yours), but set up some easily used diagrammatic system. And use it, not only to plan with, but as a budgeting and monitoring means.

Orchestrating Plans

So far, we have discussed planning a project. But the leader of the innovation organization must plan the work for an entire cast of characters as a cluster of interlocking activities. The cluster may in fact consist of a single project, as often occurs in captive R&D organizations or in a skunk works dedicated to a single innovation goal. But there are many cases when numerous simultaneous unrelated programs exist, with each investigator participating in several of the activities within a multiplicity of plans. The leader, with the help of the administrator, has to mesh all activities together effectively. Together they must orchestrate a department plan.

When a good leader is confronted with this problem, he or she recognizes that there are many advantages and will plan to exploit them. Here are some examples.

Multiple Simultaneous Programs Sustain Each Other

An investigator may get stuck in one program, and creative inspiration may dry up. The best thing to do is to turn to the challenge of creating some other new product or new process and allow one's unconscious to continue to battle with the dilemma posed by the first problem. Within a week, the elusive answer usually pops into the innovator's head. Sometimes a new development may be stymied when delivery of a crucial material or part is delayed. How fortuitous that there are some other new developments to work on while waiting. A third benefit is synergy. Program F will often suggest an answer for Program K. Good innovators are shameless in the practice of stealing from Peter to aid Paul.

A strong case can be made for multiple simultaneous programs, and the case becomes even stronger when the innovation organization is a center and applies its creative talents to many different businesses using many different technologies. In such cases, each innovator, whether specialist or generalist, usually participates in at least four simultaneous projects. This poses no problem so long as you plan for it.

Multiple Programs as Insurance

In my own experience, it was not unusual for all 15 engineers in our organization to engage in a total exceeding 60 separate innovation programs—each with its own plan and budget—in any given year. How well I remember my different bosses through the decades saying, "Why so many, George? Why not do just one, and do it right?" That suggests another reason for multiple programs: If some fail, it is not a disaster, because others will succeed. Multiple programs are a kind of insurance.

Budgeting

Throughout this book I continually make two points: Innovators are different from everyone else, and innovators are the same as everyone else. Insofar as budgeting is concerned, they are the same. Budgeting for an innovation organization is essentially similar to that for any other organization of that size within a company.

Budgeting is a discipline. It sets the scale of an activity and it does it from bottom up and from top down, with both answers coming out the same in the end.

Bottom-up budgeting addresses each innovation project, breaking it down into tasks, then fine-graining those into subtasks. It then determines the magnitude of resources to allocate to each as a function of the passage of time. The most important resource allocated in an innovation organization is people, or portions of people. Knowing their salaries and the hours they will give to each task, numbers can be derived, in units of dollars and man-days. Add up those numbers, supplement them with the costs of materials and other outside purchases, services, and overhead items, and there you are: You have generated a bottom-up budget.

But who is "you"? It is the innovators themselves—with some help in the mechanics from the administrator. A key to success in budgeting is to involve those who generated the project plans in the first place and who must ultimately carry them out. Indeed, what could be more bottom-up than their involvement?

They generated the plan, now they realize the consequence of that act. They become aware that they have had a role in determining a particular set of funding levels. Maybe in the end those funds aren't of the exact magnitude they might have desired, but they are usually in the right ball park, and the innovators can agree to them as reasonable. As the year goes on, how can they complain? They made their bed. . . .

Those who provide the funds know how much they consider reasonable too. This brings us to top-down budgeting. Anyone running a business knows how much he or she should (or, perhaps, will) allocate to the R&D budget, and somehow, regardless of the detailed care taken in constructing the final total with the bottom-up budget process, it is the CEO's number that tends to prevail.

The correct level of commitment to innovation by an executive office for any business is a subject in itself, related as much to questions like "What is it worth?" as it is to "What will it cost?" Unfortunately, the CEO decides too often on the basis of the answer to the latter question rather than the former. All I will say at this point is that R&D budgeted at .15 percent of sales is too little for any business, and that budgeted at 15 percent is probably too much, unless the money comes from an outside source such as the government.

In the end, however, there is a kind of reconciling. A single sum appears for the total budget, and everyone starts the year committed to it.

The Single-Program Case

For innovation organizations that pursue only one new product or new process goal at a time, as do many captive R&D groups and almost every skunk works, there is only one project and only one plan. The budgeting process for such a program is simple and conventional—so simple and conventional that it requires no further discussion here.

The Multiple-Program Case

When many simultaneous programs are involved, even for a small group, budgeting is far from simple. Then, not the least of one's problems is making it self-consistent.

"Self-consistent" is a term used by Wes Teich of Raytheon's New Products Center. As chief engineer, he had to allocate the time of between 15 and 20 professionals and as many technicians, shop workers, designers, and drafters over almost 100 charge numbers. (Each charge number represents an innovation program with a plan and a budget.)

Self-consistent means that every working hour of every direct-labor person for a defined time period, like a month or a quarter, is allocated in rational proportion to all programs in which that person will engage—and those hours must come out just right. If a month has 176 working hours, all 176 have to be allocated to projects for each employee. In the same way, and at the same time, the funding for each program must be allocated. Those funds must neither be overspent or underspent.

The administrator goes through the exercise of assigning the correct dollar value to each man-hour. In the end, every hour and every dollar are allocated in a way such that every program proceeds in accordance with its plan. How is it done? In the old days, I'm sure we used witchcraft. Now the computer is our salvation. A personal computer (PC) in the administrator's office performs wonders. A program like LOTUS 1-2-3 still looks like witchcraft to me, but it works better by far than the old way—and faster. Using the keyboard, one can easily shave a fraction of a person from here and compensate with another fraction from there. The printout, which is generated in December for the coming year, is really the first draft of the budget. It spews forth before one's eyes, usually at a speed of 160 bytes a second. Based on such a budget, and varied slightly to compensate for actual expenditures as the year goes on, a single month's activity can be programmed (as shown in Figure 5-5).

Having such a budget in such a form, one has created a tool for the entire upcoming year. One can see how one is doing against budget and make instant corrections when required by perusing the weekly updates after keyboarding in the numbers from that week's charges. This brings us to monitoring.

Monitoring

With our plan diagrams and with the budgets that correspond to them, we have set up a framework of specific tasks for each program, with target dates for their achievement and targeted costs for each. At the same time, plan diagrams provide a convenient mechanism for monitoring whether the targets are indeed being striven for and met.

One monitors by constantly checking status. The plan—bar chart, PERT chart, or other chart—says that by this date, such and such subtask or event should be completed. Otherwise, we are falling behind, which we do not want to do. The best way to stay on target is to become aware *early* that a target date is in jeopardy. This checking process is facilitated by simple exercises like slashing out events on a PERT chart and comparing the actual date of completion with the projected date. At the same time, we compare actual expenditures with planned expenditures, as detailed in the budget. Everyone is involved in the checking process: the boss, the administrator, but most important, the innovator himself.

Figure 5-5. Computer printout of allocation of hours of direct labor for multiple programs in an innovation center.

Technology Center, Dept. 13—1

Forecast Direct Labor Hours for November 1987

Name	R&D Programs (by Charge Code)							
	811	834	835	867	876	888	889	Total
Professionals								
Allan	50	10	30	4	10	26	46	176
Bischoff		36		100		40		176
Bailey	20	20	80	12		28	16	176
Cowen					176			176
DuLac	80					40		120
Fishbein		20		62	20	24	50	176
Foley			152					152
Gianno								0
Gundelach	50	20		40	24		42	176
Horrigan		150				26		176
Musto	16		80		80			176
Rosenberg		26				80		106
Richards	40	20	40		56		20	176
Sung		36		40			100	176
Werther	10	30	4	12	42	78		176
Total Eng./Sci.	266	368	386	270	408	342	274	2,314
Support Personnel								
Bally	20		100		30	20	6	176
Castiglione				48				48
Co-op Electronics		16	80		20	60		176
Co-op Mechanics	40			80			56	176
Fisk		30	40	20	72	12	2	176
Gide						176		176
Monelle								0
Quade	100		30	12	30		4	176
Sligo								0
Winston		150						150
Total Technical	160	196	250	160	152	268	68	1,254
Ellovitz		10	40			90	36	176
Wu		50		60	26	30	10	176
Total Drafting		60	40	60	26	120	46	352

I have used bar charts like the ones that U.S. government programs use to monitor schedules. Such charts employ some convenient symbols (see Figure 5-3), not only for measuring performance and compliance with targets but also for comparing actual costs with budgeted ones. (Symbols are shown in the keys accompanying each chart.) To monitor, you simply write them on the chart as you proceed.

In monitoring performance, it is usually adequate to check once a week and to take corrective action as necessary. Don't leave those corrective actions to verbal statements. Record them right on the planning document so that they become new targets that will, in turn, be monitored. Thus, the plan becomes a dynamic document, each change having been agreed to as "revision 1," "revision 2," and so on.

Innovators, like other employees, must be managed. The monitoring process, religiously adhered to, is an important element of that management process.

Strategic Issues

Now that the plan has taken tangible form as a set of diagrams, we are ready for the next step. Does that mean we are ready to start to perform activities, complete events, and to monitor them? Not quite. We'd better show this plan, in bar chart form, to all concerned.

With pride in a planning job well done, the director organizes a slide show, complete with handouts, and describes the meaning, the cost, and the time scale of each task. He concludes with a summary statement: "In three years, we'll have it on the market." The director waits for applause. It does not come.

"I told you, Jack" says Geraldine, director of marketing, "that we needed this in two years at the outside, but I was wrong. Our latest scuttlebutt is that if it takes us more than a year, we're done for." (She is obviously talking about timeliness.) "But to do it right, there is no way to do it faster than the time I said—three years," sputters Jack, who is always a stickler for doing things right. "Sorry," murmurs Geraldine, "that won't do."

The plan has already been useful. It has shown—graphically—that it does not fit the newest conception of competitive reality. What had better be done? There is only one thing to do: Change the plan. The most common ways to change it are to decide to compress the plan (so as to satisfy Geraldine while giving Jack heart failure) or, sadly, to decide not to proceed at all. There are other possible options, but let us concentrate on these.

Compress the Plan: The Sushi Approach

Jack has already made it clear that to do the program right will take three years. Does doing it in one year mean that it will be done wrong? Not necessarily; but it does mean that the shorter time scale will entail more risk, and the commitment to risk is an executive decision. The CEO, or at least "someone important," has to decide. Should the decision be made to proceed on a one-year instead of a three-year time scale, the plan will be redrawn and will become an example of what the Japanese call the "sushi approach" or "sushi treatment."[1]

Perhaps you've eaten sushi in a Japanese restaurant. It consists of tastefully cut and arrayed geometrical figures, and you must admire the way it looks, even if the idea of raw tuna or octopus may not appeal.

For sushi, the food is deployed in little slabs in a row, each resting in part on the preceding slab, like shingles, or like a collapsed row of dominoes. Consider each sushi slab to be a task in the plan. Note that as set out, they extend in a line for about 10 inches. So we can say that it is a 10-inch long plan. Too long? There is a way to shorten it without reducing the size of each slab (which corresponds to the time given to each activity). Just grab the two at the end, and squeeze. You want 4 inches? Easy. You need but squeeze until the row becomes 4 inches long. How did it take on that new length? By more overlap of each shushi piece with its neighbor on each side.

More task overlap means beginning the next task before the preceding one is finished—maybe too soon before. That is where the risk comes in. (How different this is from the linear program of Figure 5-1). But if you feel the approach to be taken for Task 3.0 will be a "sure thing," why wait till it's finished before starting Task 4.0? In fact, since Task 4.0 is a pretty good bet, you might as well begin Task 5.0 at the same time. And it will do no harm to muster the ingredients of Task 6.0 while you are at it. . . .

This could mean that you will begin to build the new product or the new production machine from formal drawings, before the engineering models, the EMs, have evolved to their final iteration, and well before a formal prototype is created or a pilot run is conducted (even though they too have been started with a guessed-at design). The guess is based on what the final innovation is *likely* to be, but you can't know whether it will ultimately be the best for yield, cost, and so on.

Even so, you don't wait. You rush (perhaps imprudently) ahead. Accepting and launching the final version so early may mean that millions of dollars must be spent at once for something that may not work. Go ahead, if you want to take the risk. It is a judgment call. It depends on your skill as a guesser.

If it works, what a hero you will be! And if it doesn't, you might still be a hero, if the ratio of number of good judgments over time in your career exceeds the number of bad ones. It is called "aggressive imaginative leadership" when it wins enough times and "stupidity" when it fails too often. For the Japanese, it is the approach that brought them to the position they attained in the automobile industry—outclassing and outmaneuvering American car makers—during the early 1980s, when the exhibited both timeliness and quality.

Figure 5-6 is Figure 5-3 after it has received the sushi treatment. That's the bar chart. What about the working plan, the PERT chart or its equivalent? If you have drawn that up for the three-year plan and you must now make things happen in one year, you have no choice but to redraw it. Remember, each activity will still require the same amount of effort; no matter how you rush, the laws of nature remain inviolate. Making each event happen within the new time scale means increasing the number of bodies working on the program at any time by an average factor; in this case, by three, because you are compressing a three-year project into a one-year time scale.

Turning Off the Project

Sad to say, there is another value to the plan in both its original and compressed versions. It might show that the change is not worth taking, either because the risks of compressing the program are not warranted in light of the poor chance of meeting the time goal and the product and process goals at the same time, or because doing it in the three-year period could mean that the achievement, while almost risk-free in terms of project goals, will be, as Geraldine pointed out, devastatingly untimely. Shutting down the program could mean going so far as getting out of the business altogether; maybe it's time to sell that division. But without the formulation

Figure 5-6. Schematic bar chart after "sushi treatment."

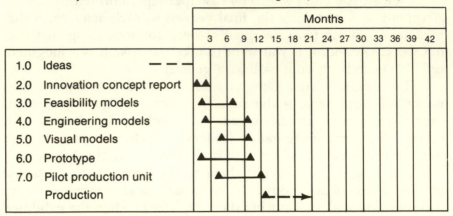

Project Title: A One-Year Innovation Program (The Seven Steps)

of those well-thought-out bar charts, you would not have been confident with any decision.

Planning Beyond the Seven Steps of the Innovation Process

Those who plan innovation must plan for success, and, as mentioned throughout, must *involve the client very early on.* That way, the client can do what is required to exploit the innovation so as to maximize new revenues and profits.

The Client Swings into Action

Sometime during the course of performing the seven steps, and well before they are completed, the client has to plan to put the innovation into production. If it is a product to be made on a production line, that line must be generated. What may be required could be millions of dollars worth of assembly machinery, all with long lead times, and tooling (more millions and more months). In addition, floor space has to be made available for this line, which may require special facilities to satisfy new insurance liability standards. Mr. Murphy lurks and enforces his Law, and this production line will have to conform to standards that old products made on old lines with old processes did not have to meet. Maybe the wisest thing would be to buy or build a new factory for it. Then there will have to be new workers hired and trained, and new engineers, and new salespeople. . . .

The role of the innovation organization is fading fast. At this point, its most valuable service might be to remind its clients no later than when final engineering models are produced, "Hey, you guys, this is probably going to work. Better start preparing for it." (Translation: "Better dig up a lot of money.")

Comparative Costs

Even if our client is not in the sushi mode, the amount of money being spent as we get close to the prototype and the pilot run steps is increasing rapidly. As discussed in Chapter 4, it is now not the innovation organization that is doing most of the spending, it is the receiver of the innovation. But even the money spent in Steps 6 and 7 are small compared with the investment that is justified by the successful completion of this innovation process. Then a manufacturing facility outfitted with all required tooling for volume production will be established, and the amount of money needed should be included in the planning and budgeting process too.

Reference

1. H. Takeuchi and N. Ikujiro, "The New Product Development Game," *Harvard Business Review*, January–February 1986, pp. 137–146.

6

Generating Patents and Know-How

During the time that a company has been going through the tortuous steps leading to the creation of an innovation, but well before the innovation appears before the public in the marketplace, it has been methodically creating equity, a little more each day. The patent attorneys call that equity "intellectual property," and the term is apt.

Much intellectual property appears during the earliest period of R&D in the innovation organization, much during the internal transfer process from innovation organization to manufacturing, and some even after the innovation has been announced to the outside world. Indeed, the portfolio of intellectual property continues to grow for as long as someone—anyone—has an original idea and implements it.

Intellectual property has value. The proof is that people are ready to pay money for it—by licensing it. Sometimes you may be the seller; other times it may be to your strategic advantage to be the buyer of another firm's intellectual property, which embodies its innovation. But even if one of your innovations doesn't generate license income, it can achieve results that are tantamount to income, as in negotiations or other interactions with companies that do not possess your property but wish they did.

In the ownership of property there is power. Power to protect your innovations and to contest the validity of innovations of others. Either action has the potential to increase revenues and profits. When innovators transfer their creations to production entities within their own organizations or outside it to licensees, some of that power is being transferred at the same time.

Whichever course you choose, one message is clear: *Treat your intellectual property in a manner that maximizes its potential value.*

Strategizing: Innovation as Battle

We will use the power represented by our intellectual property as a resource in doing battle with the competition. Let us begin by exploring the nature of that resource. Then let us consider how best to decide strategic issues like those regarding profit. Should we sell the innovation? What portion of it should we sell? What should we do about inhibiting the competition from using it? What is the best timing for all these actions? But before making any of these decisions, we must define the nature of our property.

The Property Package: Is It Patentable or Is It Know-How?

Sometimes we have no choice. The innovation is "not patentable." Examination of the achievement, remarkable though it might be in terms of new sales revenues, leads to the conclusion that it was "merely" of an ingenious nature. Indeed, as described by a phrase beloved of patent attorneys, it could have been done by anyone "skilled in the art." Yet, no one else ever thought to do it. Only we know what was done to make it happen. And if we keep that information secret, it becomes "proprietary." Nevertheless, it is still intellectual property having value, and in that case, it is called "know-how." It is not impossible for know-how, used right, to have more value than a patent.

Sometimes we have a choice and our innovation can be the basis of a patent. But our strategy may be not to apply for one, for reasons that will be given. Then that innovation too, by default, will fall into the know-how category. The point is, it is up to us whether our patentable intellectual property will be a candidate for patenting or will reside in a portfolio of know-how. That is a strategic issue to be settled as we build our strategy.

Basis for Patent

For an innovation to be patentable it must satisfy some criteria so meaningful that innovators recognize them as such without qualification. There are two major ones:

1. *There must be a concept so dependent on a unique act of creativity that it would "not be obvious to one skilled in the art."* We now see why innovators love to have their names on patents and why they can easily be persuaded to join forces with the patent attorneys who help write and file the documents. To be the author of an issued patent is to be able to show documentary proof that one has superior talents, an ability that goes beyond competence. The patent is proof that someone can create at a level above that of the merely skilled. This leads to an action item. The inventor/attorney team collaborates in writing a scholarly exposition of the "not obvious" concept. It is the major element of the first part of the patent document that will be issued by the patent department of whatever nation agrees to its validity.

2. *The concept alone is not enough; it must be "reduced to practice" (that is, demonstrated as being workable).* Reduction to practice means that a model has been constructed, usually a tangible structure that can be examined physically (intangible models, such as software, can be constructed too, but that kind of invention is much more difficult to patent). Then that model has to be operated, shown to work as claimed, and at least one example of performance data given. And that is the second major part of the patent document.

All this should be quite familiar. The first part of an issued patent summarizes our idea and innovation concept, Steps 1 and 2 of our seven steps to efficient innovation. The second part describes the results of Step 3, the feasibility model. If we wrote an innovation concept report—as we should have—we already have a head start. (It is not necessary to go through the other four steps to innovation before applying for a patent, except when they too generate invention.)

Time Scale for Patent Award

The data for proof of reduction to practice are not commonly challenged for truthfulness, for they can always be confirmed by reference to validated records, such as patent notebooks. But they can be challenged for technical soundness. An expert in the field may suggest that the experimental data might have been incorrectly derived, as with faulty equipment or measurements. Or the whole invention may be questioned in terms of chronological dating, as when someone else can show (using a patent notebook) that he or she did it first. In this case, the patent attorney calls the other person's work "prior art."

The patent offices of most nations are very good at making these challenges and in the end setting to rest all doubts. But that takes time. It takes at least three years from the date a patent attorney begins an assignment to compose a patent application of an innovation to the date it is officially issued. But five years is probably average, and seven years is not uncommon. No one can accelerate the patenting process, for no agency of the United States government is so immune to outside pressures of any sort and so universally acknowledged to be incorruptible as the U.S. Patent Office.

What does a company pursuing patents do about this time lag? It must construct its strategy with that long time requirement as an ingredient. Make a plan for the exploitation of patentable intellectual property. If it is a bar chart, the time-to-patent bar should be at least five years long.

There is only one comfort. At least you know, if you have indeed given the patent attorney a go-ahead, that you have started. As Chairman Mao said, "The longest journey starts with a single step." When the statement "patent applied for" is attached to any item of intellectual property, it has some legal significance and thus affords you some negotiating power.

Basis for Value of the Patent: The Claims

We have established the foundation of our intellectual property, but it has little tangible value until we get to the third part of the patent document: the claims. They proclaim to the world: Here are each of the items that make up this property, defined so clearly that there can be no challenge of ambiguity. Now let each one go out into the marketplace and rise to its respective value.

These claims are always introduced by a phrase that is a marvel of simplicity—probably the only simple one the patent community allows itself to indulge in. It is: "I (or "We," if there is more than one inventor) claim . . . ," followed by the claims.

Another way to look at a patent's claims is implied in the lawyers' phrase "claims allowed." If they appear in the patent, they have indeed been allowed, which means they have survived all challenge. There can be dozens of claims in a single patent, or only three or four. Any one of them could be worth millions of dollars.

Percy Spencer's historic patent on a microwave cooking apparatus, shown in Appendix 2, is a good reference. With close to two thirds of the nation owning microwave ovens, think how valuable those claims could be. While you are at it, here's an exercise for you: Identify the statement of the concept that is beyond the state of the art and point out the statement of reduction to practice. Then identify the claims.

Because the claims are property, no one else can legally use them for their own benefit without paying for them. Of course, should another company use one of our claims, we can challenge that use (thereby implying that the people involved are thieves). The challenge can take the form of a lawsuit, and the resolution of the controversy may take place in a courtroom. Someone will gain, and someone will lose. (But one group will never lose: the patent attorneys for both sides.)

The Know-How Package

Like a patent, know-how takes on added value when it has been committed to document form. But different from the patent, it is a private document. As long as know-how remains in the possession of its owner, it belongs to that person and that person alone, and he or she may want to keep it that way.

But it retains proprietary status only for as long as it is not revealed to others. The minute it is seen by strangers, it essentially is theirs too, because it is not "protected by a patent." (Lawyers may still "make a case" against others who claim it, but their task is orders of magnitude more difficult than if a patent exists or has been applied for.)

Know-how has its greatest value when it remains secret. "Do you want to know my secret?" you may say to some firm. "Then pay me, or buy my license." It is here that know-how can take on a value that a patent can never have. By their nature, patents are the opposite of secret. They are public. (Of course, one licenses patents too. In fact, most license agreements cover both and describe what has been contracted for with the all-inclusive phrase "covers patents and know-how.")

The difference between patents and know-how is this: The instant a patent is published, you have blown your cover. "See," you say, "this is what I have done, and this is how you can do it too." Your rival can use that information, not so much to copy you as to circumvent you—which means, literally, to "get around your patent." Someone can do that only if you have a "weak patent," but not if you have a "strong patent." Obviously, strong is better intellectual property.

The Battle Plan

We have now defined our resources, our intellectual property. Now, how should we make the most of it? I will not presume to advise you in this regard. You know your industry and are best acquainted with its environment and practices. Go to it, but watch that timing, especially as it pertains to patents. After the half-decade or so it requires to get one, a patent lasts for a mere 17 years. After that, it becomes "public domain." That time span seems too long when your competitor owns the patent, and too short when you own it but won't attain significant sales until the eighteenth year.

That actually happened in the case of the microwave cooking patent. It became operative in 1950, but volume sales did not begin until the countertop microwave oven was announced by Raytheon's subsidiary, Amana, in 1968. What should Raytheon have done? Should they have kept the knowledge under wraps for a decade (not so easy to do, people being such blabbermouths)? If they hadn't entered the marketplace with what we now realize were very primitive restaurant ovens, would the art have progressed as it did so that the home oven would have been now technically ready by 1968? Those are tough questions.

Tough questions must be answered by tough people, and wise ones, and even those people can't ever be sure they are doing the best thing. It is an exercise in predicting product life cycle. You'll have an edge if you understand the cycles in your industry and construct a patent and know-how strategy accordingly.

Keeping Good Records

To maximize the value of intellectual property, do not be haphazard about how you accumulate it. If you are careless in this regard, you may find years later, when the chips are down, that you have far less than what rightfully should be yours. Establish procedures for keeping good records, and then follow those procedures without deviation.

The good manager or leader of innovation never stops saying, after becoming aware of an event that has an ingredient of newness, even if seemingly trivial or modest, "Did you write it in your notebook?" Underlings respond by doing it, or by agreeing that they will and then forgetting. It is here that nagging becomes an art form. You must be unrelenting.

That notebook entry, once made, becomes property, and the act of writing it down it is an act of creating value. If the new thing never gets recorded, it is not property, it is vapor—and vapor is hard to sell or otherwise exploit.

How Much to Write Down

Where should the line be drawn on how much to record? There is no question that a description of any new concept and of any crucial experiments that prove that concept's correctness must be committed to paper. But what about "noncrucial" experiments? What about "unimportant" data? Write it all down without being judgmental. Who knows today what will take on importance five years from now? This means that innovators should make a habit of inscribing something in their notebooks on a daily basis. It is a good habit. Think of it as writing in a diary; you usually don't omit a day if you keep a diary. This means that notebooks will proliferate. So what? Notebooks are cheap.

Who Should Record Innovation Information?

Who is an innovator? Everyone working on the innovation program. Notebooks are not part of a caste system. We don't hand them out only to the senior conceiver. The juniors and the non-professionals get them, too.

It is common for an innovation organization to have more discipline in this regard than its clients or licensees do. But the clients' and licensees' notebook entries can be every bit as valuable as intellectual property. There should be no compromise when it comes to dedication to the daily task of recording intellectual progress by everyone involved.

The Attorney Knows

The innovation is property only if the law of the land recognizes it as property. It is also property in other lands, but only as *their* laws define property—which may be different from our way. If you wish to do business in faraway places, you had better know *all* the laws, ours and, on a nation-by-nation basis, theirs, because laws differ from country to country. There is only one way to treat such matters effectively: Call in the specialists. You need the advice of attorneys with special expertise in patents and licensing.

I recommend that you organize a session or two per year of a tutorial nature in which the patent attorney stands before the entire staff and explains (and for those who have heard it before, re-explains) the concept of intellectual property and discusses how to maximize its value. The result is that the whole procedure acquires credibility and everyone is sensitized.

One of the most important things that the attorneys discuss is what notebooks to use and how to use them.

Notebooks

The patent attorney will specify the construction of the notebook in which we write. We quickly learn that any old notebook won't do. Looseleaf is not permissable because new pages, with falsified old dates, can be inserted. That means it won't stand up in court as property. In court, the question (phrased with a Watergate lilt) is, What did the innovators create and when did they create it? The lawyer's term is "reduce to practice". Who did it first? Only the records can provide proof, and those records lie in the notebooks.

As court documents, innovators' notebooks will be closely scrutinized. Make sure they have been witnessed with words like "read and understood," and date those witness signatures (in ink, not pencil). Beware of statements inserted at the margins or elsewhere as overwriting. Those actions may have occurred in all innocence and on the same day as the original entry, or they may have been added yesterday, which would be bad news.

Notarizing

Notebooks are actually not the only records that can be used. Anything that can be validated qualifies as a record. But if it is not in a bound notebook, it is less valid as a testament about the date of a particular event. Still, there are things one can do. I have always insisted that at least one administrator in the department become a notary public. Then he or she can impress every page of any report with the official seal and thereby attest to the date it was recorded.

Disks

Computer disks would not have been a matter of discussion a few years ago. But today, most people build their records while sitting at a computer keyboard. This poses a dilemma that has not yet been solved, since computer text can be so easily and clearly altered. Maybe what is needed is a way to notarize disks (there's a new product challenge for you, reader), but until such a way is developed the best compromise is to notarize the printouts.

Teaming Up with the Patent Department

I have just skimmed the surface of good documentation practice. I hope you interpret these statements not so much as a guide explaining how to keep innovation records, but more a plea that you obtain the services of a good patent attorney and then follow his or her advice. The patent community, like any professional group, knows the rules. Let us not examine too deeply its motives in making those rules so convoluted; we have no choice but to adhere to them.

It is astonishing how many innovation organizations, even those in large companies that have an in-house patent department, will forget to involve that department until it is too late to maximize the value of their intellectual property. You must take the initiative. Don't expect a patent attorney to give you a call with the question, "Anything patentable today?" For an active innovation group, the property should be reviewed every two or three months. Waiting longer can do damage.

7

The Impact Statement

We've done it. The innovation has progressed through its seven steps and entered the marketplace.

There have been primitive first operating models, and later more refined models. Then there was transfer out of the laboratory. In the course of this process, those who have participated have grown older, having invested more than mere dollars. They have invested parts of their lives—the process has taken years.

Once transferred, the innovated products have been manufactured and sold to the public in quantities numbering in the hundreds or thousands. Something that never existed before—a product, a process, or a system—has been added to the world.

There are sales that otherwise would never have existed. There are workers with jobs who would otherwise be employed elsewhere, or not at all. There are organizations with facilities and staffs and identities. There is return on investment and profits. There are also patents, already in existence or pending, ready to provide license income or a position of industry exclusivity. Yes, useful innovation has taken place.

All this means that an impact has been made—on our company, on our competition, even on society. That impact should be delineated and declared so that all may know it.

It is strange in light of the significance of this class of achievement that new elements often intrude here: modesty and shyness. Reject such tendencies. During the lifespan of every person and every organization, there is a time for blowing your own horn—and now is the time.

If you don't blow your own horn, those who deserve praise might not get it and, as a result, may miss out on increases in salary, bonuses, and company status. Their managers deserve to receive information on the magnitude and implication of subordinates' innovation strategies and actions. If managers don't receive that feedback, is it any wonder that they often consider the whole idea of innovation to be of secondary importance? To prevent such harm and misconceptions, allow a reasonable interval to elapse and then generate an impact statement.

The key is the word *impact*. Everyone in business understands incremental sales and profits, so the impact of an innovation on a company must be drawn up in those terms—quantitatively—and must be presented periodically in a formal manner.

It is the responsibility of the leader of the innovation organization to organize the impact document and to arrange to get it before the eyes of management at the highest level of authority in the company. In so doing, leaders fulfill their obligation not only to their boss, but also to those they lead, who have the same need for such treatment as any other deserving employee. A leader who does not do this is doing a poor job.

Some managers present their impact statements on the day of their yearly funding request (see Chapter 3), but a better strategy is to give it its own hearing about a month before, so that its implications have a chance to sink in. In either case, innovation will get the attention it deserves.

This chapter has a threefold message. First, the statement, in incontrovertible, unbiased terms, must be generated. Second, the innovators can depend only on themselves to take the initiative to put the statement together. Third, upon persuing the impact statement, almost everyone is surprised. It is rare that the impact of innovation does not turn out to exceed expectations of all concerned.

Everything in Money Units

If there is a *lingua franca*, an *esperanto*, a common language in a company, it is dollars. Not everyone in a position of authority understands the other languages being used in the firm, such as the scientific terminology in the chem lab or computerese in the software lab, but it is always easy for all to comprehend what appears on the bottom line. Yes, there is more in life than just money, even in a corporation; but for a first approximation of how well one is doing, the language of dollars will do. Thus, the impact statement must translate the effect of the innovation into financial terms.

The best way to do this is proceed as good innovators always do. When a special expertise is required, do not hesitate to enlist the services of experts. In this case, controllers are the ones who are most knowledgeable about a company's money.

Which Controllers?

Involving the controllers is no problem for a small enterprise with a single department that handles the company's financial affairs. Then there is only one place to go to for impact data. But a large diverse company with many divisions, subsidiaries, sectors, operations, or P&L centers generally has a separate controller for each corporate unit. If your innovation group is a center, serving many of these at the same time, you'll need to go to each respective controller. The more the better! You can be more impressive when the report is a summation of multiple inputs, each contributed by dispassionate, unbiased, expert authorities.

Set Up Consistent Impact Criteria

You'll quickly learn that the controller wants some ground rules. First, he or she will say, we must define "impact."

"Impact of an innovation" can have a number of definitions, but the most simple is: incremental sales for the preceding year measured in dollars. This should be supplemented by a statement of incremental profits (or losses) associated with those incremental sales.

The difficulty with the preceding definition is that, while it is easily applied to new products, it doesn't work as well for new processes or other new procedures. In those cases the impact of the innovation may not result in increased sales so much as in increased margins. Yet increased sales may nevertheless be tabulated if, for example, a strategic decision is made to pass the benefit on to the buyer in the form of lower prices, thus trading off increased margins per unit with increased numbers of units at lower prices.

Although it can become complicated, the challenge of defining the impact can nevertheless be dealt with. All the controller has to do is to say, "Let us compare A with B. A is the old way, B is the new way." Admittedly, what the controller comes up with may be his or her interpretation of how best to carry out the comparison. That means it may be rather arbitrary; but so long as the same rules are used consistently, the amount of impact will be perceived correctly from year to year.

There are other interpretive definitions that the controller must devise for cases when the innovation results in incremental license income, profits from minority positions in other companies, or joint ventures. With a little imagination, a good controller can come up with a valid measure of dollar impact in each of these cases, a measure that is understood and accepted by top management.

Payback Calculations

Payback* calculations are also worth doing and including in the impact statement. Again, the controllers will know how to set these up so as to provide useful, easily understood data, even when the situation is complex.

For example, how much was invested in the innovation? If we consider only the funds spent in the innovation organization, that might result in spectacularly swift payback ratios, because most of those investments are dedicated to only the first five steps of the innovation process. Not only do such numbers not cover the other two steps, usually far more expensive and usually performed by the client organization, but they leave out the costs of facilitating and tooling and promoting the new creation. All of these costs can be much higher. (In Chapter 4, Figure 4-2 showed how widely the levels of spending can differ between the innovation organization and the receiving organization.)

The best way to handle this dilemma is to make two sets of calculations. Show payback numbers first for the innovation organization by itself and then as part of a larger investment that includes what the client had to contribute. Let management mull over each set of figures. The result will be a broader and more honest

* Payback is defined as the number of years required to accumulate a sum of money equal to the sum of both the investment in an innovation and the venture that results from it from net cash generated from operating that venture.

presentation that will lead to a more inclusive and deeper under-standing of what has been accomplished than if payback were shown for only one class of expenditure.

Giving and Taking Credit

Who deserves the credit for the financial impact an innovation has had? That should be in the impact statement too. The right principle is, "Give credit where credit is due."

Nothing is more irritating to the client organization than innovators claiming all the credit for an accomplishment—especially if the impact statement testifies to its great value. Give credit right in the impact statement to all who deserve recognition.

Credit, justly allocated, implies rewards, also justly allocated, for those responsible for the salubrious impact. Management has responsibility for giving rewards to all deserving employees and for doing it in a manner compatible with the magnitude of the achievement. (See Chapter 9 for a complete discussion of this matter.) The impact statement should leave no doubt about the magnitude of impact and about who contributed which portion. It is officially documented and therefore has credibility.

What if the impact is negative? That has to be recorded, too. As with any other activity in business (and in life), truthfulness is the best policy. Waffling or leaving out negative facts is a bad practice not just because it is immoral but because it won't work. The truth always comes out. Innovators know that failure is not a sin—so long as it is tempered with a reasonable proportion of successes. So they are not ashamed of it. The challenge is to have a management that views the situation with the same broad per-spective. Telling the truth in the impact statement, the whole truth, only aids in raising its level of credibility.

The Impact of the Statement

People engaged in the demanding tasks of running a business do not automatically make a point of investigating what their own innovation investment means to them. They tend to ride year after year on superficial impressions, and that goes for both the good and the bad consequences of an investment. As a result, only superficial attention is paid to including consideration of technology and innovation in the formation of company strategy. To improve the situation, innovation managers must increase the depth of knowledge their superiors receive about the R&D operation and its effects on the company's bottom line.

"Are you trying to tell me that 21 percent of last year's sales from our transformer division were due to that new model S1711 developed by their research group and introduced three years ago?" the CEO asks, incredulous. "I didn't know that. And the increase of 18 percent in margins in the graphics division comes from that new ink the technology center came up with last year. I knew they had come up with a new ink, but I didn't know it had improved margins that much." It's time *your* CEO knows these types of things. As I stated at the beginning of this chapter, those in charge are often favorably surprised.

Only with a periodically prepared, well-researched, well-organized, highly quantitative, well-presented research statement can the company feel confident about what actions to take in the future, both in the long and short term, in the area of innovation.

Part 3

Company Policies— Company Support

8

How Can Management Facilitate Innovation?

Up to now, this book has dealt with how to set up autonomous innovation entities and how to manage them to achieve their goals with efficiency and timeliness. Innovation was shown to be a process, as pictured schematically in Figure 1-1 of Chapter 1, which informs us that while these organizations are "implementation means" leading directly to the achievement of "goals" there are still several factors, represented by the blocks entitled "support groups" and "the executive office," that can facilitate the process. The facilitating roles of management and staff is the subject of the three chapters that make up Part 3.

The support groups are strongly interdependent and provide ways in which significant back-up can be supplied by company managers, the subject of this chapter, and by the human resources department, discussed in the following one. If it chooses to be, the executive office is the ultimate support system. From it emanates the company philosophy and culture that gives thrust to the flow of innovation. It empowers the innovators, giving them the credibility required to achieve their mission. That empowering environment is treated in Chapter 10, the final chapter of Part 3.

Figure 1-2 (see Chapter 1) shows the master chart of innovation. It lists the following five support functions that link the company's strategies for attaining a variety of growth goals with the means of attaining those goals by using innovation organizations.

1. Sponsor.
2. Champion.
3. Encourager/facilitator.
4. Human resources department.
5. Idea groups.

Of these five functions, the sponsor is the most important.

Sponsors

American Heritage Dictionary defines *sponsor* as: "One who assumes responsibility for a person or group during a period of instruction, apprenticeship, or probation" and "one who vouches for the suitability of a candidate for admission." Both definitions imply a kind of rite of passage involving a mature authority figure and an unproved candidate for respectability and eventual maturity. How do these concepts apply to a business?

Required Status of a Sponsor of Innovation

Sponsors, to be effective, must have clout. They must be "mature authority figures" indeed. In a company, this personage is a company officer or at least a division manager. In either case, the sponsor holds a position of power.

What does power consist of in a company? Two things: First, such a person can, in the normal course of a workday, engage in dialogue with the chief executive officer or, in a large company, with someone almost as exalted, like a group vice president, and thus influence the course the company, or a major segment of it, will take. (In fact, the sponsor may possess the ultimate intimacy with the CEO or the group vice president, for he or she may be that very person. There is no reason why the top executive in a company cannot be a sponsor.) Second, such a person, one way or another, commands a purse, for which he or she holds the purse strings. With these two attributes, a person can fit into our definition of sponsor, for they are the minimum required of "one who assumes responsibility."

There may be individuals in a company who are eager to assume the role of sponsor but who do not possess these powers. Enlist their aid. Everyone who favors innovation is a force for good. But don't fool yourself—such a person is not a sponsor, for to qualify a person must have the boss's ear and the means to establish and finance innovation. Nevertheless, he or she may be a champion, another function that is dealt with later in this chapter.

The Sponsor's Job

One might think that the need for sponsorship is obvious and thus does not require detailed treatment here. But the fact is, innovation is not a trivial activity for any firm to engage in, and any nontrivial activity cannot come to fruition without executive approval. However, approval and sponsorship are not the same thing, the former is merely a head-nod, while the latter implies wholehearted active support.

The role of sponsor, once undertaken, cannot be passive or even reactive. Sponsors have a job to do. They must convince superiors, in some cases the board of directors, of the wisdom of the course to be taken. They may not have to do that in the earliest days of the program, when the sponsor can provide support without approval from others, but the time eventually comes when the innovation program must receive its hearing from top management.

The sponsor must similarly convince both peers and staff of the value of a particular R&D project. Of course, it helps if the innovation sells itself because it is irresistible. But we must expect those not involved to find it remarkably easy to resist, and that is all the more reason to have a persuasive and powerful sponsor.

In addition, money must be found to pay for hours to be expended, and materials to be consumed, and a place to work in. Permission to borrow equipment and workers from other areas of the company must be granted. (These issues should be familiar. They were the subject of Part 1 of this book.) None of this will happen without a powerful sponsor.

Sponsors have still another important role. They cut through red tape. In all companies, some rules exist that will muddy waters, slow movement, prohibit passage—in short, frustrate innovators. It's not that they are bad rules; they are useful for dealing with what has already been established. But they can damage what is about to be established. A sponsor knows how to get around them, and a good sponsor can do it gracefully and tactfully so as to minimize the number of noses knocked out of joint.

Sponsors are vital to creating a new innovation organization. But they are needed just as much in launching a major new innovation program or a new venture by an already existing R&D organization. The requirements and the rules—and benefits—are the same. When there is a sponsor, the program's chances for success improve significantly.

Finding and Enlisting Your Sponsor

Sponsors are rare. Most executives attain the upper reaches of a company hierarchy by steadfastly grinding away through their careers, imbued with an ethic that combines minimization of risk with the goal of meeting monthly or quarterly fiscal goals. They tend not to favor innovation, which entails risk and diverts employees from the primary tasks of making and selling established products. Those executives understand only too well that risk and diversion can seriously erode sales and profits.

But take heart. There is always someone among the company officers who is listed on the last page of the annual report and who is infected with the innovation bug (even though that fact may be carefully hidden from public view). Innovation is more a part of American culture than of any other national culture. As we grow up, we embrace and idealize Edison as much as the current popular music star; we admire the inventors of the transistor and new software languages and those who manipulate genes as much as we cheer on a sports hero. Those who are bent on innovation, either to found and build an innovation organization or to launch a particular innovation project, must identify and win over that uncommon, but not nonexistent, person.

How is it done? By bravely doing it. The person with the innovation vision (usually a member of middle management or a principal investigator, either of whom has conceived a new way to implement a new idea and who is *consumed* by that idea) manages to summon up the guts or *chutzpah* (guts fortified with gall) to knock on every door in executive row until he or she finds the vice president who is infected with the fatal weakness: the up-till-now dormant bug.

Once found, the susceptible executive must be thoroughly sold on the project. When the sponsor is a believer who's ready to go out on a limb even while fellow executives jeer, the innovation activity is on its way. It has stepped onto the first rung of the process; making that first step might be the hardest job the innovators have to accomplish.

I have checked with innovators in dozens of firms through the years, and I have never unearthed an innovation program that resulted in viable incremental business which reached that state without a sponsor. If I were to ennoble any company employee with the title of "hero," it is the person who emerges as sponsor.

Sponsors Finding Innovators

It can work the other way, too. The sponsor can be the initiator of the relationship, finding worthy innovation programs and organizing dedicated people to pursue them. Indeed, that is the way it should be, for such an action is an expression of leadership. Are not sponsors in a company position from which leadership should be expected? Alas, it is overwhelmingly the case that that someone from the lower ranks persuades those with higher status.

But even though sponsorship is usually born in a bottom-up process, a top-down route is sometimes taken. In the end, the nature of the process doesn't matter, because true sponsorship is true commitment regardless of how it was initiated.

The Life Cycle of a Sponsor

The need for sponsors changes with time; in fact, it can disappear. This happens when the innovation organization, by virtue of its track record of accomplishments, one day emerges as a full member of the establishment and no longer needs a sponsor. So long as it continues to fulfill its role, it will maintain that independent status. That becomes its challenge, because what it has to watch out for is that, like any mature organism, it not drift with time into impotence. (But that is another problem entirely, requiring other skills than those of sponsorship.)

Champions

Turning again to our dictionary, we learn that a *champion* is "one who fights for, defends, or supports a cause or another person." Insofar as innovation in business is concerned, I can add that champions are those employees who inject emotion and obsession into a program or an organization. Unbusinesslike though those terms may seem, they are necessary ingredients of successful innovation.

R. T. Ossman of Michigan Bell extends the definition:

> Product champions [are] . . . those individuals who contribute entrepreneurial spirit and initiative. . . . When executive support for innovation is diffused or lacking, product champions are unable to provide the type of leadership needed to successfully implement innovative ideas. . . . Strong executive support and sponsorship is the single most important factor that enables product champions to overcome the bureaucratic roadblocks of a large corporation.[1]

Here is one more extension to our definition, derived from a summary statement by a panel made up of a group of ten R&D managers:

> The key characteristic of the product champion is the tension between the individual and what the organization wants. Thus . . . the collective wisdom of the organization would have killed the idea without the emergence of the product champion. . . . It doesn't matter where in the ranks that individual is.[2]

The Rank of the Champion

An effective leader of an innovation organization should be (at least one of) the champions of the group's projects. In the same way, the principal investigator, who could be the primary source of the idea and the concept that will make it real, may also be a champion. There is nothing wrong with having two champions—the more the merrier. These working-level innovators are what may be characterized as internal champions, in the sense that they rank below the high executives who make up top management.

Of course, high-ranking managers can be champions too. In view of their position of authority in the company, they are often much more effective. Let us call them "executive champions." Sometimes a sponsor is also the champion—which makes the situation better yet.

The Qualities of Champions

A. K. Chakrabarti provides a list of the personal traits of good champions. These are:

Technical competence.
Knowledge about the company.
Knowledge about the market.
Drive and aggressiveness.
Political astuteness.[3]

The panel of R&D managers added another trait, intuition, saying: "In a sense . . . a product champion's behavior represents a movement away from the traditional economic rationality that governs most modern bureacracies."[4] The panel went on to comment that there could be too much of that rationality; sometimes "one of the product champion's personal strengths was that he or she did not recognize the 'irrationality' of what they were doing. . . . More than likely, champions are following intuitive conclusions that make good sense to them." They conclude that without such intuitive input, great opportunities might be lost.

Those Who Break Through

Some innovators loom larger than everyone else. They are the elite of the pack, the people who "did it all." That type of person is often simultaneously the creator of the idea, the conceiver of the concept on which to base its development, the implementer of the innovation process, the sponsor, the champion, the project manager, the business manager, the chief executive officer, and more—to the point of becoming a captain of industry of our nation. Such people are like the rare baseball player who "hits for the circuit" and who ends up owning the ball club.

Thomas Edison was just such a remarkable person, as is Edwin Land, who invented the instant camera and founded and managed his own multi-billion-dollar company, Polaroid, while he was at it. Percy Spencer, who held more than 100 patents, among them the one for microwave cooking (see Appendix 2), and who finished his career as Executive Vice President of Raytheon Company, belongs on this list. Stephen Wozniak of Apple Computer is another.

If these stars have a single quality that outstrips all their other stupendous qualities, it is as fervent champions, of themselves and of their causes. In most cases they end up in positions of top management. Nayak and Ketteringham tab them as innovators who have broken through conventional practices, hence the title of their book, *Breakthroughs!* and its subtitle, *How the Vision and Drive of Innovators in Sixteen Companies Created Commercial Breakthroughs That Swept the World.*[5] Included are the sagas of the creation of VCRs, microwave ovens, Federal Express, and 13 other innovations.

Managing Champions

It goes without saying that emotionally motivated employees like those who assume the roles of champions may pose management problems. They deserve the incentive rewards described in the following chapter, especially if what they champion succeeds. If it doesn't succeed, they still should be rewarded in some rational fashion.

Champions can devote their considerable energies as passionately to innovations that are fated to fail as to those that will make it. Here the executive office must take a hand. Sponsors must be so blessed with wisdom as to know which program of which champion to sponsor. (I never said innovation was going to be easy, only that it can be more exhilarating and interesting than anything else a company can engage in.)

Some champions have meager leadership qualities and even fewer managerial qualities. Again, the executive office must take action to save the company. It must know when to challenge the vision and enthusiasm of the champion and when to transfer management to managers (even those who are not so visionary or enthusiastic, who bring no more to the scene than their capabilities for orderly management).

Encouragers/Facilitators

No company deserves the benefits of innovation if it does not encourage it to happen and if it does not facilitate its progress. Those businesses that consciously take actions to find and aid their innovators will greatly improve their chances to reap a flourishing crop of new products, new processes, and new ventures.

Company Culture as Encourager/Facilitator

Some encouragement for innovators derives from a positive company culture. For example, at 3M, a star among large firms when innovation is the criterion, company culture mandates that a new idea cannot be rejected unless management generates a convincing case showing its deficiencies. The burden of proof resides with the executive office. Such an attitude shows (encouragingly) how deeply sad the firm feels when it has to reject what one of its employees has conceived. How different that is from the usual position adopted by most managements, which begin consideration of a new innovation idea with an automatic rejection and then might allow themselves to be persuaded of the opposite by the champion pointing out the new idea's good points. It is the difference between starting with a positive or a negative attitude—exemplified by the classic questions: Is the glass half full or half empty? Is the person on the dock innocent till proven guilty or guilty till proven innocent? But more of culture in Chapter 10.

Organizing the Pre-Program Phase

There is a stage in innovation that precedes the emergence of the champion and the introduction of the sponsor. It occurs before we even know what the innovation might be and who will work on it. It represents a step or steps prior to the seven steps to efficient innovation. If the first step of the seven is the idea, this has to be "pre-idea." I will dub it the let's-find-and-nurture-an-idea stage.

The pre-program stage can be left to chance or it can be organized to optimize what one derives from it both in quality and quantity. There is no question that leaving it to chance can work. In most companies, ideas generated by motivated and creative employees simply surface. Many bosses would say, "Who needs more than that? We can't even find time to consider most of those ideas." Our response to that position is that "surfacing" must necessarily have aspects of randomness, if not capriciousness. So, even for those who take that position, why not invest this pre-program stage with order and control and, even to a degree, with predictability? If there is an increase of quality and quantity, so much the better, for then one's options are improved. Indeed the real blockbuster idea may emerge thereby, an idea that would never have seen the light of day since the person who would be its champion happens to be shy and nonassertive. It can be done, and more and more companies are doing it.

Organizing the stage of finding and nurturing an idea consists of two major elements. First, generating a formal program to mine the minds of the employees for new concepts and second, aiding the new concepts through their first moments of existence (George Seifert, Vice President of Corporate Planning and Development at Ameritech Publishing, calls such aid "incubation").

Chapter 17 describes how Eastman Kodak uses these "facilitated" ideas, nurturing them to the point of skunk works status. Bob Rosenfeld, Kodak's Director of Innovation Network Development, is also the founder of his company's Office of Innovation Network; there are 18 separate encourager/facilitator offices, one in each major EK operation worldwide. Rosenfeld coined the expression "encourager/facilitator" and has written illuminatingly, with co-author Jenny Servo, about how it works.[6]

Essentially, employees are invited to come up with ideas for new products, businesses, or ventures. Submission of an "idea memorandum" (IM) implies that the ideator intends to be identified with it, possibly even to the point of being willing to change his or her career path. This differs from submission of a suggestion to Kodak's Suggestion System, which implies that the suggester typically remains on the sidelines as someone else picks the idea up and implements it.

The facilitator now undertakes to study each submission by sending it for appraisal by selected internal consultants. This procedure provides feedback, on the basis of which the originator can redraft the idea to improve it, or choose to abandon it. What remains is truly worthy of further consideration.

Those ideas may warrant further action in the form of market analysis (Is there a need? Will it sell? Who will buy it? For how much?) and determination of likely manufacturing procedures and costs. Such information will provide the basis for the generation of a preliminary business concept draft, which management requires and deserves if it is to go on to exploit the idea. The facilitator will make sure that such a plan will be formulated and that it will be credible. How can this happen when the prospective innovator is a mere neophyte in such matters? The encourager/facilitator will provide or recruit help and tutelage. Any gap in the innovator's capability will be filled.

The facilitator has to do this because many of the neophyte innovators simply do not have the needed experience. They don't know how to conduct a market analysis or how to survey possible manufacturing procedures. They often have little awareness of costs. But the facilitator provides, from someplace in the company, just the right expertise, and pays for it with funds from the facilitation budget. It is a case of "sanctioned" bootlegging. That is facilitation indeed.

The innovator has to participate too. But where does the time come from? Some of it is the new innovator's own time, at nights and on weekends. Some more may be cajoled, by the originator or the facilitator, from the innovator's boss. That may not be easy and usually generates some resistance, for to the innovator's boss, a heretofore loyal employee now has divided loyalties and new priorities. (The facilitator's job is definitely not an easy one.)

If the idea still looks good, it can go on to the next stage, and the next; as it progresses, others fall by the wayside. In talking with people from several companies that engage in this facilitation process, I have discovered a set of statistics, common to all. For every 1,000 submitted ideas (actually for a range of between 500 and 1,500), perhaps 100 are selected for developing a preliminary market and manufacturing analysis plan. Of those, 20 are designated as being worthy of launching as feasibility programs (which means entrance into our sequence of seven steps of innovation). By the time the third step, feasibility, has been demonstrated, four ideas have survived.

The facilitator now leaves the scene, but not before performing one more essential act. He or she finds a sponsor for each of these surviving innovation ideas.

A system like the one at Eastman Kodak has had good success at many other firms, Owens/Corning Fiberglas (OCF) among them. John Zaloudek, who managed the OCF program during its early years, kindly submitted the documents that make up Figure 8-1; they are examples of the kinds of literature and forms employees had been given to initiate the encouraged, facilitated idea on its path to company commitment. Another example is Ohio Bell's, shown in Figure 8-2.

Ameritech Publishing, which I visited in early 1987, has a facilitation program called GENESIS. It provides a good example of executive office support for innovation.

Genesis at Ameritech Publishing

Ameritech Publishing is a subsidiary of American Technologies, Inc. (Ameritech, Inc.), one of the seven regional Bell companies formed when ATT was reorganized. (Ameritech, Inc., is the holding company of those telephone companies that provide telephone services to the northern Midwest and includes other subsidiaries, such as Illinois Bell, Michigan Bell, Indiana Bell, Wisconsin Bell, and Ohio Bell.) Ameritech Publishing is in the business of publishing and marketing directory advertising products and services, such as various kinds of yellow pages. Each kind constitutes a separate product, many of which are highly innovative in basic concept. Ameritech Publishing has yearly revenues in the $1 billion range. It has 2,000 employees and is located in Troy, Michigan.

The Solicitation Document
Each employee receives a handsome bound booklet, whose frontispiece says:

> The President of Ameritech Publishing, Inc., is pleased to announce GENESIS, a program designed for your participation as we answer the challenges of the future which will assure the continued success of our company.

On page 10 is the exhortation:

> The basic principle is simple: We are seeking ideas which suggest ways in which to grow. Major ways in major markets.

I can do no better in describing how Ameritech Publishing proceeds to implement its quest for ideas and to turn them into reality than to extract a few more quotations from the pages that follow:

> An individual conceives the idea that Ameritech Publishing could enter market X and produce product Y. They believe

(Text continues on page 163.)

Figure 8-1. Owens/Corning Fiberglas documents for in-house solicitation of "facilitated" ideas.

New Product Concept Idea

Idea Title _____

Submitted By _____   Phone _____

Location _____   MOD Ident. No. _____

MOD Skunkworks Philosophy
Our skunkworks is intended to be a step, or series of steps between an idea and the implementation of a full-fledged product development program. This hands-on, free-wheeling, plan-by-doing, low-level technical/mechanical feasibility effort is designed to replace endless discussion about the benefits and shortcomings of an idea. Using this "learn by trying" process, we will determine the workability of an idea, learn more about potential applications, and do both more quickly at minimal cost.

MOD Innovation Board
There are four members of the MOD Innovation Board:
- MOD Planning Manager, Toledo
- TOD/MD Portfolio Director, Granville
- IOD/NCP/FRPC Portfolio Director, Granville
- MOD Manager New Business Development, Toledo

You may contact one of these people about your idea anytime. Upon receiving an idea, one of the board members will contact you about your idea. The purpose of this contact will be to discuss what *you* want to do with *your* idea and what help *you* need to pursue *your* idea. The emphasis is on *you,* the individual employee!

The Innovation Board member will help clarify the idea and identify the support you need, including money to purchase materials or to obtain technical help in Granville. The Innovation Board will discuss your idea to determine the best available resources and respond to you promptly with two things: (1) the amount of financial support you will receive and (2) who your "mentor" will be. Your mentor will serve as coach and a resource as you develop your idea.

Send to: MOD Manager, New Business Development, Fiberglas Tower (OB/8), Toledo, OH 43659

Courtesy of Owens/Corning Fiberglas

(continued)

Figure 8-1 *(continued)*.

Problem/Need
Describe the problem or need as you see it—What is it; who has it; when, where and why does it occur.

_____
_____
_____
_____
_____
_____
_____
_____
_____
_____
_____
_____
_____
_____
_____
_____
_____
_____

Current Product/Solution
Describe how the problem or need is currently satisfied. Also describe what's wrong with current product/solution.

_____
_____
_____
_____
_____
_____
_____
_____
_____
_____
_____
_____
_____
_____
_____
_____
_____
_____

Costs

What are costs for the current product/solution. Consider all parts of cost - unit cost, freight, installation and maintenance or replacement.

_____

_____

_____

_____

_____

_____

Identify the source(s) of your cost information _____

_____

_____

_____

Product/Concept Idea

Describe your idea and how it solves the problem or satisfies the need. Attach pictures and drawings. Use back page for sketches.

_____

_____

_____

_____

_____

_____

_____

_____

_____

_____

_____

_____

_____

_____

_____

_____

_____

_____

_____

_____

_____

Have you disclosed your idea to persons outside OCF (including OCF subsidiaries, affiliates or licensees?) ☐ _yes_ ☐ _no_

(continued)

Figure 8-1 *(continued)*.

Sketches/Graphs - pertaining to idea.

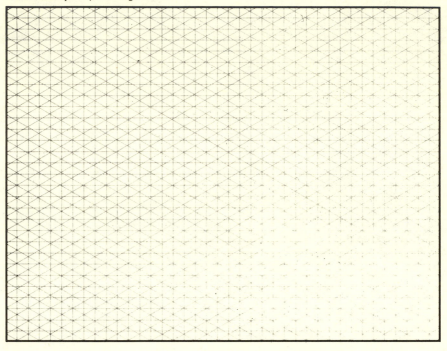

Other Information Sources - include customers, experts, publications and organizations.

Name   **Address**   **Phone**

_____
_____
_____
_____
_____
_____
_____

I understand this idea belongs to Owens-Corning Fiberglas Corp.

Intrapreneur(s) Signature   Dates

_____   _____
_____   _____
                                                          _____

Read and understood by

_____   _____
_____   _____

Pub. No. 15-MO-12985   Litho in U.S.A., January, 1985   Copyright © 1985 Owens-Corning Fiberglas Corp.

SUGGESTED APPROACH TO GAIN SUPPORT FOR YOUR IDEA,
PROJECT OR BUSINESS VENTURE

GENERAL CONCEPT

Create and develop stakeholders by sharing your idea. Obtain support for
your idea from others. Connect with several customers or users. Ask for
advice and evaluation from customers and inside supporters.

SUGGESTED APPROACH

. Identify ten potential "inside" supporters. For each person, identify
  the area, function or facet of your idea where each of these ten
  potential supporters is probably (a) most in support of you; and (b)
  least in support of you.

. From this analysis of possible supporters, select the three "that now
  seem to be most accessible" (and ideally "most powerful") as a
  stakeholder.

. Approach these three possible supporters <u>personally</u> to:

  (a) Educate, inform and involve them so that they understand your idea.

  (b) Seek their advice about how to "sell" your idea or project. Make
       them a stakeholder - ask each to help you. Have specific needs
       identified so they can select an area of interest to give you help.

  (c) Ask each one who else might be willing and able to help with and
       support your idea.

. Continue to build support. Contact newly identified supporters.
  Continually update supporters previously established about your progress
  and new needs.

. Find a way to expose your idea to one or more potential customers or
  users - <u>they are the only people who can truly evaluate an idea or
  concept</u>. For product ideas work with prototype or scale models. Use
  your network to find supportive marketing and sales people who can
  become a stakeholder and help make customer connections.

. Suggested criteria for identifying customers are: 1) OCF dedicated
  customers with strong relationships; 2) innovative "triers" and "early
  adopters" - like to be involved in new things; 3) knowledgeable of the
  market, it's products and factors that are important for new products;
  4) willing to "invest" in a new idea by trying the idea and sharing in
  the cost.

. Determine your next steps - small, fast and cheap - to utilize the
  support base to advance your idea.

                          6/6/86 (R2)

Adapted from presentation by:
  Gustaf Delin
  The ForeSight Group
  May 1985

Figure 8-2.   Ohio Bell's "Invitation to Innovate."

AN INVITATION TO INNOVATE

You are cordially invited to use your knowledge, insight, and creativity to find new ways to help Ohio Bell continue to earn the respect of customers and the loyalty of employees. Enter-Prize wants your ideas. Your creativity can help Ohio Bell reduce expenses, bring in additional revenue, and develop new lines of business. Enter-Prize is eager to help implement your best ideas and reward you for furthering our company's success.

If you need some suggestions to get started, we interviewed Ohio Bell's executives to determine where they would like employees to focus their efforts. Some of their recommendations may get you thinking:

- Reducing the costs of ordering, provisioning and billing our services.

- Reducing the costs of delivering employee benefits.

- Pinpointing management plans or procedures which could be marketed to other companies or organizations, within the telecommunications industry and beyond.

- Preparing for future demands for new service without undue expense or delay.

We hope these ideas can be springboards to innovation. We urge you to use an Innovation Form 9694 to submit your ideas to Enter-Prize. For more information, call:

216-822-IDEA   **ENTER-PRIZE**
                   Excellence Through
                   Employee Innovation

Courtesy of Ohio Bell

> this is a good potential for entry for several different reasons, but always because market X or product Y is related to Ameritech Publishing's business.
>
> In conventional systems, an innovative idea could be squelched early in the game by one's immediate supervisor. We have designed a scenario which avoids politics, levels, and bias.
>
> It is crucial if a creative idea is to grow into reality, that it be planted in a conducive environment.
>
> At Ameritech Publishing this environment has a home in the Corporate Planning & Development organization. Corporate Planning & Development reviews the idea.
>
> If a thought created meets the corporate objective and appears to have the potential impact and significance which is needed, the employee and his or her idea are brought into a specifically designed structure which is . ... affectionately referred to as the "Incubator."
>
> Designed exclusively to plant and cultivate product ideas, the "Incubator" has a staff available with the expertise needed to direct an innovative idea from a concept to a working reality.

The text goes on to outline what could happen if the idea is considered worthy of company investment. The originator of the idea may take the equivalent of an internal leave of absence from his or her present job in a time frame expected to be about six months. But should that employee wish to return to his or her previous status and department, the original position will be preserved so that option will be available. Additional compensation for outstanding contributions will be made, and it will be supplemented by corporate recognition and "the opportunity to use even more of one's talent."

The Incubator

The incubator's staff consists of some 15 employees of the corporate planning and development staff, all of whom are available to aid the originator on a part-time or full-time basis. They possess expertise in many disciplines, including marketing, financing, and statistics. These experts participate in the incubation process for each selected candidate by devoting significant time and effort to each.

During incubation, a feasibility study is made and a business case is developed. After review by management, the business case is the basis for the formation of a business plan. That plan is detailed enough to act as the blueprint for the new venture.

The business plan is presented to the company's top management (usually by the originator, also known as the "product champion") and the GENESIS booklet concludes with the statement:

If support is given, you have just begun a new business.

Prospects

Ameritech Publishing's vice president of corporate planning and development informed me that after only three years, five ventures have been started and are producing revenues—four are profitable and one is in a loss position. The company is pleased with progress to date in using this technique of encouraging and facilitating innovation, and expects that significant positive impact on the bottom line will occur in most of these, because no new product or venture is accepted that has lesser prospects than to grow to $10 million of sales per year.

Mechanisms for Building an Environment Hospitable to Innovation

Does the company *really* want its employees to be innovative? Only by its actions will the firm demonstrate the extent and sincerity of its commitment. Employees will know whether these actions are just "for show" or whether management means it.

Some of the procedures for demonstrating corporate commitment are so obvious as to seem corny, but they're still effective. Almost every business circulates a company organ. Does it have a column entitled "Innovation" or "Intrapreneuring" or "New Venture Status"? If it has, and if that section documents how the company is building incremental business, the impact on employees is real.

Another technique that works with similar good results is to hold publicized ceremonies ("The Inventors' Dinner") once or twice a year. Everyone who matters is invited, including spouses or live-in friends of honorees. It takes place in the best hall in town and the master of ceremonies is no less than the company president. Such activities are always encouraged by the human relations department.

Another very effective encouragement mechanism is an innovation fair. Such fairs are very like the science fairs that most innovators starred in when they were high school students. It worked then and it can work now. Ohio Bell's fair is one of the best.

Ohio Bell's Innovation Fair

Cyndi McCabe, a member of Ohio Bell's support services staff, has been designated "Enter-Prize Administrator," and I thank her for providing the information in this section.

Figure 8-3 shows the front page of the announcement of the fair and its floor plan for the two locations in which it was held on two sequential weeks, and Figure 8-4 is an "action photo" taken at the Cleveland event. Each fair began with a kick-off breakfast attended by more than 100 employees and company executives. At the event in Cleveland, the president and vice presidents of Ohio Bell were joined by a top executive from Ameritech, Inc., Ohio Bell's parent company.

Ohio Bell employees flocked to the fair in substantial numbers. Long lines of employees had used their breaks or lunch periods to attend or, in some instances, had been given time off for this purpose. They viewed the fair not as a lark away from their desks or work benches, but as a chance to view an impressive group of accomplishments by their fellow workers, accomplishments that would one day rebound to their benefit as employees of this forward-looking company.

As for the exhibits, many were quite impressive. They conformed for the most part to Step 4, engineering models, although some were no further along than Step 3, feasibility models. Some were visuals (Step 5), and a few had reached prototype level (Step 6).

The Enter-Prize program, begun in July 1985, was set up to meet the needs of Ohio Bell's new post-divestiture environment. Ohio Bell felt that success in the telecommunications industry—with rapid changes taking place in technology, markets, and customers' demands—would come to companies that could capture initiative and run with it. So it set up a program that gives employees

Figure 8-3. Announcement and floor plans of Ohio Bell's innovation fair.

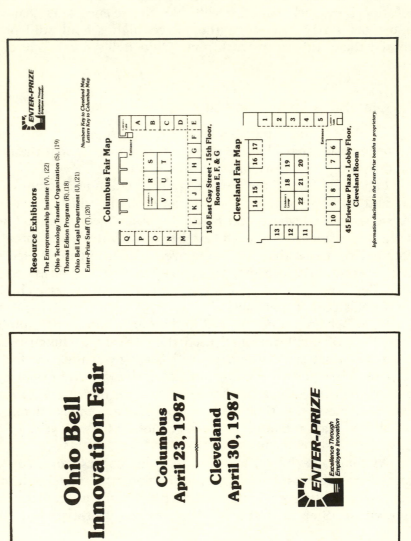

Courtesy of Ohio Bell

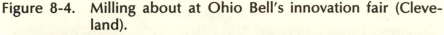

Figure 8-4.   Milling about at Ohio Bell's innovation fair (Cleveland).

Courtesy of Ohio Bell

power to implement the cost-saving, revenue-producing ideas that they are in position to see most clearly.

Ms. McCabe informed me that next year's innovation fair is already in the initial phase of organization.

One side comment: Ohio Bell brought these innovations to their present state of fruition without benefit of having set up any of our eight kinds of innovation means.

Thus, Ohio Bell is starting almost from scratch. As evidenced by the exhibits in the fair, it has accomplished much in a very short time in terms of building motivation among its employees to become innovators. How did it do that without formal technology centers or new products centers—or even captive R&D groups? The way most companies begin. By piggybacking innovation within existing line operations. But I venture to say, having come this far, that this company's next step will be the creation of at least one kind of formal innovation organization of the sort described in this book.

Those who won encouragement were given seed money and permission to take time off from their daily assignments, when needed, to pursue their extracurricular tasks. Such ad hoc procedures smack of sanctioned bootlegging, and maybe they qualify as a ninth mode of innovation. For like unsanctioned bootlegging, they can achieve meaningful results. But I steadfastly hold to the primary position that is the theme of this book. Organizing for innovation—purposely and with intent—is, if done right, faster and more efficient. But having made that statement, let us examine one more ad hoc approach to facilitating innovation: idea teams.

Idea Teams

Instead of polling the entire body of employees for suggestions for new products and new ventures, the same kind of result can be obtained by setting up temporary teams of selected middle- and upper-level employees to engage in high-intensity off-site programs. It is not a new idea; 3M and IBM do it. Our example is Signode.

The keys to success are incorporated in the phrases "selected" and "high intensity." We can add others: "with relief from normal assignments," which amounts to virtual "total commitment." As for the important jobs these people have been performing, they must simply be assigned to other capable employees.

I have served on many committees for determining which new products to develop and which new ventures to embark on. I can report that, unless the course to take is obvious, wise choices rarely derive from a one-hour meeting once a week, even if the committee members are experts. Good decisions, that is, those leading to potential blockbusters rather than to modest and mundane programs or enterprises, can emerge only after in-depth and unfettered study, which requires total dedication.

In effect, the team members are locked up in a room and told not to come out until they come up with an idea for a new venture that fits their company. This can go on for months. The Signode division of Illinois Tool Works (ITW) calls such teams "V-Teams" ("V" for *venture*) and gives them six to nine months to produce.

V-Teams at Signode

Signode, prior to its acquisition by ITW in 1986, was an old-line company, founded in 1913, which is recognized as a worldwide leader in a basic industrial product, steel strapping for industrial packaging and materials handling. It is located in Glenview, Illinois, and had 1984 sales of $751 million. The new combined company has sales approximately double this of $1.5 billion. The description of the operation of idea teams to promote innovation and new venture development deals with activity that took place prior to the time of that acquisition.

V-teams at Signode have received good press.[7] It is clear on reading the literature, and on talking with Jack Campbell who was vice president of new business development when these teams were organized and operated, that the company had many reasons to enter the 20th century, if not the 21st, with new products and ventures. Because of its overcommitment to a nongrowth business, it set the goal of cutting reliance on strapping systems from 75 percent to 50 percent in five years.

Signode already had a sterling set of employees, many of whom had demonstrated imagination and drive. Those people would be the resource whereby such change would be accomplished. In other words, why go outside? All that had to be done was to organize capable loyal workers into task forces that would come up with the answers.

In late 1983, Signode identified six strategic areas in which to build new business. It then "assigned a half-dozen innovative people to each of six groups to exploit these areas. Each group, operating without an official leader, scoured markets seeking unsatisfied demand. . . . The packaging team, for example, spent six months in basic market research, interviewing 2,000 food industry employees ranging from CEOs to production-line people. Team members traveled in pairs, usually one marketing and one technology expert."[8]

Who are the team members? No less than the company's best and brightest. Dr. Schaffhauser, executive vice president and chief executive officer, describes them as consisting of "interdisciplinary groups of six or so employees, usually volunteers, who are brought together to tackle a special mission. Typically, the employees are 'borrowed' from operating divisions. Team members may be full-

or part-time, may or may not have an official leader, and may work on- or off-site."[9]

When the venture is launched, the members of the team tend to shift their careers into managing it. But if they prefer, they can return to their previous assignments or into the next venture team. It is "success" that motivates them. Schaffhauser goes on to say that "as volunteers on a new capital investment opportunity, V-team participants are enthusiastic entrepreneurs." Which is what a company wants when it engages in new ventures. And as entrepreneurs, they expect and will receive concomitant rewards.

No venture is considered for company commitment unless it has the potential for $50 million in yearly sales in five years. It must also stay within such additional guidelines as: It must build on Signode's strengths in marketing to industry, utilize existing technology, have the chance to become an industry leader, and involve an initial capital outlay not exceeding $30 million.

After a follow-up discussion with Mr. Campbell, just as this book goes to press, I am pleased to report that eight ventures formed out of the V-team approach now exist as small business entities for ITW. Several of them, for example, the operation that manufactures art-leading "dual-ovenable" polyester trays used as packages for frozen food and suitable for heating and cooking in both conventional and microwave ovens,[10] give good prospects of attaining the original goal of sales exceeding $50 million.

References

1. R. T. Ossman, "Product Champions: an Endangered Species," *Intrapreneurial Excellence*, August 1986, p. 9.

2. W. A. Fischer, W. Hamilton, C. P. McLaughlin, and R. W. Zmud, "The Elusive Product Champion," *Research Management*, May–June 1986, p. 13.

3. A. K. Chakrabarti, "The Role of the Champion in Product Innovation," *California Management Review*, 17:2 (Winter 1974), pp. 56–62.

4. Fischer et al., op. cit.

5. P. R. Nayak and J. M. Ketteringham, *Breakthroughs!* (New York: Rawson Associates, 1986).

6. R. Rosenfeld and J. C. Servo, "Making Ideas Connect," *The Futurist*, August 1984, pp. 21–26.

7. R. J. Schaffhauser, "Charting the Future with Venture Teams," *Plastics Engineering*, February 1985; J. Hyatt, "Strapped for Ideas, Signode Learns to Listen," *Inc.*, July 1985; B. S. Moskal, "Inventing the Future," *Industry Week*, September 30, 1985, pp. 45–46; D. C. Brown, "In-House Teams Broaden Firm's Business," *Business Marketing*, April 1985.

8. Brown, op. cit.

9. Schaffhauser, op. cit.

10. "Huge Emphasis Placed on CPET Food Trays," *Packaging*, September 1985.

9

Personnel Policies and Initiatives

While the previous chapter explains how management can further the cause of innovation, this one attempts to show how company staff—specifically the human resources department—can engage in the same endeavor. What is being undertaken is supporting, bolstering, encouraging, and facilitating of extraordinary achievements by out-of-the-ordinary people, which means that, in the final analysis, the challenge is in the field of human relations. That is why every forward-looking company must have a strong human resources (HR) department (sometimes called a personnel or human relations department).

Using the Human Resources Department to Improve Innovation

The HR department handles union negotiations and pension benefits and writes job descriptions and sets pay scales for each job. It awards sick leaves and provides hospital benefits and may even send flowers to funerals. It also doles out parking spots and makes sure that the local radio station announces "no work today" when blizzards or hurricanes descend. While all those functions are "human" ones, they represent the mechanical side of humanness. Those matters are part of doing business, and the human resources department generally handles them with unchallengeable professional competence. Many companies consciously or otherwise consider that that's enough for HR to do, and do not involve the department in other responsibilities. That is a mistake.

There is much more that HR people can accomplish with their special expertise. Experts are needed who can handle the complexities of human motivation and psychology. As far as achieving success in innovation is concerned, that sort of role by the HR department is more important than the mechanical "routines" listed in the preceding paragraph.

When I visited Dr. Thomas MacAvoy, vice chairman of the board and technical director of Corning Glass Works, to discuss how his company innovates, I was struck by the fact that he was not accompanied by his research director or his technology director. Rather, he chose to have me meet Marie McKee, director of executive personnel planning, because he considers what she does to be a major positive force in the support of creative achievement by the employees of Corning's Technical Center. "Innovation is a social problem," he said.

Ms. McKee is a member of Corning's executive personnel department, which is a component of its human resources staff. The present role of that department in supporting research and development (R&D) at Corning has evolved over the last decade and resembles what one observes today in an increasing number of large companies that have a commitment to innovation. "The role of human resources in innovation is to understand how the process operates and to be supportive of it and the innovators," said Ms. McKee. "This includes recognizing the most creative people and helping the company to utilize their talents to their fullest potential, and that in turn means linking people and ideas— a critical part of the innovation process. That's another example of where a human resources department can help. All this comes together in the development of an environment that encourages creativity as well as rewarding and motivating the team, without which successful innovation will not occur."

Ms. McKee went on to say, "An effective human resource person can help develop the appropriate experiences and career paths in these people to develop their innovation skills." But that is not enough. She concluded with the point that "the role of human resources is also to be part of the business team and to encourage a philosophy in management that balances both short-term and long-term results."

If one must describe the human resources role in a short phrase, it is "be supportive," not only to innovators but to those who supervise innovators and the innovation process as well, and there are many ways to fulfill that role.

Easing the Way to Accomplishment

One way the HR department can support innovation is based on the fact that it knows how to cut red tape and how to "bend the rules." The human resources professional knows the limits of such action within each company and will not go too far—but will go far enough to make a difference.

I told Ms. McKee that in my travels I came across an occurrence that typifies the kind of problem that HR people can address with happy results. A young, highly regarded scientist in an R&D department was accruing credits for a graduate degree by attending night classes at a local university. One crucial course was not offered in the evening curriculum, but it was available two days a week at 3:00 P.M.—during working hours. He went to his boss and asked permission to take the time off and make it up by working Saturdays or evenings. "Sorry," he was told, "we have rules against going to school during working hours, even if you make up the time." So he quit and went to work for a competitor in the next town— who let him have the time off for that class. When I visited his former employer, gloom lay heavy. "Not only have we lost an outstanding guy with great potential," wailed the manager, "I can't bring myself to think what he is telling our competition."

Marie smiled when I related this tale. "I could have headed that off," she said.

Counseling

If you talk to people in the psychology business, they will tell you that *everybody* needs therapy—so many times a week at so much an hour. That's going a bit far, but, without question, some people do. Perhaps certain of those who use creativity as a way to make a living need therapy more than most.

A good boss can supply much useful "amateur" therapy, just by virtue of being a good boss, which includes being sensitive to what goes on in the minds of his or her subordinates. But a boss never feels more helpless than when a problem goes beyond his or her capabilities. If the problem's not solved, the star innovator may retreat into ineffectiveness, if not downright destructiveness. The chance of rescuing the situation improves when the HR people get into the act. They can put the troubled person in touch with counseling, which sometimes, but not always, mitigates the crisis.

A more subtle but related role for HR professionals addresses the issue not of alleviating crises, but rather of improving performance and professional growth. If HR people are warm and intelligent and motivated by a sincere drive to serve, you can get underachieving innovators to talk to them. We all like to talk about ourselves. Where someone may be inhibited or embarrassed about "letting it all out" to the boss, the private office of the human relations person, who sees listening as a mission, is another matter entirely. It can have salutary results.

Performance Appraisal

Periodic performance appraisals are often done as rote exercises by the boss filling out a form, or not done at all. Yet this discipline is potentially a means to achieve much good: better motivation, better teamwork, better performance in all its aspects. Also, while the leader of a group may not look forward to engaging in it, lower-level employees often do. So performance appraisals must be done, and with sincerity and care.

While the form that is used as an appraisal guide often has standard blanks to fill in, the information provided is rife with meaning for the person being appraised. Each blank can be the basis for deep discussion, with the potential for revealing problems that can be set right. As with so much we do professionally, good communication is the basis for accomplishment. The performance appraisal offers a unique opportunity for dialogue. In fact, sometimes it should be a "trialogue" or a dialogue with an "outsider." For a human problem is revealed. Enter the HR department.

Training: Formal Programs

Most human resources departments employ a director of training whose job might include organizing a four-hour course to instruct bench workers in how to assemble a product. There are also many other courses of greater sophistication, and the director of training sets those up, too.

Such courses may go far beyond mere instruction in skills. Many companies, for example, give formal management training courses, some of them so elaborate as to turn out people with what amounts to mini-MBAs. Other specialties are similarly addressed, depending on the firm's unique interests. One that should interest us is creativity training.

As I read the article by J. Gordon and R. Zemke,[1] I realized that I had devoted my entire professional career to creativity without ever having had a course in it. Although I managed quite well, I probably would have done better using techniques the article describes.

Training: Ad Hoc Programs

A bigger challenge to HR departments is to generate training programs or workshops that deal with unusual one-time problems. Such a need arose at New York Telephone when a reorganization of the marketing department resulted in the creation of 40 new positions for product managers. Dominick DeAngelo, the division manager for this function, called on the management and organization department group in human resources to design an introduction, orientation, and initial training experience for new product managers. Most of these neophyte product managers, while high achievers in other assignments, were totally unfamiliar with product management.

Miriam Cohen and Edward Dwyer, internal consultants, developed a three-week program (see Figure 9–1) that combined outside speakers who discussed topics on the telecommunications industry and marketing subjects (including one on the third day on "Innovation/Creativity"), presentations on the corporate and departmental contexts of product management, and specific job-related course work.

Another function of the HR staff is to exercise initiative. The idea of giving courses like this doesn't have to come from those who must confront the problem of gaps in understanding on the part of their employees. Such ideas can arise from human resources specialists. However, they cannot know to make such suggestions unless they know what direction the company is taking. That means that it is good policy to include the senior HR person as a participant in high-level staff and policy meetings. Many companies blunder by not doing this.

Figure 9-1. New York Telephone's training workshop (over one month) for product managers.

SUNDAY	MONDAY	TUESDAY	WEDNESDAY	THURSDAY	FRIDAY	SATURDAY
			1 9:30-10 Breakfast 10-12 #1 Expectations 12-1 lunch with top team 1-3 #2 Vision and Mission of Mktg./Tech. Org. 3-5 #3 Visit Offices	**2** 8:30-9 Coffee 9-11 #4 Trends 11-12 #5 Integrative discussion 1-3 #6 Marketing Overview 3-4 #7 Integ. Disc. 4-5 #8 "Mktg. Imag."	**3** 8:30-9 Coffee 9-11 #9 Info/Commun. Overview 11-12 #10 Integ. Disc. 1-3 #11 Innovation/ Creativity 3-4 #12 Integ. Disc. 4-5 #13 "Mktg. Imagination"	
	6	**7**	**8**	**9**	**10**	
	#14 Product Management Course for Groups A and B				#15 PROFITS course for Groups A and B	
	13 #16 Corporate Environment Overview - Day 1	**14** #17 Personal Computer for Group A Mktg. Imag. Planning Group B	**15** #16 Corporate Environment Overview - Day 2	**16** #17 Personal Computer for Group B Mktg. Imag. Planning Group A	**17** AM #18 Data Bases	
	20 AM #16 Corp. Env. - Pricing Services & Costs PM #19 Marketing Imagination Presentations	**21** #20 Quality	**22** Institute	**23** AM #21 Assimilation Workshop PM #22 Bridging the Gaps	**24** 9-10 #23 Integration and Preparation for Open Forum 10 - #24 Open Forum with Division Team	
	27	**28**	**29**	**30**		

Courtesy of New York Telephone

Executive Development

High-level executives can also benefit from counsel and training in the field of interactions with their subordinates, peers, and superiors. They too must master skills and must increase their levels of sensitivity.

Many who attain the upper reaches of a company organization are so gifted in their personal endowments that they know instinctively how to advance their own careers and, by that token, the health of their companies in these regards. But many others, equally talented in other regards, have deficiencies that can be eliminated by direction offered by HR professionals. As a result, some "great" executives can emerge who might never have risen to that status. Even those who approach greatness can improve their effectiveness significantly.

This extends to the CEO. Every CEO can be better, but who will tell the top person how? When a good director of human resources has a pipeline to that exalted creature, much benefit can accrue to the company. As will be discussed in the following chapter, there is often a real need for such improvement in the area of consciousness raising directed to top management. Especially with regard to what concerns us, innovation.

The primary subject of this part of the book, Part 3, is the support, encouragement, and facilitation to be provided by top management. But top managers often do not know that they should provide these. Also, they may not be aware of the fact that they are too "present-oriented." Some of their focus should be shifted to the future. Human resources personnel can have a good influence in this area.

Motorola has a program initiated and managed by its HR department that addresses this problem effectively. It runs intensive six-day "senior executive programs" for groups of about 20 people. This is described in an article with the intriguing title, "Vision Improvement for Senior Executives at Motorola." External experts are engaged for this purpose from the worlds of education, business, and politics. As a result, "Motorola reassessed and in some cases changed its strategic assumptions." The article concludes with the statement that this kind of workshop creates a process that is a "powerful . . . agent for creating vision and/or change."[2] The process itself then becomes as important as the programs that result from it.

Special Personnel Practices for Innovators

Innovators are personnel. Thus we should strive to treat them as much as possible like everyone else who works for the company: with fairness and with concern and sympathy for their personal growth and welfare. When done right, this should lead to agreeable reactions on their part, such as sincere loyalty to and identification with the firm, good performance, and high productivity.

But innovators have unique qualities, and there is always a special packet of personnel practices, expressed or not, that should be tailored and applied as supplements to general employer/employee procedures. The evolution and establishment of such practices is the responsibility of the managers of the departments for which these employees work, operating in conjunction with the human resources department.

We may divide the personnel practices tailored for innovators into two groups: (1) those facilitating employee performance and (2) those concerned with recruitment and rewards. The preceding chapter and this one to this point have dealt with the first of these. The remainder of this chapter will treat the second.

Recruitment of Innovators

The kinds of people required in autonomous innovation organizations have been described in Chapter 2. When we list them with job descriptions like the ones human resources departments generate, they may not seem especially unlike anyone else in the company in any other job in related fields. But either spelled out or implied are the additional qualifications of "creative," "ingenious," "inventive," and "innovative," to which must be added "skilled in implementation," "skilled in networking," and "dedicated." How does one write such requirements into a want ad?

Previously "Unknown" Candidates
Advertising is one course to take, but the results are usually lean. Nevertheless, newspaper ads can produce good candidates and

should not be rejected. What happens is that the resumes appear—and pile up. The human relations people can put them through initial culling and submit the remainder to the manager who initiated the new employee requisition. That manager subjects them to further sifting and requests certain selected individuals to appear for interview. One of those may fit.

You can also use recruiting agencies. The best of them are very good. The key to success is to head off their tendency to bombard you with hundreds of resumes. Rather, insist that they come up with a few, very carefully selected potential employees who come close to meeting your needs. The agency must therefore invest time and effort in researching each candidate before presenting that person. That justifies their fee.

But the best approach is for the personnel department in your own company to approach the problem exactly as a good recruiting agency does, with the difference that it uses existing employees as a reservoir of candidates. Unfortunately, internal human relations departments would rather provide listings from their files of requests for transfer, or personnel from eliminated departments, or employees "deemed not to fit" their present assignments. This is no worse a source than the gleanings from want ads. In fact, it's better, because credible histories of interesting individuals can be obtained by any department manager who wants to make the effort. The more that manager probes and learns, the further the candidate moves from the "unknown" into the "known" category.

"Known" Candidates

It is saying the obvious to point out that uncertainty diminishes when the job candidate has already interacted with his or her prospective boss in a professional capacity and has come through with flying colors. It is then easy for the manager to say, "I know Rita can do this job because in the last ten years she has done similar work successfully, some of it in her department's joint projects with our group. She already has an impressive portfolio of achieved innovations. Furthermore, her present boss says she's cooperative and hardworking. I want her for my department." If Rita is available, there is no need to look elsewhere.

That's my point. Usually, the best candidates for an innovation organization are already company employees, already part of the family. They are best because they are knowledgeable about the company: its products, its processes, its markets, its way of operating. And you know about them, or you can find out by asking, not a single person, but half a dozen people. Because those you ask are going to remain your co-workers, they tend, more often than not, to be honest in their appraisals.

When innovators are homegrown, I consider the benefits derived to outweigh the possible negatives of inbreeding. We can draw an analogy with baseball. The teams that most often win pennants and have the best morale are the ones with the best farm systems.

It pays to know your company. Know where talent resides and who the talented individuals are. That pertains to the building of permanent staff for an innovation organization as well. Think of the already-employed creative people as a pool. You can fish in someone else's pool if you're not careless or capricious.

There is a special circumstance that operates advantageously for innovation organizations. If they are put together right, they are what is known as "a unique environment for unique individuals," which the other kinds of environments in the company may not be. When an innovative employee offers a creative new idea to the boss of a department that does not see newness as its mission, the employee is often squelched. The boss is having trouble enough with oldness, and has no need for any new approach, with its risks and deviations from immediate goals. That is a formula for frustration, and frustrated employees are relatively easy to transfer to other departments.

In my experience, and in the experience of others, virtually every star of innovation came from within. Almost every skunker in Xerox's East Rochester skunk works was a born-and-bred Xerox employee, transferred from other departments in the company. And Eastman Kodak's New Opportunity Department, with its assemblage of 14 infant enterprises, was also staffed by "old hands" who formerly had other EK identities.

Some (certainly not all) may even have been "problem employees" because they always took routes different from the channels in which their bosses tried to place them; they could never stop themselves from pursuing novelty. As a result, they may have been tabbed as people who were not going to rise in the company hierarchy. But that may have been because they were in the wrong organization.

Of course, if you engage in this practice of identifying and uprooting someone else's people for your own benefit, you can get into trouble. But that's a function of how tactfully and skillfully you do it.

There are other avenues for recruiting "known quantities." Word of mouth does a lot of good. Ask present employees of innovation organizations questions like, "Are there any others like you back where you came from?" If there are, they'll know—and their judgments are usually trustworthy. Another approach that has worked for me has been to visit the alumni placement office of my alma mater. Or one's former professor who now works as a consultant for the company. Because one has a personal link to such people, they can be trusted to listen and to generate an awareness of exactly the kind of person required—and they often come up with sterling candidates—with proven credentials.

Criteria for Selection

I wish I could provide a guide on how one should detect and select potential star innovators. I am not referring to competence in the general and specialty fields described in Chapter 2, with which there can be no compromise. Rather, I am talking of personality—attitudes and traits. After 40 years in this business, I can do little more than list the following generalizations:

- Innovators have a better sense of humor than other people (except for some brilliant ones who have zero wit or inclination to smile).
- Innovators have broad interests in fields outside of their professional expertise, as witness the chemist who plays the bagpipes or the physicist who raises pigs or the computer programmer who doubles as town selectman (except for some brilliant innovators who have no perceptible interest in life away from work other than to plunk down with a beer in front of the television set).
- Innovators are disorganized and sloppy (except for many who are organized and neat).
- Innovators are nonconformists (except for those who are painfully conventional in every respect).
- Innovators are optimistic (except for those who are pessimistic).

- Innovators are arrogant and stubborn and not easily diverted from their approach to solving a problem (except for those who are diffident and easily discouraged—and they are the ones who blossom in a favorable environment like one of our innovation organizations).
- Innovators are bright and alert and have flashing eyes (except for many I know who have heavy eyelids and frequently drop off during fascinating moments).

Rewards

What motivates good innovation? Rewards. Most people work for pay, not for rewards. How sad for them. It is reward, in the sense of satisfaction, that makes work a pleasure. If there is no satisfaction, compensation for work is no more than a kind of manifestation of the first law of thermodynamics, the conservation of energy. Assuming that levels of pay are fair, the worker expends energy and is compensated with legal tender that can be exchanged for goods and services representing corresponding amounts of energy.

Such pay—at a minimum—has to be given for work. It is a necessity, if only to maintain life with food, shelter, and so on. This "first law" level of pay is established for each kind of job at a rate determined by the free market. Let us call it "basic pay."

Satisfaction is the pay—the reward—that may be added to basic pay. Ideally, compensation is made up of the sum of basic pay (BP) and reward in the form of satisfaction (S). We can express this:

$$\text{Compensation} = BP + S$$

or we can think of compensation as incorporating a "satisfaction ratio" that takes the form S/BP. The higher the ratio, the better.

In the literature, when personnel specialists address the question of compensation for employees engaged in creative or entrepreneurial work, they call the satisfaction term by another name: "incentive." Incentive is considered by the employer to be a tool utilized as a means to derive increased value from certain selected workers. As far as truly innovative or entrepreneurial employees are concerned, incentive is considered to be no more than their just reward. The remainder of this chapter will deal with these two factors: BP and S (or I).

Basic Pay

As employees, innovators must fit into the company's pay structure. This means they are given titles like junior engineer or principal scientist and assigned job levels with numerical designations like Job Level 9. Every level carries with it a nonspecific (in the sense of not relating to a given field of expertise) description of responsibilities for subordinates and for importance of decisions that can be made without recourse to supervisors. With each such level comes a specified pay range extending from a minimum to a maximum and generally overlapping the ranges of the two job levels on either side of it.

Basic pay and the salary structures like that described above have to be acceptable and comparable to what is offered by local competition. That level is the baseline from which we can start to consider added-on incentives. Indeed, incentive is not absent from basic pay structures. It is incorporated into the chance to receive higher annual pay raises than one's co-workers as a result of superior performance and the chance to be promoted to the next-higher level for the same reason. For many employees, those are the only incentives required to perform outstanding work. But there are other incentives a company can provide to those who create new business for it that can be more productive yet.

Additional Incentives

If providing incentive means to satisfy, we must define that term. According to my dictionary, its meanings include: "to gratify fully the wants, wishes, desires of; to give what is due; to make content."

Creators of incremental new business for their companies "want, wish for, and desire" two things beyond the rewards provided by basic pay: psychic satisfaction and a piece of the action. They feel both are their "due." If they get them, they will feel as "content" as they ever can get.

Of course, no employee is ever gratified "fully." But for the company to attempt to gratify selected members of an innovation organization even partially could produce good results otherwise unattainable, and thus constitute good business practice.

Nonmonetary Incentives

Not only do nonmonetary rewards qualify as incentives for innovators, there is a body of research that maintains that performance can actually decline when money is offered for creative work as a substitute for praise and pleasure in the work itself.[3] In other words, for creative people, work is an end, not a means.

Much of the pleasure in the pursuit of innovation derives from what might be considered a less than admirable human quality: ego. Not everyone has a strong ego, but innovators do. Creation is an ego trip. A creation is an extension of oneself, whether what is being created is a new gadget for the marketplace or a new baby for the family. So people who get paid to be creative are getting paid double when compared with other employees. They get salary (basic pay) just like everyone; but in addition, they get ego gratification, which is worth as much to them as money.

Please don't rush to cut their salaries in the assumption that they will probably stay on and continue to produce anyway. The matter is more complex than that. Rather, do what you can to gratify their egos by formal recognition of their accomplishments.

You cannot recognize accomplishment if you have no way to measure it. J. T. Coe points out that "output from [innovation programs] is usually submerged in the financial statistics of a business. Accounting conventions . . . do not readily reveal what R&D contributes to a business." Furthermore, evidence of the magnitude of their contributions is generally not immediately apparent. Because of the nature of innovation, that sort of data is subject to lag. Coe goes on to suggest certain accounting procedures that may be of help. (Those suggestions are essentially extensions of this book's recommendations for an impact statement in Chapter 7.) Coe concludes his article with some statements of the beneficial consequences of good measurement (impact) data:

> Perhaps the greatest leverage from these . . . measurements
> was the stimulus they gave to the R&D organization.

Healthy internal competition evolved between R&D units with respect to new product sales.

Productivity in the laboratory can be significantly increased when creative scientists are given a clear measure of their business objectives (new product sales and margins) and when the results of their work are continuously recognized.[4]

The key word is "recognition." The measurements alone provide it, but for the best gratification for ego, the innovators have to feel that their peers and their bosses appreciate those measurements (another term for which is "feedback") just as much as they do. In his article entitled "Managing the Goldcollar Worker," Goldstein describes the value of rewarding innovative people by arranging for them to meet notables in their fields—even if this means trips to pleasant places. He calls it warranted special treatment.

Another kind of special treatment is independence. Goldstein says that "a strong corporate bureaucracy of inflexible organization structure is likely to send most creative people packing—or, at the very least, substantially reduce their productivity." He goes on to quote Professor Hakmiller of the University of Connecticut, who states that "to these people work is an extension of themselves, and they don't take well to trivial interference." And another quotation, from Peter Drucker: "The best thing you can do for creative people is just get out of their way. Give them a task and leave them alone." I go along with those statements, while averring that planning, budgeting, and monitoring of innovators, as described in Chapter 5, is still necessary and, done with intelligence and restraint, is not inconsistent with them. Indeed, Drucker further points out that a deadline should be imposed and the resources allocated before the supervisor "walks away."[5]

All this should be supplemented by a chance to shine in public, but especially in the eyes of top management. If innovators deserve to receive public praise, let them have it. Foster advises CEOs to be sensitive to how positively innovators respond to such actions:

Your task, is to get all "users" and potential users of innovation to understand that the more gratitude (recognition) for innovation they express, the more innovation they will see. . . .
All the company's communication media should be employed. Trade and local community media should also be exploited.

. . . We sometimes jokingly refer to recognition systems as "Atta boy" programs.[6]

That is the message. When innovation is achieved, conquer your natural reserve. Say "Atta boy" (or "Atta girl").

Monetary Incentives

Emotional satisfaction is not quite enough. It is necessary, but not sufficient. There have to be incremental tangible rewards as well. If the company makes a bundle on an innovation, it should share some of this with the innovators.

There is temptation not to do this, for reasons extending from stinginess on the part of management to its fear of the possible explosions that may occur with other employees (non-innovators, non-entreprenuers) that could result from venturing into what is undeniably a minefield. This is exacerbated by the danger of rewarding the wrong people or allocating the wrong proportions of rewards. Furthermore, the record tells us that there are many instances of outstanding innovation achievements where extra monetary incentives are never given. But there is more to the record than that.

Kanter tells us of a study of 105 Boston-area high-tech firms that tended, "on average, to pay a lower base pay [than their traditional counterparts] but offer more financial incentives of other kinds, such as cash bonuses, stock options, and profit-sharing plans."[7] That led her to quote the results of a study by Schuster of 66 high-tech companies. It concluded that the 24 "best" of these in financial performance were the ones that had the greater reliance on financial incentives for its innovative employees. Schuster's data shows a very significant profit improvement correlating with significant levels of incentives to innovators.[8]

I must confess that my own experience does not qualify me as an expert. In fact, my feelings lead me on a path contradictory to the arguments given here. I recall how my associates and I worked with frenzy for a half-decade to establish our company at the forefront of transistor business in the 1950s. Our opposite numbers in Silicon Valley got "a piece of the action" and today probably must contend with the burdens of managing enormous bank accounts. When I asked my boss, back then, what I would get for my efforts, he responded that I would get to keep my job.

Would we have worked even harder had we owned part of the enterprise? My firm conclusion is "maybe." I can only say, read the literature and benefit from the experience of others. For the situation is not a black-and-white one.

If we do accept that monetary incentives will improve the results of investments in innovation, how should we go about implementing a fair system? Hurwich advises us to set up an incentive compensation program in advance so that all employees, those in the program and those outside it as well, know its implications and its dependence on the achievements of certain individuals. If it honors principles of equity and fairness, the minefield will have fewer unexploded hidden bombs.[9]

Foster cautions that these incentives must be significant; that is, not too small. He makes the point that small incremental financial rewards are perceived by innovators as being "nice to have, but not really incentives."[10]

Kanter gives us the best summary of present practices, even those that are still experimental. They include the creation of shares in phantom companies.[11] Participants have a chance, if the new venture succeeds, of becoming almost as wealthy and powerful as though they had left the company and established themselves with venture capital. But if they fail, their risks are less. They will still be employed, albeit with the penalty of having lost some years in pursuing their career tracks.

Some firms (for example, AT&T) even offer internal entrepreneurs the privilege of increasing the numbers of their shares by allowing them to "invest" a portion of normal pay increases or bonuses, simulating even more realistically what they would have encountered in "the real world."

The royalties derived from intellectual property can similarly be used as a basis for incentives. Some firms give inventors a share of royalty income.

Then, there is the simplest form of incentive—bonuses and/or stock options. You can hardly go wrong with these.

In all these cases, attention should be given to the issue of time span. The innovation may not be a success until seven or eight years have passed. How can you provide incentive during that period? Hurwich's approach helps. He recommends defining milestones before the innovation program is embarked on. Then it is possible to provide rewards as these goals are met.

These are rational courses to take, but surely there are others. Innovation is dependent on imagination, so apply yours. In so doing, you will be well advised to hark back to the recommendation of Foster. He says that, in providing your employees with incentives, follow the Golden Rule: "Do unto others as you would have them do unto you." In addition to being a course with high moral value, it is good business—and might even produce more of another kind of gold.[12]

References

1. J. Gordon and R. Zemke, "Making Them More Creative," *Training, the Magazine of Human Resources Development,* May 1986, p. 30.

2. "Vision Improvement for Senior Executives at Motorola," *The President,* October 1986, p. 3.

3. A. Kohn, "Studies Find Reward Often No Motivator," *The Boston Globe,* January 19, 1987, p. 43.

4. J. T. Coe, "Measuring the Success of R&D Innovations," *The National Productivity Review,* Summer 1982, p. 330.

5. M. L. Goldstein, "Managing the Goldcollar Worker," *Industry Week,* September 2, 1982, p. 33.

6. W. K. Foster, "Innovation Success Quality #4: Innovation Incentives," *Intrapreneurial Excellence,* July 1986, p. 9.

7. R. M. Kanter, "From Status to Contribution: Some Organizational Implications of the Changing Basis of Pay," *Personnel,* January 1987, p. 12.

8. J. R. Schuster, *Management Compensation in High Technology Companies* (Lexington, MA: Lexington Books, 1984).

9. "Evidence of a Change in Thinking," *Intrapreneurial Excellence,* May 1986, p. 6.

10. Foster, op. cit.

11. Kanter, op. cit.

12. Foster, op. cit.

10

Company Culture and the Executive Office

Calvin Coolidge said, with characteristic terseness, "The business of America is business." When we consider the political and philosophical foundations of the ideas "America" and "business," we perceive that his pronouncement incorporates a contradiction. While the United States is a democratic nation, its businesses are not democratic at all. Rather, they are dictatorial. One hears that there is a similar contradiction in certain nondemocratic societies, such as the Soviet Union, Rumania, or China—but in reverse—where business and operating decisions are often arrived at by democratic votes of the employees. So, every day as we walk in the front door of the office building or laboratory in which we work, or through the gate of the factory in which we spend the most productive hours of our existence, we leave behind many of the splendors and blessings of our "democratic way of life."

Some elements of democracy do not really disappear—for example, the union retains its right to collective bargaining, and employees can sue the company if they are the victims of racial discrimination or work hazards. But you can still be fired. You can still be transferred against your will to another department or to another location thousands of miles away. You can be misclassified into a dead-end job below your capabilities and with unfairly low pay and status, while reporting to a superior of inferior capability and motives—and thus give up your best years to a misdirected career. (You are still "free," for you can always quit. But until you land the next job, it doesn't feel like freedom.)

Admittedly, you can appeal to management, asking it to change its judgment, and you might win your case. But even as you win, you are overwhelmed by the realization that much of that victory was in the nature of an "indulgence" by a "reasonable" management. And you know that it would have taken little reordering in the spectrum of prevailing whims among certain executives for the decision to have been the opposite, with no further appeal. (For more on this subject, read any short story or novel by Kafka.)

But we are so accustomed to those restrictions on our freedom of choice and to these limits to our liberty that we never think of them (until they impinge on us unpleasantly), for they are part of "The American Way." There is one other class of (dictatorial) restriction that remains and to which we will now turn our attention, for it underlies the subject of this book. It can be phrased as a question: How well and how much can we engage in innovation in our place of work?

The answer lies within the minds of the top executives in the nation's businesses, especially the CEO (not without reason does the "C" of that acronym stand for "Chief"). In the role as company dictator, the CEO's use of his or her brain in a rational fashion—combined with a willingness to erode that rationality by waves of emotion, bad habits, misplaced values, caprice, and bias—will determine whether the company acquires a reputation as "innovative" or not. What results from this sort of executive-office direction is a corporate way of life that innovators will find either hospitable or hostile, or something between. It has a name: "company culture."

Culture is power. Whatever happens in any human organization, good or bad, useful or wasteful, awkward or graceful, is empowered by the culture that underpins it. Thus, a culture based on the American Constitution is "good" and, by that token, has made our actions during the last two centuries more good than bad. A culture based on Hitler's Nazism was evil and empowered evil actions. Japanese culture is orderly and conforming, empowering their manufacturing organizations with efficiencies and quality unheard of in our philosophy. Balinese culture is relaxed and affectionate and empowers its inhabitants to become great dancers—but not to create industrial empires.

Yet, all the inhabitants of those nations are inherently the same. Let them be immigrants into each other's lands, and they will, with time, be "remade" into people who conform to their adopted cultures.

But returning our focus to innovation in business, we refer again to Chapter 1 of this book, specifically to Figure 1–1, which

Table 10-1.
Empowering policies/company culture.

1. Acquisitions (full or minority positions in art-leading businesses).
2. Streamlining.
3. Enriching (facilities, procedures, technologies).
4. Licensing (in or out).
5. Support of new business analysis and market research.
6. Support of innovation.
7. Combinations of above.

shows how empowering company culture determines the effectiveness of the innovation process. We have already discussed the major factors required to attain the goals: implementation means and support by management and staff of the implementors. But those factors can be meaningless, and in some firms nonexistent, depending on what hovers over all, in what looks like a parallel path emanating from the executive office. It is the arch entitled "Empowering Policies/Company Culture" that is the spirit—consciously or unconsciously dictated from above—that activates the flow of innovation. Without a positive and supportive culture, the process is never consummated because there is no driving force to empower it.

Figure 1–2 depicts the same flow process, but in expanded detail. The first of the four sets of factors, labeled "Empowering Policies/Company Culture," is what concerns us in this final chapter of Part 3. It appears here as Table 10–1.

It is those seven factors, and how effectively they stimulate employees into action (as a function of employees' perception of the sincerity of the executive office's belief in them), that create the part of company culture that empowers the innovation process. Surely the list is not complete, but it comprises the driving forces I can identify. If you know of others, just add them. As we examine these building blocks of company culture, we recognize that they may be given another, less intimidating designation than "culture." They are the company's strategies for growth.

Growth Strategies

There are two kinds of growth strategies. The firm may, consciously or otherwise, create an atmosphere for no growth. Or, very consciously, it may create one for growth.

The No-Growth Strategy

The easiest growth strategy to discuss—and dispose of—does not appear in Table 10–1. It is associated with companies that have no strategy for growth, and by that token for innovation. In Chapter 11, I refer to Professor Vesper's research among some 200 representative companies in which he inquired whether they engaged in innovation programs. About two thirds replied that they did none. How could they innovate, they intimated, when they had more important things to do, such as making a profit this year!

Those companies have a culture that mandates that innovation is unnecessary and irrelevant. Innovation is not empowered and therefore is absent. What better case can one make for the power of company culture?

Continuation of Existing Growth Strategy

In firms that believe innovation is necessary and relevant, the direction given to innovation activities is determined by what policies they select to follow from Table 10–1. Having given direction, they must next decide how aggressively to pursue it. Those are decisions for which we cannot make generalized statements. They are different for each company operating within its unique environment.

Such decisions may be of a nature that are not upsetting, because they conform with the way the company has always done business. Or they can be traumatic because they introduce new values and goals. In the former case we observe a continuation of a traditional company culture, in the latter we confront the challenge of creating a new one.

Creation of New Growth Strategy

Company cultures—like national or ethnic ones—cannot easily be changed, especially for large firms with elaborate, entrenched, empowered organizational entities. But it is not impossible, and every year we hear of companies that have experienced "turn-around" because a new virtuoso CEO has taken charge and imposed his or her "new ways" (for which we substitute the expression "new culture"). It is here that the status of dictator helps. (I didn't say dictatorship is all bad; in fact, it is a way to achieve immediate change with high efficiency, and it gives gratification—at least to the dictator.)

Let us take the Allen-Bradley (A-B) company as an example of changing a company culture and its impact on innovation activities. These changes took place in a period starting in 1983 and have taken hold with increasing strength as this book goes to press. A-B was acquired by Rockwell International in 1985 and is now a subsidiary of that firm, but that change from independent status has not slowed its momentum in the matters discussed here. Please note as I relate what occurred at this company that its management has used almost every one of the options listed in Table 10–1 and has employed many of the innovation modes of Figure 1–2 (see Chapter 1).

A *Business Week* article[1] (quoted from throughout this section) describes how this $1 billion, 81-year-old business—"the epitome of a conservative, privately held" firm, engaged in the manufacture of "a multitude of switches, relays, and electrical devices that have controlled U.S. production machinery for decades"—was being threatened by the emergence of new electronic and computer technology for automating the American factory. Clearly, the company faced the classic dilemma of a mature industry leader threatened with going down the drain because of lack of participation in the development of new products and technologies. It engaged a new CEO, Tracy O'Rourke, who "turned Allen-Bradley upside down almost as soon as he walked in the door."

The first thing he did was to "waste no time in paring . . . entrenched management." Three hundred old-timers went, and half of the 150 top managers were replaced by recruits from outside the company. Such action appears in Table 10–1 as "stream-lining."

Then he engaged in "acquisitions." "O'Rourke went shopping," says *Business Week,* and "snapped up 15 companies," all possessing art-leading technology in the field of computers. Additionally, A-B invested in several high-tech start-ups, establishing minority positions in those new firms.

These actions have "enriched" the firm with higher capabilities than it previously had, even while simultaneously streamlining it (those two seemingly contradictory courses often go together when a company rebuilds). The article makes no mention of whether Allen-Bradley at the same time engaged in internal streamlining/enriching by closing down some of its obsolete facilities and retiring old production machinery, replacing these with up-to-date and more relevant tooling and facilities; but such activity is inevitable under these circumstances.

The article further explains that "O'Rourke is also trying to turn the company into a more efficient marketer and developer of new products" and has "set up 12 special business units that are responsible for devising marketing strategies and bringing new products to market." (These sound much like what we call "skunk works.") Evidence that he has already succeeded, at least in part in changing the company's product lines is this statement from C. R. Whitney, A-B's chairman: "We used to be a company that sold bits and pieces of electrical hardware. Now we are selling intelligent boxes." Clearly, the firm has supported new business analysis, market research, and innovation. Only licensing, from Table 10–1, does not appear on O'Rourke's list of action items—but for all we know, he did some of that too.

It is not surprising that the article concludes with the statement that "O'Rourke has already left an indelible mark on a company that only a few years ago sold its line of electrical relays and switches from a catalogue that rarely changed." I would rephrase that sentence by saying he changed Allen-Bradley's culture, thereby empowering innovation in many modes to levels not previously known in that company.

But that article was written in 1984. When I recently discussed the events that followed with a company spokesperson, it became obvious that in 1984 the stage had indeed been set for a new technology innovation as well as for a new product that have propelled the firm far ahead of its competitors—and probably was the single most important factor that influenced Rockwell to join forces with it. This innovation is "CIM," described below. The tale is fascinating; so much so that a *Time* article refers to it with a phrase, "the soul of new machines."[2]

Allen-Bradley's chairman, C. R. Whitney, and CEO, Tracy O'Rourke, put together a planning team of company executives to conceive the outlines of this innovation program; then they gathered a group of "30 engineers, technicians, accountants, and other specialists [to] tackle the factory-of-the-future project."[3] Having the power that comes from being the boss, O'Rourke courageously committed $15 million to the program. That power may also account for the fact that the whole company was put at the service of the innovators. Organizational barriers were breached and the services of technical specialists from throughout the firm were made available as required.

Twenty-four months later, CIM appeared. The acronym stands for computer-integrated manufacturing. What is integrated are the office, engineering, and manufacturing phases of production.

This means that orders are received (by the office) and the unique product requirements of each are keyboarded directly into the production line. At 5:00 A.M., computers at the line program that day's production, coping easily with its changing complexity and day-to-day variety. That program starts machine operation. Using bar code symbols on each item to determine its identity, each contacter or relay is made as programmed, with its own unique materials and geometries—and at breakneck speed.

As shown in the photograph in Figure 10–1, only a few attendants oversee operations at the company's automated assembly line at the Milwaukee headquarters. The line requires only 14 employees to turn out 600 units per hour, as compared with conventional labor-intensive practice requiring many dozens of assembly workers for the same output. Products, made to order, are shipped to customers within 24 hours of the sales call. Such expedition means that inventories are kept to a minimum and warehousing is almost nonexistent. The remarkable thing is that what is shipped are the same products Allen-Bradley has made for decades—but made more inexpensively, more swiftly, and with greater quality control.

The firm has changed its technology for making its own products. But it has achieved more than that. It is now a powerful factor in the business of marketing automation machinery systems

Figure 10-1. Allen-Bradley's computer-integrated manufacturing (CIM) line.

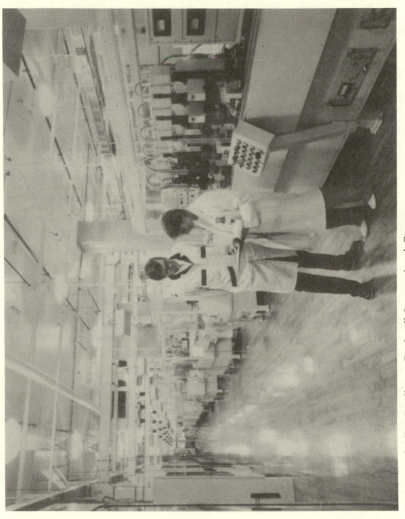

Courtesy of Allen-Bradley, a Rockwell International Company

based on CIM principles. It thus has a new product too. In large part, this is due to "the manufacturing zeal of Tracy O'Rourke."[4] One more point about this gentleman: He has been quoted as saying, "I guess I have a reputation that I'll listen to about anybody and you can't hurt my feelings, but when the quarterback says, 'run left,' you run left." Is a quarterback a dictator? Close enough.

The Strategizing Function

Most companies have a company officer with the title (or at least the function) of vice president, strategic planning. Whatever document he or she periodically creates ("The Plan") becomes a statement of company culture for the coming year or five-year period. Sometimes it goes on to strategize for the "distant" future, like the year 2013, which is always a good thing to do—and an exercise too many firms omit.

It is interesting that it is always easier to predict next year and 25 years from now than the five-year point. But that does not mean that one shouldn't attempt all of these. Trying to think ahead has to be better for the company than not trying.

The only advice I have to offer for how to do it is: Involve the managers of innovation. Too often, the strategizing process focuses only on "business matters," with emphasis on fiscal issues, and fortifies its predictions with the forecasts of economists. If it supplements the basis for its plans by including its speculations of future "market pull" forces, I can only applaud the inclusion of such thinking. But what about the influence of "technology push"? Why neglect that when planning for the future?

When that year's assemblage of strategies is declared official, the identities of those who formulated them are unimportant; for if one name is to be associated with them, it is that of the CEO. It is with the establishment of the company strategy and with the implementation of it that the CEO justifies his or her considerable salary.

The Mission

It helps to summarize the assemblage of strategies in a single sentence or paragraph and to circulate that statement to every employee, regardless of job assignment or status. How better to establish the basis of a company culture with official credentials?

I would think (although I'm not certain) that a company like Allen-Bradley might have a mission statement similar to the following:

> It is our mission, while continuing to serve our traditional markets, to update all our electro-mechanical technology and products—creating new technologies and products in the process—so that they incorporate electronic and computer features both newer than and superior to those offered by any competition. We will then aggressively address our customers with these products, in the process participating with them in significantly advancing their capability for automatic manufacture.

Sometimes mission statements sound obvious or even corny. Everyone believes in motherhood, so why bother saying you too are for it? Yet, it's worth doing. When such principles are included and given credibility by company actions over the years, it contributes positively to clarifying and establishing a desirable company culture. A firm states in its mission that it believes in integrity. So what—don't we all? Sadly, not all of us. Several of this company's competitors have been caught in unethical practices, such as attempting to bribe government contract officers. But the one with "integrity" in its mission statement has always scorned such practices. As a result, its market share has soared, in the process eroding that of those who were unable to resist temptation. The mission statement worked.

If just declaring something is part of the company mission helps to make it happen, why not then include a commitment to innovation, along with all the other good things?

Style and Atmosphere

If strategy is part of company culture, so are style and atmosphere. Those are the qualities of a company that impress a visitor or employee more than the elegance of the buildings, offices, and laboratories or the sophistication of the individuals one meets. What lasts in our minds about a company is the "impression" it gives—and that impression is based on less tangible matters, including style and atmosphere.

If, after spending a few days or even a few hours on a company's premises, you get a feeling that it is innovative and committed to it with a kind of undefinable upbeat sincerity, you are usually right. Watch that company; other things being equal, it is a good prospect to flourish in its industry. Several stylistic and atmospheric factors will contribute to such a favorable impression.

Failure Is Not a Sin—A Style

In a company that pursues innovation effectively, everyone up the hierarchical ladder, even to the CEO, recognizes that predictions by strategizers are unsure. After all, no one can really predict the future. Predictions have a batting average, and the better one is at it, the better the average. Only a few times a century is the year's batting champion able to attain an average of .400. Sometimes being right only one-third of the time is better than what anyone else can do.

The same is true for innovations. If one in ten makes it as a commercial success, you are already exceeding the national average. The challenge to effective management of innovation is to raise that average to something like one in five. If your innovations succeed one-third of the time, consider yourself blessed beyond all reasonable expectation.

There is a feeling in a company with a real commitment to innovation that the fact that something failed is almost a positive event. It means that someone had the courage to try something new and what was learned in the process will serve to improve the chance for success the next time around. That feeling is an essential ingredient of the style of an innovative company—to understand that failure is not a sin.

The Executive Champion—Creation of Atmosphere

We have discussed champions in several places in this book, and in the process noted that it is just as possible for such people to commit themselves with passion to programs that ultimately fail as to those that ultimately succeed. It's the successes that get written up in the business journals, so we often get a biased picture about how many champions should be considered geniuses—for batting averages operate as much with a champion in the act as with merely a dispassionate program manager. But this much we can say: With the added spirit that a champion imparts, the batting average goes up. It goes even higher when the champion is a top-level company executive, preferably the CEO. The fact is that any innovation program benefits from having a good expediter. No one performs that task better than a boss—and the CEO is better at it than any lesser boss.

The atmosphere created in a company in which the CEO is a champion of innovation is unfortunately not common. But when one encounters it, it is exhilarating.

References

1. "Allen-Bradley Races to Catch the Factory of the Future," *Business Week,* October 15, 1984.
2. J. S. DeMott, "In Old Milwaukee: Tomorrow's Factory Today," *Time,* June 16, 1986, p. 66.
3. G. Bylinsky, "A Breakthrough in Automating the Assembly Line," *Fortune,* May 26, 1986, p. 64.
4. F. McGrail, "The Manufacturing Zeal of Tracy O'Rourke," *Electronic Business,* September 15, 1986.

Part 4

The Eight
Innovation Modes

11

The Nature of
Innovation in
U.S. Industry

The remaining chapters of this book describe the following eight varieties of autonomous innovation groups, each of which exemplifies a particular innovation mode:

1. Technical centers.
2. Research centers.
3. New products centers.
4. Captive research and development (R&D) programs.
5. External teams.
6. Internal ventures centers.
7. External ventures centers.
8. Licensing arrangements.

Using specific examples, the chapters illustrate how each type characteristically operates within a business enterprise. The eight types break down into a number of loose categories, as well as into several different kinds of activities. Before we treat the eight, one by one, let us set the stage by defining these categories and functions, showing at the same time how they relate to each other and how they fit into the larger context of the national scene.

Either Inner or Outer—or Neither

First, some are inner-directed and some are outer-directed. That is to say, there is a difference between client-oriented organizations, which serve to aid existing businesses within the parent enterprise, and organizations that address themselves to the creation of new ventures, also for the benefit of the parent. Professor Karl Vesper of the Graduate School of Business Administration of the University of Washington calls these "non-entrepreneurial R&D" and "entrepreneurial activity," respectively.

In 1984, Vesper conducted an investigation of 198 representative companies in this country and found that two-thirds of them did neither. When asked what mode of innovation they engaged in, their answer was "No mode. We don't innovate, we don't have time for that, we're too busy running our business." That is a staggering statement! But I think it represents the true state of affairs in our country. (Perhaps we can take solace in knowing that most other countries do worse.)

But that leaves the other third—actually, 60 companies that engaged in 77 formal innovation programs (some doing more than one). These were essentially equally divided; 38 were internal client-oriented operations and 39 were entrepreneurial.[1]

Experimental R&D vs. Administrative Organizations

In five of the eight innovation modes, the staff engages in experimentation and handles the new product, process, or system through all the steps of its birth, much as parents, obstetricians, and pediatricians handle the birthing and nurturing of a baby. These are true R&D organizations. The other three groups, in the same sense, handle nothing. Staff personnel sit in offices and "arrange" eventual births, as though they were in the cattle-breeding business. It follows that a descriptive name for them is "administrative."

Table 11–1 shows how different types of innovation organizations fit these categories. Note that there is some overlap and that the boundaries are fuzzy. For example, in the internal ventures center, the individual skunk works groups administered by the center are in fact performing research and development. In the ventures centers, both internal and external, new enterprises meant to stand alone may at some crucial moment be absorbed by existing business entities in the parent company, and it turns out they were client-oriented all the time. Such secondary roles are indicated in the table with parentheses. Nothing in innovation can be kept in neat boxes. There are always deviants, even within the organizations themselves, who will address projects not strictly within the mission of their group. Who is going to stop a determined innovator from creating a new product, even if he is a member of the technology center, which is not charged with new product development? The researcher who persists in working in technology and the new product developer who engages in basic research will prevail if they are committed to pursuing new ideas.

Tangible and Intangible Innovation

There are two kinds of innovation that occur in business. The first is the one that automatically comes to mind, namely that which results in new products that are three-dimensional and solid— tangible—in the sense that they are manufactured. But there is another kind, which provides new procedures or systems or services that are intangible in that they are not factory-made and there is essentially nothing—or little—to hold on to or plug in. But both kinds are equally significant and both can affect our lives. Not only that, both have the same prospect for contributing to the health and growth of the companies that develop them.

Consumers Union (CU), the nonprofit product-evaluation organization that publishes *Consumer Reports,* provides us with as good a set of examples of these two kinds of innovation as we can formulate. On the occasion of celebrating its 50th anniversary in 1986, CU undertook to list the innovations that most changed our lives in the course of the half-century of its existence (Table 11–2). Indeed, those items overturned old ways of getting through the day, as anyone who was around and aware in 1936 can testify.

Let's see how some of the items in Table 11–2 fall into our two categories of tangibility. Air conditioners are certainly tangible. So are color television sets, detergents, disposable diapers, refrigerators, and transistors. But credit cards are more than those wallet-sized rectangular slabs of plastic; they are only one small element of a service, one step in an innovation process. So credit cards are intangible. The same holds for paperback books, health insurance, pensions and social security, shopping malls, and fast foods. I would add some personal choices to each group as numbers 51 and 52:

Table 11-1.

Categories of innovation organizations.

Innovation Mode	Inner-Directed, Non-Entrepreneurial, Client-Oriented	Outer-Directed, Entrepreneurial, Venture-Oriented	R&D	Administrative
1. Technical center	✓		✓	
2. Research center	✓		✓	
3. New products center	✓		✓	
4. Captive R&D program	✓		✓	
5. External teams	✓		✓	
6. Internal ventures center	(✓)*	✓	(✓)*	✓
7. External ventures center	(✓)*	✓	(✓)*	✓
8. Directorate of licensing	✓	✓		✓
Skunk works (May be incorporated into items 4 and 6 above)	✓	✓	✓	

* Secondary role.

Table 11-2.
Fifty items that changed the way we live.

Air conditioners	Paperbacks
Air travel	Pensions and social security
Antibiotics	Personal computers
Austin/Morris Mini (1959)	The Pill
Automatic transmissions	Plymouth Voyager (1984)
Black-and-white TVs	Polio vaccine
Color TVs	Power mowers
Compact discs	Refrigerators and freezers
Credit cards	Running shoes
Detergents	Safety belts
Disposable diapers	Shopping malls
Enriched bread	Smoke detectors
Fluoridation	Dr. Spock's *Baby and Child Care*
Ford Mustang (1965)	Standardized dining (fast foods)
Frozen foods	Suburbia
The "G.I. Bill of Rights"	Supermarkets
Health insurance	Synthetic fabrics
Hi-fi's	Tampons
Jeep (1941)	Toyota Corona (1965)
Latex paint	Transistors
LP records	Transparent tape
Magnetic tape	VA and FHA mortgages
Nash 600 (1941)	VCRs
Oldsmobile/Cadillac V-8 (1949)	Volkswagen Beetle (1951)
Oldsmobile Toronado (1966)	Washers and dryers

SOURCE: *I'll Buy That! 50 Small Wonders and Big Deals That Revolutionized the Lives of Consumers.* Copyright 1986 by Consumers Union of United States, Inc., Mount Vernon, NY 10553. Excerpted by permission from Consumer Reports Books.

microwave ovens for tangible and new versions of yellow pages of telephone books for intangible. While we are at it, throw in some that you like. Certainly there are some new candidates; 1986 is already a long time ago in terms of new products and processes.

CU's list breaks down into about 35 items that are manufactured and 15 that are not. (Some overlap and are borderline.) All went through a process of R&D, and thus through some of our modes of innovation.

R&D

What does that common and overworked term "R&D" really mean?
Let's define it and see what it consists of for both manufactured
and service/system products, and then turn, for the remainder of
Part 4, to each innovation mode and see how it employs research
and development.

R&D in Manufacturing Businesses: Tangible

The U.S. Department of Commerce has definitions generated
by its agency, the National Science Foundation, that are as good
as any we will find. Pertinent excerpts from these are as follows:

Scope of R&D. Pertains to advanced work in the fields of "the
sciences (including medicine) and in engineering, and design and
development of prototypes, products, and processes. It does not
include quality control, routine product testing, market research,
sales promotion, sales service, research in the social sciences or
psychology, or other nontechnological activities or services."

Basic research. ". . . projects which represent original investigation for the advancement of scientific knowledge and which do
not have specific commercial objectives (although they may be in
the fields of present or potential interest to the . . . company)."

Applied research. The same as basic research except with "specific commercial objectives with respect to either products or processes."

Development. ". . . technical activity concerned with nonroutine
problems encountered in translating research findings or other
general scientific knowledge into products or processes."[2]

R&D in Nonmanufacturing Businesses: Intangible

This definition is easy. Simply extend the preceding definitions
from the Department of Commerce to include what it left out.
Namely: quality control, routine product testing, market research,
sales promotion, sales service, research in social sciences and psychology, and other nontechnical activities or services.

Is there really a common ground in each of the innovation
modes for manufactured and nonmanufactured products? For ex-

ample, there is no question that manufacturing involves technology—but does nonmanufacturing? Although the technology of system/service products is, by its nature, less tangible, that does not mean that it doesn't exist. Consider credit cards. They depend on computer technology.

How Does American Industry Choose What to Innovate?

The biggest challenge facing the innovator, and that person's employer, is that of choosing the right thing to innovate. The achievement of a brilliant result is meaningless if no one buys it or uses it. The right choice is usually connected with life cycles—of both the technology that addresses existing products and the products themselves.

What better examples of making the right choices can we have than the Consumers Union listing of the "Top 50"? Let's use hindsight to consider what the inclusion of certain items on CU's list implies about product/process life cycles and the impact of innovation on those life cycles:

Air conditioners. We can infer that innovation devoted to refining the freon cycle was a better investment 50 years ago than the same effort devoted to electric fans, which haven't changed much since.

Air travel. Train travel was maturing; for a company in the transportation business, R&D investments into advanced airplanes 50 years ago would pay back better than R&D into advanced deisel engines.

Antibiotics. Investigation into the chemicals manufactured by molds would have been wiser than investigation into improved forms of epsom salts.

Austin/Morris Mini. Developers of this product were more "with it," in view of the maturing of the market for large elaborate cars, than their rivals at Rolls Royce, who persisted in developing costly, even more elegant, vehicles. The Mini's developers perceived that a new life cycle was starting in automobiles; consumers were ready for small, affordable mass-produced cars.

As our eight kinds of innovation organizations pursue their destinies, they must always view the selection of what they will work on in the context of how mature the market, the process, and the product are that they are addressing. Every product, every technology, every pattern or procedure, even as it flourishes and "lives," is on its way out. As with living creatures, existence does not go on forever.

Thus, innovation is, in a way, a matter of life and death. The word we use is "obsolescence." While life and death sounds grim, obsolescence does not. Americans like obsolescence—not for what it disposes of, but for what it provides as a replacement. Obsolescence sets the tone of the nation, and American businesses accepts its challenge (while not always welcoming it). The trick is to use innovation so as to be obsoleters rather than obsoletees.

As we describe an innovation mode in each of the following eight chapters, examples will be provided of specific innovation programs. Each example should be considered from the point of view of where the activity stands in the pertinent life cycle. For example, in Chapter 12 we describe how Emhart improved the technology of making glass bottles, which proved to be a wise choice of innovation program. But, if plastics and paper containers had completely replaced glass containers just during the period in which Emhart committed its R&D groups to improving glass-making machinery, the innovation approach would have been irrelevant. Emhart would have been in the same boat as watchmakers who invested in improving jeweled watch bearings just as low-cost good-quality digital systems came in to take over. The lesson is that wise companies don't invest in improving technology for a dying product if it is truly on its death bed.

By the same token, they don't invest in improving a dying technology. An example is the manufacture of plate glass. The traditional way to make quality plate glass two or three decades ago was to grind both surfaces to a wonderful smoothness. Anyone in that business might, with good reason, have been tempted to invest in better automation of the grinding process or in developing a new and superior grinding compound. That would have been right had not the Pilkington Plate Glass Company of Great Britain developed the "float glass" process.

Someone at Pilkington underwent a superlative creative spasm and realized that hot viscous glass floating on a pool of molten metal (tin) is automatically flat, for it floats on a flat liquid interface. If no one jiggles the liquid, all that needs to be done is to carefully

Figure 11-1. Life cycles of products and technologies.

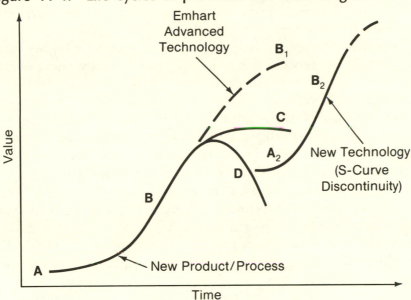

withdraw the glass and cool it. Grinding is unnecessary. That, too, was a winner—no one grinds plate glass anymore.

What we are talking about is perceiving where any technology is at the moment we pursue it and placing it in what L. J. Thomas, director of Research Laboratories of Eastman Kodak, calls the "technology maturity curve"[3] and what Richard Foster, in his book *Innovation,* points out is the classic S-curve of life cycles.[4]

Figure 11–1 illustrates such a curve, along with other possible courses. It shows that the value of a new product or technology is almost flat with time during its early life (region A). It gathers momentum and reaps profits as the curve steepens (regions B and B₁). As competitive products and technologies emerge, euphoria ceases and the curve may either flatten (region C) or undergo a reversal in value (region D). The question to be asked for any technology is, what region is it in today?

It is easy to ask that question, but it is not always easy to come up with the right answer. I fear I have no guidelines for you. You know your industry. Just guard against overzealous loyalty to the old and familiar, for you can count on at least one of your competitors possibly beating the pants off you in a year or two with a new technology. If you begin to perceive that a new way to do something has appeared, pay attention. It may turn into what Foster calls a "discontinuity."

As shown in Figure 11–1, a discontinuity adds far higher value to a product or process, for it is a new technology addressed to the same class of end product. The introduction of float-glass technology to the plate-glass industry illustrates such a discontinuity.

Yet a flexible attitude must be maintained. Emhart improved conventional bottle-making machinery so well as to extend its value into region B_1. It did this in the face of more common experience in mature industry, in which extensive investments in old technologies result in only marginal increases in slope (region C). That's too bad, because once a technology matures, it costs much to attain little, while in the early days the reverse is the case. The diminishing-returns law is now in effect, and it is characteristic of region C.

There is a message here. The best choices of innovation programs are those that are based on a perception of where resulting achievements will fit on life-cycle S-curves. If innovators expend their efforts and resources in products or technologies that are already recipients of the kiss of death of excessive maturity (regions C and D of Figure 11–1), that could be an investment wasted. But if the work results in revivifying and thus prolonging the steep portion of the curve, as Emhart did in region B_1 or in launching a totally new approach as represented by a discontinuity, then that will pay off. Region A_2 shows such a case; and indeed region A, years ago, must have been the same.

A Demography of American Innovation

If we consider innovators to be a human population segment, they should be describable, as are other such segments, using demography, or "vital statistics." The figures that concern us are the moneys consumed, the numbers of people involved, and the floor space they occupy. Part 1 of this book describes funding practices, staffs, and facilities in terms of their unique, often very personal, characteristics; here, in contrast, let us summarize a few of the quite impersonal quantitative aspects of innovation.

The most meaningful way to think of spending on innovation is to characterize it as a proportion of sales dollars. It is the percentage of today's gross income devoted to future business. Thus, it is a kind of optimistic insurance premium, the purpose of which is more than merely to provide for survival; rather it is to lay a basis for a company to flourish.

There are other measures. An interesting one, not normally cited, is the percentage of the total technical personnel reservoir in any nation that is devoted to R&D. We can break these numbers into the proportions devoted to government or commercial end uses and into the R&D categories of basic, applied, and developmental.

R&D Spending: Some National and International Statistics

National Science Foundation data inform us that in 1986, our nation spent 2.8 percent of its gross national product on research and development. West Germany's rate was 2.7 percent and Japan's for 1985 was 2.8 percent. Thus, all three major Western industrial nations are tightly clumped in terms of level of commitment to innovation. Russia's 1986 rate is much higher, at 3.8 percent, but we can bet that little of that was invested on breakthroughs in videocassette recorders or microwave ovens. (It is interesting and distressing that the United States also gave little attention to these. But Japan and Korea mounted significant efforts in advancing the sophistication of such products and their technologies, which explains why they "own" those markets today.)

R&D spending in this country, according to the National Science Foundation, has been increasing rapidly, totaling $108.8 billion for 1985, which is triple the spending rate a decade earlier. The number for 1986 is $117 billion, and a projection for 1987 is at the $125 billion level.[5] These sums reflect the total of the three categories of innovation, the ratios of which remain roughly the same with time (although basic research has lost a percentage point or two to the other categories in recent years). Basic research consumes roughly one-eigth of the total, applied research one-fifth, and development the remainder about two-thirds.

As for the percentage of R&D funded by the government, in 1985, at $50.5 billion, it was 46.4 percent. Of this, $34.3 billion was for national defense. Projections for 1987 show federal funding increasing to 47.8 percent.[6] Please note that these sums include both industrial and nonindustrial expenditures. Most of the data that follow will be designated for the industrial portion only.

Numbers of Individuals Engaged in R&D

The U.S. Bureau of the Census through National Science Foundation publications is a good source for personnel information, even though the currently available data may be a few years old. In 1983, the total complement of employed engineers and scientists was 3,137,000 (about 1.4 percent of the nation's population). Of these, 529,900,* or 16.9 percent, were engaged in research and development. This adds a dimension to our consideration of how significant our innovation effort is. While we give one out of every $36 of revenue to it, we go much further in terms of talent. We give more than one-sixth of our technical professionals to it.

We can add to this the number of skilled helpers and support personnel. The Bureau provides a 1983 statistic for the category of "engineers and scientists in industry," whether in R&D or other technical activity (leaving out those in universities, foundations, government laboratories, health sciences, and so on). There were 1,560,400 such engineers and scientists, and they were supported by 1,303,600 drafters, technicians, and computer programmers. This comes to .85 supporters for every supportee.[7] In the absence of other figures, and on the basis of a career of observation, I would judge that about the same ratio holds for those engaged exclusively in R&D.

Cost per R&D Employee

The Bureau of the Census 1985 data for the yearly costs to support an engineer or scientist, including all materials, technician support, and overhead expenses, is given for major industries in Table 11–3. The average for 1984 was $127,600 per year. This increased by 7.4 percent to $137,000 the following year (shown in table). From here on, the Bureau supplies no quantitative data, but I have an estimate of my own for 1987 of $175,000. It is not

---

* Exact figures for more recent years are not available, but this number probably approaches 700,000 for 1987.

Table 11-3.
Cost per scientist or engineer, 1985.

Industry	Cost ($000)
Chemicals and allied products	$125.2
Machinery	136.4
Electrical equipment and communications	146.2
Motor vehicles and other transportation	227.5
Aircraft and missiles	167.6
Average*	137.0

* Calculated on basis of *all* industries, including those not listed.

SOURCE: National Science Foundation, 1987.

for the nation as whole, but for the one third of national R&D spending represented by the "100 biggest spenders" of Table 11–4. It is consistent with recent discussions with my peers in the innovation game, most of whom work for *Fortune* 500 companies. They all cluster in the ball park of this number for 1987.

Note again in Table 11–3 the costs per professional year by industry for 1985. Why the R&D cost per person working in the auto/bus/truck field should so far exceed the cost of workers in all the other fields, even the aircraft and missiles industry, is a puzzle that I leave for the reader to solve.

On the other hand, Table 11–5 shows that the *total* spending for aircraft and missiles for 1985 is more than double that in the motor vehicles category, but that should be viewed with respect to the portion of their respective R&D efforts that is self-funded compared to that which is government funded. From the point of view of self-funding, the aircraft and missiles companies make the smallest investment of any category.

Floor-Space Utilization

According to another similarly derived index, each R&D professional with his or her helper occupies 2,000 square feet of R&D facility. My measure of floor space used is admittedly more open to challenge than my 1987 cost-per-professional number. The Bureau has not tabulated any data for occupancy. The figure is a

Table 11-4.
The 100 biggest R&D spenders in U.S. industry, 1986.

Rank 1986	Company*	R&D Expenditure ($ millions)	R&D Sales (%)
1	General Motors (1)	$4157.7	4.0%
2	IBM (5)	3975.0	7.8
3	Ford (3)	2305.0	3.7
4	AT&T (7)	2278.0	4.2
5	General Electric** (6)	1300.0	3.7
6	Du Pont (9)	1156.0	4.3
7	Eastman Kodak (26)	1059.0	9.2
8	United Technologies (17)	852.8	5.4
9	Hewlett-Packard (51)	824.0	11.6
10	Digital Equipment (44)	814.1	10.7
11	Boeing (16)	757.0	4.6
12	Chrysler (11)	732.0	3.2
13	Xerox (32)	650.0	6.9
14	Exxon (2)	616.0	0.9
15	Dow (27)	605.0	5.4
16	3M (39)	564.0	6.6
17	Monsanto (55)	523.0	7.6
18	Johnson & Johnson (53)	521.3	7.4
19	McDonnell Douglas (23)	504.8	4.0
20	Motorola (60)	492.0	8.4
21	Lockheed (30)	491.0	4.8
22	Merck (91)	479.8	11.6
23	Procter & Gamble (18)	479.0	3.1
24	Allied-Signal (25)	459.0	3.9
25	Unisys (46)†	440.8	5.9
26	Lilly, Eli (101)	427.0	11.5
27	Rockwell (24)	407.5	3.3
28	Texas Instruments (72)	406.0	8.2
29	Northrop (64)	378.3	6.7
30	SmithKline (99)	376.9	10.1
31	Pfizer (84)	335.5	7.5
32	NCR (75)	320.7	6.6
33	Upjohn (162)	314.1	13.7
34	Control Data (119)	313.9	9.4
35	Bristol-Myers (76)	311.1	6.4
36	GTE (NL)	291.0	1.9
37	Goodyear Tire & Rubber (29)	290.4	3.2

Rank 1986	Company*	R&D Expenditure ($ millions)	R&D Sales (%)
38	Abbott Labs (96)	$ 284.9	7.5%
39	American Cyanamid (94)	278.3	7.3
40	General Dynamics (36)	268.2	3.0
41	Raytheon (48)	254.0	3.5
42	Honeywell (52)	246.7	4.6
43	Westinghouse Electric (28)	246.0	2.3
44	Shell Oil (15)	246.0	1.5
45	Mobil Oil (5)	229.0	0.5
46	Intel (256)	228.3	18.0
47	American Home Products (74)	227.1	4.6
48	Chevron (10)	225.0	0.9
49	Deere (111)	224.7	6.4
50	National Semiconductor (227)	222.4	15.0
51	Martin Marietta (77)††	218.9	4.6
52	Amoco (13)	217.0	1.2
53	Schering-Plough (157)	212.1	8.8
54	ITT (41)	208.0	2.7
55	PPG (78)	203.5	4.3
56	Baxter Travenol (63)	203.0	3.7
57	Wang Labs (146)	202.8	7.7
58	Warner-Lambert (127)	202.3	6.5
59	Tektronix (242)	198.2	14.7
60	Advanced Micro Devices (436)	181.4	28.7
61	Caterpillar (47)	178.0	2.4
62	AMP (185)	170.0	8.8
63	Squibb (153)	163.0	9.1
64	NYNEX (NL)	160.0	1.4
65	Texaco (8)	160.0	0.5
66	TRW (58)	159.7	2.6
67	Emerson Electric (73)	151.7	3.1
68	Union Carbide (42)	148.0	2.3
69	FMC (131)	145.8	4.9
70	Data General (255)	143.1	11.3
71	Syntex (NL)	143.0	14.6
72	Aluminum Co. of America (79)	137.9	3.0
73	Eaton (95)	134.1	3.5
74	Rohm and Haas (172)	132.8	6.4
75	Apple Computer (190)	127.8	6.7
76	Polaroid (211)	126.6	7.8

(continued)

Table 11-4 *(continued).*

Rank 1986	Company*	R&D Expenditure ($ millions)	R&D Sales (%)
77	Standard Oil (35)	$ 125.0	1.4%
78	General Foods (NL)	122.2	1.3
79	Amdahl (372)	119.2	12.3
80	Litton Industries (83)	118.1	2.6
81	Harris (166)	117.9	5.3
82	Ingersoll-Rand (139)	111.1	4.0
83	Kimberly-Clark (90)	111.0	2.6
84	Textron (69)	107.0	2.1
85	Perkin-Elmer (251)	105.0	8.1
86	Corning Glass (193)	103.5	5.6
87	Sterling Drug (177)	102.9	5.2
88	Zenith Electronics (191)	99.7	5.3
89	General Signal (214)	98.0	6.2
90	Gould (235)	97.9	10.8
91	Colgate-Palmolive (71)	95.0	1.9
92	W. R. Grace (56)	94.2	2.5
93	Atlantic Richfield (20)	94.0	0.6
94	Prime Computer (337)	91.9	10.7
95	Phillips Petroleum (31)	89.0	0.9
96	Firestone Tire & Rubber (102)	88.0	2.5
97	Cray Research (421)	87.7	14.7
98	Cummins Engine (160)	87.5	3.8
99	Tandem Computers (364)	86.6	11.3
100	Teledyne (124)	84.6	2.6
	Total/Average	$41,254.6	6.08%

* Ranking in *Fortune* 500 industrial survey. GTE and NYNEX are considered service companies. General Foods is a subsidiary of Philip Morris, but its R&D figures are reported separately. Syntex is registered in Panama.
** Includes RCA.
† Merged Burroughs and Sperry.
†† Omitted from last year's survey.

SOURCE: Adapted from *Inside R&D,* a publication of Technical Insights, P.O. Box 1304, Fort Lee, NJ 07024. Used with permission.

rough average of what professionals I talked to use, and, within that limitation, is valid as a ball park number.

Table 11-5.
U.S. industry investment in innovation in 1985.
(in $ millions)

Industry Category	Government Funded	Self-Funded	Total
Aircraft and missiles	$13,421	$ 4,198	$17,619
Electrical equipment	6,887	10,194	17,081
Machinery	1,536	9,334	10,870
Chemicals and related products	316	8,352	8,668
Motor vehicles and equipment	978	6,080	7,058
Other industries	3,346	13,536	16,882
Total for all industries	$26,484	$51,694	$78,178*

* This is for industry investment only. Total including nonindustry is $108.8 billion.
SOURCE: National Science Foundation.

The 100 Biggest Spenders

The 100 biggest spenders on R&D in our nation expended $41 billion in 1986 (see Table 11–4), or in excess of one third of total innovation investment. All other firms in the country plus all nonindustrial research and development account for the other two-thirds. (Some of that two-thirds is funneled through the same 100 firms as contracted R&D, which is not included in Table 11–5. Those moneys are of the category represented by the "Government funded" column of Table 11–4.) Keeping our attention on self-funded innovation only and using my estimated rate of spending per engineer and scientist of $175,000 per year, these 100 big spenders employ around 220,000 of these (and more than 400,000 if technicians are included) or close to half the total R&D reservoir in the country. As for portion of sales dollars committed to R&D, it averaged 6.08 percent. That is more than double that of all industries of the nation as a whole, and a most impressive number. How impressive it is can be conceptualized if we apply our indexes for resources of innovation organizations in this country.

The median company in this list, spending about $400 million on innovation yearly, has an R&D staff of professionals and aides exceeding 4,000 and occupies facilities consisting of around 100 roofed acres. That is a tremendous commitment to innovation. As for the biggest of these biggies, General Motors, the mind boggles. That company has about 800,000 employees, or almost triple the population of the sovereign nation of Luxembourg. At $4.16 billion invested on innovation, its R&D staff probably exceeds 40,000 (highly trained) people!

Some Rules of Thumb

We can come up with some rules of thumb from all this. For the 100 biggest, we can calculate that, at $175,000 per, there is an average of about one engineer for each $4 million of yearly revenue (although the spread runs from $25 million per engineer for the oil companies to $2.1 million for the pharmaceuticals).

For companies in the nation as a whole, I estimate that on average, for 1987, $6.3 million sales supports one team of R&D professionals plus an assistant.

If you have a company doing sales of $100 million per year (obviously not one of the "biggest"), and if you run a typical R&D activity, then:

- It would have a professional R&D staff of 16 people.
- Those people would be supported, at .85 per, by 14 semi-professionals.
- They would occupy a facility of 32,000 square feet.

Performing Innovation Eight Ways

Chapters 12 through 19 contain a discussion of the distinctive features of each of the innovation organizations and descriptions of how they operate. As you proceed through each description, it should be instructive to relate it to the issues discussed in this chapter: how closely each is bound to existing clients within the company or committed to venturing into new fields, how tangible or intangible the results of the actions taken will be, whether the innovation is of an R&D nature or administrative, and finally, how much of company resources is apportioned in relation to the others and with respect to company revenues.

Most of the chapters include at least one example derived from a combination of personal visits and information from the literature. I was gratified to find that they were pursued with an awareness of how these related to life-cycle S-curves for each respective new process or product, and that all were at the forefront.

I am indebted to the following companies for having allowed me free interchange of information with their executives, their directors of innovation programs, and most important—with their innovators themselves. Technical center: General Motors, Emhart Corporation, Corning Glass Works; new products center: Raytheon Company; research center: Hoechst Celanese Corporation; captive R&D department (skunk works): Xerox; captive R&D department (technology in a small company): Repligen Corporation; external team: Contex Graphics Systems, with faculty team from Carnegie-Mellon University; internal ventures center: Eastman Kodak; external ventures center: Continental Can, Raytheon Company, Venture Captial Journal; licensing: MIT Technology and Licensing Office.

References

1. Karl Vesper, personal communication with author.
2. "Research and Development in Industry," *Surveys of Science Resources Series* (Washington, D.C.: National Science Foundation, 1984), p. 2.
3. L. J. Thomas, "Technology and Business Strategy—the R&D Link," *Research Management*, May–June 1984, pp. 15–19.
4. R. Foster, *Innovation* (New York: Summit Books, 1986).
5. "$125 Billion for R&D in the USA in 1987," *Research and Development*, January 1987, pp. 68–70.
6. Verbal communication with the National Science Foundation.
7. "Statistical Abstract of the United States 1986," *U.S. Department of the Census*, 106th ed., p. 582.

12

Technical Center

A technical center advances the state of the art in its industry and specifically in all parts of its company (each part constituting a "client" in our terminology) in either or both of two major areas:

- Materials used to construct final products.
- Methods and tools of fabrication.

The results of the efforts of such an organization are the upgrading or replacement of existing materials or practices so that products can be manufactured with less cost while at the same time improving their performance, visual design, and useful life and reliability. The work of a technical center does not purposefully address the creation of new products. Nor does it, with intent, lead to the formation of new ventures. But it is not uncommon for new products and new ventures to "fall out" of its activities.

There are no limits to the level of sophistication of the work performed by a technical center. It could involve basic research, applied research, or straightforward development based on such research.

Mature Industry: The Most Comfortable Environment for a Technical Center

Established companies' instinctive reaction when considering innovation is that it is not for them. Like the Boston dowager who, when asked where she got her hats, replied, "I don't get hats, I have my hats," mature companies *have* their products.

Consider the automobile industry. Albert Sobey, senior director of Energy and Advanced Product Economics at General Motors Corporation, pointed out when I visited him that the industry produces essentially only one product, the one it has made for most of the last 100 years: some chambers in which to explode gasoline that are placed in a box mounted on four wheels (one in each corner), with a fifth wheel to steer with. GM isn't planning to change now, so their innovation activity does not focus on devising a wholly new vehicle based on a wholly new principle. Rather, they seek to develop new ways to make the present one, ways to produce a better car more economically. That is achieved by means of technological innovation, much of it carried on in a technical center (or, in the case of the huge GM, in a number of these).

General Motors employs about 14,000 engineers and scientists engaged in the process of advancing present states of knowledge, with close to 2,000 of them in basic and applied research and a similar number in design, which leaves most of the remainder to engage in technological advance, both in centers and in captive groups.

The accomplishments of technical innovation in the automobile industry in the last year by GM, and by its competitors as well, are of major magnitude. In the field of materials alone, we note that the average 1987 car weighs 100 pounds less than 1985 models, and that is in addition to as much as 1,000 pounds eliminated over the last decade. Weight saving is due in large part to the fact that plastics now account for 10 percent of all materials used.[1]

These are not ordinary plastics; rather, they are engineered specialty materials like "injection-molded carbon-fiber-reinforced polyetheretherketone," referred to by its intimates as PEEK. It is resistant to high temperatures and wear and does not corrode in oils, greases, and most chemicals. It has replaced metal in the construction of oil pumps, turbo inlets, and turbo impellers. Car and truck manufacturers have replaced metal bumpers, front grills, hoods, and cabs with plastic.

In other kinds of materials, Ford claims a first in 1987 with an all-ceramic combustion chamber in a diesel engine. Chrysler and GM have introduced similar advances in materials encompassing new metal alloys, ceramics, coatings, paints, and fabrics. The list goes on. Be assured, it will be added to next year, and every year after that.

And I have not even mentioned new automated assembly machinery for forming, welding, gluing, finishing, and otherwise handling all these materials.

A few words about the development of manufacturing machinery: It is not enough for a technical center to devise a model of a machine based on a new concept; in many cases it must go on to build the final operating version that will be installed in a production line. Such special, proprietary, one-of-a-kind equipment is often impractical to "order" from an outside firm. While other kinds of innovation lead to transfer to another organizational entity, technology transfer for a technical center more commonly occurs within the center itself. This accounts for the large size of technical centers in certain kinds of large firms.

I have already indicated the impressive work force General Motors devotes to technical R&D. Many other companies also conduct this kind of business on a grand scale. The technical center at Eastman Kodak, for example, employs many hundreds of people, who not only develop advanced models of the machinery that accurately and cost-effectively apply light-sensitive coating to film, but who then go on to build and install production equipment based on those models. Consider the tobacco industry, another mature one. Essentially, cigarettes today are the same as cigarettes years ago, the same brown shreds wrapped in white paper. The best way to innovate in that industry is to develop innovative manufacturing machinery. As an example, the technology group at Philip Morris has developed and built a machine that produces cigarettes at the rate of 133 per second!

On the other hand, Emhart Corporation, a company that ranks about 200 in the *Fortune* 500 list, built a small technical center that best fits its (mature and diverse) divisions.

I offer below two examples of technical centers, one large and one modest: General Electric's, which serves its home appliance business, and Emhart's. This chapter concludes with a description of a representative of a very new, and currently very small, kind of business, Repligen Corporation, a biotech firm, for whom "tech" looms large.

A Large-Scale Technical Center: General Electric

General Electric is the nation's fifth-largest company, with sales in the $35 billion range. It is a multi-business company, and one of its businesses is home appliances, a field in which it ranks first for dollar volume in this country. That sector of GE is designated as MABG, Major Appliance Business Group; it is managed by a senior vice president, to whom John C. Truscott, the vice president and general manager of technology, reports.

In a recent article from which much of the information for this example is derived, Truscott is quoted as seeing his mission as achieving "the highest quality at the lowest produced cost," making it "essential to optimize both the product and the process for producing that product . . . from the beginning of the design phase rather than waiting until after the fact."[2] He goes on to point out that benefits derive from allowing the process to drive the product rather than letting the product drive the process. While his first statement is second nature to any manager of a technical center, the second is rarely annunciated. Yet, if one thinks about it, it follows.

A manufacturing company's R&D capability should include two departments: a product design engineering department and an advanced production technology department. A goal, one which seems to have been attained at GE, is to remove the traditional barriers between the two. "No longer are products designed without regard for the methods of producing them," says Truscott.

A further group of organizational elements in GE's technology division involves applications centers, which will propel the company down the path to what it calls "factories with a future." These are the Automated Assembly Applications Center (AAAC) and the Plastics Applications Center (PAC). "An applications center is the center of expertise in a business whose objective is to pursue its specialty and act as an internal consulting resource for the entire company," says GE.

That consultation is not free. Operating entities must pay for the services of the applications centers. Furthermore, the centers must compete for those jobs with outside organizations, a factor that fights complacency.

GE means it when it states that the applications centers serve the entire company. In spite of the fact that such centers' primary orientation is to the appliance sector, an applications center shares what it knows with all sectors. Its resources are used by the Aircraft Engine Business Group, the Factory Automation Products Division, and others. And that sharing works both ways. The applications centers make use of the scientists in the corporate research center in Schenectady, New York, and they give credit to the aircraft engine group for significant aid in early development phases of a rotary compressor for refrigerators.

The track record is there to see. AAAC supports the entire range of assembly automation. This includes computer simulation of factory processes to anticipate any possible running condition, pick-and-place robot-based assembly, automatic in-process inspection, and many others. A recent example of one successful project is a $5.5 million system it developed and installed that automatically assembles a 39-part compressor.

The same tale may be told with regard to the Plastics Applications Center. While it is situated, as is AAAC, in GE's Appliance Park in Louisville, Kentucky, and while it is primarily oriented to serving the major-appliances business sector, it is used by some 40 other organizations in the company.

An achievement of which PAC is justifiably proud is its *PermaTuf* clothes washer tub. Here is another instance of the replacement of metal, in this case porcelainized metal, with plastic. GE was unable to find chemical suppliers that could provide just the right material to satisfy its specs, so it undertook the development itself, and succeeded. The product has had good customer acceptance and contributes to the fact that GE is number one in market share for clothes washers in this country.

When a company is as well facilitated and staffed with technology innovation expertise as is GE, and when the pursuit of new technology is supported by the CEO, as it is at GE, extraordinary turnaround results can occasionally be attained. For example, GE recently introduced at the National Home Builders Exposition a state-of-the-art model of a refrigerator that had been developed in 21 months rather than in the original allotted development time of 44 months. It did this by a process of overlapping steps, in which commitment to the next step is given before the preceding one has been completed. This is what the Japanese call the "sushi" approach (see Chapter 5), and one engages in it only when top management is sold on the quality of the facilities in which the work will take place and of the broad range of competence combined with determination of the people engaged in that work.

What accompanies all this? Big bucks—both going out and coming in. GE is using its technological innovation as justification for investing literally billions of dollars in remaking its factories, and as a result its revenues grow significantly in an absolute sense, but also in terms of income per square foot of plant and income per worker.

All of the technical advances, both in materials and in machinery, are at the forefront of their art. They demand such depth of scientific know-how that, in most organizations, only "centers" can cluster enough facilities and engineers and scientists to attack the challenges. That is what the auto companies and, in the home appliances industry, what General Electric has done.

A Small-Scale Technology Center: Emhart Corporation

Emhart Corporation engages in a variety of businesses, all of them in the mature category. "We've been building our business for more than a century," says Emhart's chairman, T. E. Ford. "We're an old-line New England company that makes unsexy products, but products that satisfy some very basic human needs."[3] The company makes high-capacity machinery for the manufacture of such commodities as footware and glass bottles. It also produces fastening machinery and a spectrum of hardware items such as door locks. Emhart had sales in 1983 of $1.7 billion and employed 29,000 people.*

Emhart is committed to the principle that for a traditional product business such as theirs, salvation—if not survival itself— lies in identifying which technologies are approaching the ends of their life cycles and then taking innovative action to update or replace them. It is management's position that integrating state-of-the-art technologies with mature technologies can prevent obsolescence in many cases (see Chapter 11, which discusses Emhart's development resulting in extension of an S-curve). The challenge lies first in providing an awareness and a competence in the new area of technology and then in superimposing that new technology effectively onto an old one.

To accomplish this, Emhart created a Center for Technological Innovation on the premises of one of its subsidiaries, The United Shoe Machinery Company in Beverly, Massachusetts. It engages in

---

* Things move fast in this second half of the 1980s. Since this was written, Emhart has undergone major reorganization, and has sold off several of its divisions.

R&D in design, process engineering, and manufacturing, and is under the aegis of the vice president for technology, John Rydz.

Rydz shares the GE philosophy that "process leads product," but his way of implementing it differs. Where a GE technical center will develop a new material or a new production machine, Emhart's technical center will perform early creative work but will turn the results of such work over to the operating entities to complete. Such actions by the divisions would never have occurred but for the stimulation provided by the technical center. But Rydz does not use the word stimulate, he prefers "catalyze."

For those familiar with catalysis, the implications for organization size are clear. It doesn't take much of a catalyst to stimulate large-scale chemical reactions. That's why the Emhart technology center is small—30 to 40 people are all it takes. Yet the center's scope is large and eclectic. The group consists of specialists who moniter some 20 advanced technologies and translate them, in Rydz's words, into "threats or opportunities for Emhart."*

The advanced technologies include microelectronics hardware and software, sensors and new microhydraulics, machine diagnostics and mechanism analysis, computer-aided vision, materials, and others. The members of the technical center are experts in these fields, but they supplement and extend their expertise with external resources in universities, consulting firms, and—this is an interesting one—vendors.

Implied in the capabilities provided by the technology group is that they are gap-fillers. The business entities (clients) they serve possess neither the depth of expertise in these areas, nor the attitudes sympathetic to substantial investment that are inherent in the makeup and culture of the personnel of the technical center. Yet they have sophisticated skills in their own right. Each company division has its own captive R&D department, led by its own director of R&D. Such a department can then look upon the technical center as a resource, an extension of itself in areas in which it is lean.

This is an essential factor in the success of any innovation center. Its personnel must be matched with people of similar capability in each division client with whom to interact. The way

---

* For more on this and related subjects, see Rydz's book *Managing Innovation,* published in 1986 by Ballinger.

Emhart is organized, it has attained this goal. It is precisely this interaction that Rydz calls catalysis. For in the end the new technology is developed (for the most part) by the client and for the client. The center serves best when it stimulates the client to finish the job.

The corporation encourages each of its business entities to avail itself of the reservoir of expertise represented by the technical center. But it is interesting that Emhart does more than urge. It maintains a new technology committee made up of four board members with strong personal experience with new technologies— background not commonly found among members of most boards. The committee meets quarterly and applies its clout to ensure that all required steps are taken to guarantee that those technology programs they choose to sponsor are implemented. Once courses of action are determined, the board continues its involvement with an ongoing monitoring process.

This lessens certain client options, but the client's positions on the wisdom of a particular course of action are given fair hearing. In many other companies, it is more incumbent on the innovation organization to sell the client on innovations than at Emhart.

Another element of the center/client relationship is that projects are co-funded. Costs are shared by the participating divisions, which means that some of the technical center share is provided by the corporation and thus amounts to a partial subsidy to the divisions for any project they engage in (see the discussion of the merits of mandated funding allocation in Chapter 3).

The results—process and productivity improvement—are similar in kind to what we observe at other companies discussed in this chapter, but are perhaps more interesting because they're applied to "grubbier" products. For example, the bottle-making machinery division found itself confronted not only with aging machinery but also with a significant trend among customers to choose plastics and paper instead of glass. Yet the technology innovations introduced have preserved this business and made it comfortably profitable.

Emhart satisfied itself that, in spite of the growth of non-glass packaging, there would always be a place for glass containers. It decided to look with "new eyes" at the venerable bottle-making process.

A bottle starts with a gob of almost white-hot jelly-consistency glass. Traditionally, bottles are shaped by craftsmen, one by one, with the inevitable relegation of bits of unused glass into the discard bin. The R&D job was to quantify: Use just the right amount of molten glass per gob, not too much or too little, and automate.

Scientifically, the problem concerned the dynamics of heat transfer. Innovators wanted to control the cooling (and resulting stiffening) rate of the gob, which meant that the problem had to be attacked using computer simulation of the cooling process and computer control of the final machine process. The team of center and captive R&D group members accomplished this and did it in the best of all possible ways: The resulting new gadgetry could be plugged into existing machines.

Botkin et al. devote an entire chapter to Emhart, and much of it consists of the glass-bottle case study. "Results were staggering," say the authors. "The gross revenue potential of this one innovation is in the order of $100 million."[4]

One final comment about this achievement. It resulted in a new product that can be independently marketed as part of a new venture (a computer-controlled bottle-making machine). New venturing is not the primary goal of technology innovation groups, but in this case, the innovation concerned itself with process improvement, a skill of the technical center, which meant that the fallout new venture improved the process technology of the firms that bought Emhart's new product. So that element of consistency still prevailed. A similar event occurred at Allen-Bradley, resulting in its decision to launch a new venture based on its CIM machine (see Chapter 10).

The Place of Technology Innovation in New Business

It is rare for new ventures to be of such a scale that a formal technical center is organized. An opportunity exists when such enterprises are spawned out of a large company with such a center already in place. Then the services of the center can be offered to the venturers—but if they are of the character of most skunk workers, they will probably reject such aid. (A bit of executive discipline is not out of place in such cases.) Whether technology is centralized or not, most new businesses tend not to give it sufficient shrift. They should change their ways.

It is common for innovators to create spectacular products that work well in the lab and then fall flat because, as a *Business Week* article states, they are "plagued by manufacturing problems, many of which could be traced to excessively hasty design."[5] It is hard to persuade a start-up enterprise to adopt at least some of the philosophy of a GE technology center and to realize that process leads product. New ventures *should* build a technology innovation activity, no matter how small.

It is interesting that there is one kind of high-tech new business that reverses the normal approach to technology and makes it primary in its innovation agenda. That is the biotechnology field. Not without reason is "technology" in its name. Dr. Thomas Fraser, executive vice president and chief technical officer of Repligen Corporation of Cambridge, Massachusetts, informs me that for his kind of business the process is everything.

Some remarkable new gene-spliced protein fragments may some day be ingredients of a vaccine to fight immune deficiency diseases. But how prosaic a typical product looks—just liter jars of milky white liquid. The challenge comes in building technology— processes and equipment—to mimic and increase the scale of processes that go on in nature.

References

1. "Detroit Unveils 1987 Models," *Materials Engineering,* October 1986, pp. 33–37.
2. "A Finely Tuned Competitor," *Appliance,* June 1986, GE-19 through GE-46.
3. J. Botkin, D. Dimancescu, and R. Stata, *The Innovators* (New York: Harper and Row, 1984), pp. 56–80.
4. Ibid., p. 67.
5. "Two Lessons in Failure from Silicon Valley," *Business Week,* September 10, 1984, p. 74.

13

Research Center

When we are born, we are handed a heritage of history and culture that shapes our lives. When we engage in our work, we should realize that our company and its industry have been presented with a similar gift. Everything in industry had its beginning in research done by someone. The reservoir of basic information derived from the research that pertains to and underlies a technology is our heritage.

You could take a snapshot of the fund of knowledge on which your company's products and practices are based. Then it is more than a heritage: It is capital, just as much as some of the items called "assets" in the balance sheet. It is on the basis of such capital that a company can engage in that form of R&D called "development."

The National Science Foundation defines *development* as "technical activity concerned with nonroutine problems encountered in translating research findings or other general scientific knowledge into products and processes." What this means is that if you have an extensive enough fund of "research findings" and "other general scientific knowledge" under your belt to carry on all the innovative development your company has planned for in its strategy, there is no need to invest in further research.

Are You Living Off Your Capital?

Of course, you can't live off your capital forever, but that doesn't mean that many businesses can't engage for quite long periods in new technology development and new product development, "fat, dumb, and happy," as the saying goes, without damage or regret. "Look at the new models in our product line this year—all winners," boasts the CEO, "and what about that robot welder we just installed, it cut labor by 80 percent. Not only that, we made history for our firm with that great ROI number." He concludes, unable to repress a triumphal smirk, "And all without one Ph.D!" But is he fooling himself? Does disaster loom? Should he set up a research organization?

To Do Research or Not?

The answer to the question of whether to conduct research is not a simple one, especially when there are ways to hedge.

Keeping Up-to-Date

There is a way for innovation to proceed effectively without in-house research. It lies with using the research of others. Most results derived from most research are available to all who take the trouble to read the literature and attend scientific conferences. Competitive products can be disassembled and analyzed. In addition, people do change jobs, bringing with them their personal inventory of research-derived information. But these approaches also are accompanied by two major penalties.

First, no matter how "recent" the published papers or the competitor's new products are, those who did the research on which they are based knew that information at least one or two years before. People who do no research have no head start. They are compelled to launch their development programs with a timing handicap—no small matter in any fast-moving competitive industry.

Second, the firm for which the researchers work may choose not to publish certain crucial results from their work; they may decide to hold back. Now they have intellectual property that their competitors do not have. Of course, someday the competitors will know about it. For example, they can become licensees (see Chapter 19). Again, the issue is that of the untimeliness penalty.

So, like everything else in business, whether or not to commit yourself to your own research capability is a judgment call that involves trade-offs. You might be so swift and efficient in knowing about and using the research of others that you may never have to do your own. But keep in mind that someday you might regret that you never accumulated some capital of your own.

Buying Research

A company can put off setting up its own research facility, maybe forever, by investing in external teams (see Chapter 16) such as may be found in universities, consulting establishments, or small, high-tech firms willing to work under contract.

Or, a company can invest in an existing firm, thus laying claim not only to that firm's research heritage, but also to its staff and facility, which constantly add to that heritage. A company may acquire another company outright, it may buy a minority position in a sophisticated firm, or it may enter into a joint venture. (All these possible courses of action are described in Chapter 18.)

Doing One's Own Research

There is one other option. It is to establish your own research center. Then your company will be in a position to break new ground in science and technology, serving its own interests—its own internal clients—first.

The Personality of a Research Center

What is so special about a research center? It has the same general mission as other kinds of R&D organizations; namely, that the consequences of its work must one day fit our definition of useful innovation. What it produces must ultimately find its way into the marketplace and must ultimately produce incremental revenues and profits. What is different about it are its direction and style.

Basic Research

It's not really a research organization unless some of the staff engages in basic research. That is the hardest fact for hard-boiled company executives to accept. "I'm not in a *pro bono* business," they say. "So why should I pay for basic research? It will result in knowledge that I can't understand and can't use. All I've done is pay the salaries of a bunch of eggheads."

The answer to those executives is that, if their company does conduct research, an aura of depth and scholarliness will enfold the organization and set the stage for progress of a sort that would otherwise be missing. Without basic research going on in-house, technical advances—attractive and profitable though they may be—will rarely rise above the superficial. Maybe that will still be the case; there is no assurance that conducting research that is more "basic" in a little lab down the hall will have monumental effects, but the chances improve.

Think about the work in solid state physics that went on at Bell Labs in the early 1940s. That was basic research; no one knew where it would lead. But the Bell System invested in it and it resulted in transistors, integrated circuits, high-speed computers—in short, the one technology that emerged in the middle of this century that most affects our lives today. Yet when they started that work, the field was so unknown that even its name raised questions (what is solid state physics?). Where would the world be today if Bell hadn't decided to put together that scientific team? Where would all those many billions of dollars of business that resulted be? Yes, there is a place for industry-sponsored basic research.

But don't go overboard. A company can fall into the trap of funding basic research too much. Then the activity begins to look like a university, which, as we all know, is a nonprofit institution. For industry, the investment in basic research should be a small part of the total research investment, but it should be a meaningful, greater-than-critical-mass investment. An allocation of 10 to 15 percent of the research center's budget is meaningful. The remainder can be devoted to applied research.

Applied Research

The applied research activity is product oriented, new-market oriented, profit oriented. In these regards, it may differ little from the directions taken by technical centers or even, sometimes, skunk works. But there is a difference. Such work going on in a research environment is, as has been said, less superficial. What is achieved takes longer, but it may come out more art-leading, more elegant.

That leads to a danger; namely, that applied researchers are tempted to be too "basic." They have to be reminded that what they are aiming for is not the writing of papers to be published in learned journals. That is a goal, but a secondary one. The real goal, as for all innovation, is the creation of new business. Thus, researchers must be pushed to create their achievements in timely fashion. How does that happen? By selecting the right leader for them, someone who shares the goals of the company and unrelentingly drives his or her people to attain them.

When I visited the Hoechst Celanese Research Company, I felt that I was in an exemplary central research organization.

A Research Center: Hoechst Celanese Research Company

When Hoechst A. G. (a West German company) and Celanese Corporation (a U.S. firm) merged in 1987, the combined organization became the world's largest chemical firm, with sales of $17 billion. The American operations, incorporating the original Celanese Corporation, then took on the new name Hoechst Celanese Corporation.

The pre-merger Celanese Corporation, with headquarters in New York City, was a worldwide manufacturer of chemical materials in both raw and fabricated form. Sales for 1985 were $3.046 billion; research and development, at $103 million for that year, represented 3.3 percent of sales.

Distribution of Business Activity

Business for 1985 was distributed in sectors as follows:

Chemicals	32%
Fibers	48%
Specialties	18%
Other	2%

At that time, Celanese employed about 20,000 people, of whom 1,200 were in R&D. Approximately 450 of these worked at the Robert L. Mitchell Technical Center in Summit, New Jersey. Those engaged in research at the Mitchell Center are organized as a separate company, now called the Hoechst Celanese Research Company, consisting of 250 scientists, engineers, and support personnel.

Strategy for Growth

The Hoechst Celanese strategy is that it will grow within the chemicals industry and that such growth "will be attained by diversifying into new advanced materials based on existing skills in polymers, fibers, organic chemistry, and materials technology." (This quotation, as well as others that follow in this section, come from a 1985 promotional brochure.) Before the merger with Hoechst, the company had stated that "Celanese believes also that coalitions with others skilled in specific product technologies and applications will support the growth strategy." (When I visited HCRC in early 1987, the Hoechst merger was taking place. I was assured that that new association would result in no diminution of Celanese's research role, but rather that it would be strengthened by access to the most powerful coalition it had had to date—with Hoechst's extensive advanced technologies worldwide.)

Innovation Track Record

This strategy has produced significant innovation results. "In the commodity fibers business, over half of the current textile and industrial products were introduced within the past five years." And new ventures have been initiated in separations materials (a kind of filter) and in nonlinear optics, which could lead to a revolution in computer and telecommunication circuits by using light (photons) instead of electrons.

Going back some 30 years to the 1950s, Celanese can be seen to have amassed an impressive innovation record. Its names for textile fibers have not achieved dictionary status, but Arnel and Fortrel are nevertheless valid American words. The flame-resistant PBI fibers used in astronauts' uniforms are also its creation. Then there are other significant new products, not so readily recognized by the public, such as Celgard microporous films used in sophisticated separations tasks and Vectra, a self-reinforcing liquid-crystal molding resin used in precision electrical and electronics applications.

Mission of the Research Center

Hoechst Celanese Research Company sees its mission as a mixture of "diversification research, interactions, . . . and staying in the forefront of core scientific areas."

By "diversification research," HCRC means providing a basis founded on exploratory research and applied research firmly grounded in core technological strengths for entering wholly new business areas for the company. This will lead to new product development, also performed within HCRC. New products are to be made available to any of the established business sectors or, if they do not fit any of these, to the Advanced Materials Technology Group, which conforms to our designation of an internal ventures center (see Chapter 17). Whichever organization provides the final home for the products based on these innovations, it will be a comfortable one if only because all of them are linked by a universal principle at Hoechst Celanese of advanced materials technology. The business area may be wholly new, but the technical area is familiar.

"Interactions" is Hoechst Celanese's term for the providing of sophisticated technical support to all divisions within the corporation, both for new and mature products. The dealings with other parts of the corporation described in this and the preceding paragraph conform to what this book designates as client relationships.

"Staying in the forefront of core scientific areas" is basic research and consumes about 20 percent of HCRC's budget, the remaining 80 percent going to fund applied research. Another way of looking at innovation activity, whether involving basic or applied research, is to determine if the opportunity comes from market demand or from discovery. By staying at the forefront of core scientific areas, the Hoechst Celanese Research Company is in a position to identify and exploit diversification opportunities that are internal and market-driven, or either internal or external and discovery-driven. Looked at from this point of view, "core research" for diversification opportunities is a significant portion of its activities.

How Hoechst Celanese Research Company Fits Organizationally and Functionally

Figure 13–1 is a version of the Hoechst Celanese Corporation organization chart. It shows that extensive R&D goes on in captive organizations throughout the separate product-line entities of that company. This is supplemented and supported by the firm's primary R&D center, the research group, which they have chosen to designate as a "company" (certainly a designation with the sound of autonomy about it), and they have chosen further to make it a subsidiary of their Specialty Operations sector, which markets the most advanced of the established products of the company. This reporting line to one sector does not seem to interfere with its function as a center for the others.

Some Unique Features

HCRC utilizes the services of a Scientific Advisory Board, described in a company brochure as made up of "members, mostly from outside the Corporation, . . . world-renowned experts in key scientific disciplines such as biotechnology, materials science and processing, electronics, polymers, and technology planning. The Board helps us to develop insights in technology issues and new businesses and to assure that science and technology are used effectively and imaginatively throughout HCRC and the Corporation."

The Advanced Technology organization, while shown in Figure 13–1 as a "sector" that, like the others, is made up of an array of independent businesses, is in reality a home for several skunk works and fledgling enterprises, most of them born in HCRC. It is an internal ventures center of the sort described in Chapter 17.

HCRC is housed with other units of the Robert L. Mitchell Technical Center in a campus-like environment on a 45-acre site in Summit, New Jersey, on which are situated 11 buildings occupying 365,000 square feet. (See Figure 3–4 in Chapter 3.) In these are situated "dozens of modern, well-equipped laboratories and offices; the very latest in computer equipment; and a Technical Information Center." The Summit site is also the location of a number of the smaller business enterprises.

Hoechst Celanese Research Company maintains a Technical Center in Corpus Christi, Texas, which provides pilot line facilities and works on R&D in the area of chemicals technology.

I was privileged to have the opportunity of exploring an interesting research project, described in the following section.

Creation of a New Tool for Molecular Synthesis

Dr. Gregory V. Nelson was the leader of the Computer and Mathematical Services Group for the Summit location until 1985.

Figure 13-1. Organization chart of Hoechst Celanese Corporation.

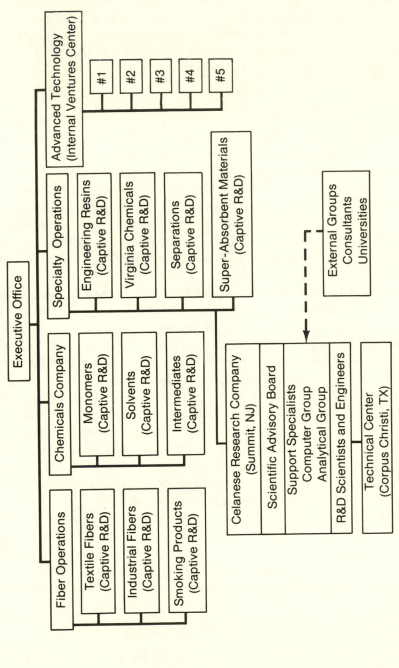

Courtesy of Hoechst Celanese Corporation

He has gone on to another related assignment in the field of molecular modeling, but the group continues to fulfill a unique function. The HCRC staff has come to depend on the group as a way to improve effectiveness in dealing with technical communications and experimental information.

Nelson is a scientist with a specialty in molecular structures who was a chemistry professor before joining Celanese. He is both a generalist/conceiver and, with his additional qualities of high dedication and initiative, a champion. He brings to his job a personal fascination with computers not common among chemists. It was this extra interest, coupled with his chemicals background, that gave birth to his accomplishment.

Nelson perceived a kind of inefficiency in traditional techniques of formulating new organic materials. It was his contention that it is wrong to go right to the laboratory bench and start making promising mixes in test tubes. Why not apply known molecular modeling tools to a description of the shape of molecules and the arrangement of atoms within them, optimize the bond structure so as to attain desired chemical properties, and perform that modeling on a computer keyboard? Then a newly hypothesized molecular structure would appear as a model on a video terminal. In short, Dr. Nelson had conceived a computer-aided-design procedure—a CAD—for designing molecules of organic chemicals with new industrial and domestic applications.

His problem was that the program to which he was assigned at the time, while a creative challenge in itself, had no room in it—no funds, no interest, no goal—for this computer application. His management had given him other direction. He did what innovators always do in this circumstance and pursued it on his own. That means he became a bootlegger, using company resources and some company time. As he proceeded, he was encouraged to find that his idea was feasible, at which point he realized that he could not go on without formal approval. He found a company executive whom he sold on the wisdom of his idea and who became its sponsor.

As a result, a formal program was launched; and now, several years later, it is correct to say that it has succeeded. HCRC's brochure features its Computer and Mathematical Services Group and separate molecular modeling capability. (Dr. Nelson was manager of that group, but has taken on the new title of senior staff associate and now devotes his activity to the molecular modeling activity.) Dr. Nelson claims that for every dollar committed to computer modeling, three are saved when compared to conventional research spending.

HCRC has recently installed a procedure for soliciting ideas for new products and technologies from its employees and for reviewing these scrupulously for exploitation of those judged to be prospective winners. That is essentially the process of encouraging/facilitating described in Chapter 8. A strong commitment to and encouragement of innovation within the Specialties Operations Sector has strengthened the recognition of other new ideas at HCRC similar to the one championed by Dr. Nelson.

14

New Products Center

A new products center (NPC) enriches the product lines of existing businesses within a company (its clients) by adding innovative features to existing products or by developing altogether new ones. Such new products are targeted to utilize existing technologies, to conform to existing product functions, and to be exploitable through existing channels to the marketplace. Thus, they represent new generation products—advances in, rather than departures from, existing products. (But a new products center will not reject an outstanding new concept that would result in a new product far different in nature from those that make up an existing product line or that would demand a drastic change in technology, so long as the market mission of its client is still addressed.)

No Research

New product centers do no research. They focus on development. But they astutely utilize—even commission—the research, basic or applied, of others.

No Ventures

What distinguishes a new products center from several of the other innovation modes is that, in spite of the fact that many of the innovations it creates could be the bases of new ventures, it does not purposely engage in new venturing. Its mission is to serve already established enterprises, which means that venturing took place decades before. Yet, it is inevitable that fallouts will occur that can only be exploited by an avenue different from that addressed by existing clients. In such cases, should management determine that the new activity is worthy of commitment, it should organize separately for that commitment—perhaps in a skunk works.

Mis(ad)venture

Sometimes the temptation to hold on too long becomes an overwhelming force. Even though the resulting venture may be a success, the attendant trauma can be so severe as to virtually cancel the benefits.

I recall when my new products center came up with a series of products that became the basis for a new venture that exists today in a healthy, industry-leading condition. It produces good revenues and growth for the company and has taken on the status of a mature, ongoing business entity (people forget that it was a new venture a decade before). In this instance, the staff of the new products center, confronted with the dilemma of having produced good new product prototypes without a company client to pick them up, decided to go into business itself. It did not transfer the new product to anyone, and the company went along with that decision. It was a mistake on both parts.

For the first two years, the incipient new venture spawned a skunk works within the new products center. It became a monster that took over the operation. No one could resist the exhilaration of the prospect of "being in business." All talent and all resources were devoted to this new overriding priority. This left little for the other new product programs—the real mission of center—which limped along with token attention, and thus with no more than token achievement.

Added to this was the fact that the first prototypes were good enough to sell to customers. That's how the business was launched. Now the managers of the new products center found that they were at the same time the managers of a business and had to answer to their bosses for profits (or lack thereof), for accumulated inventory of questionable worth, for transgressions of union rules, and all the other factors involved in a company-sponsored start-up business.

In retrospect, it is clear that for a new products center to go into skunking and from there into a new business venture is a mistake. It turned out that most of the talented creative staff of the center, outstanding as innovators, were duds as businesspeople.

In addition, for about three years the new products center produced virtually no new products. Things got back on track only when the new venture was transferred to a formally organized new ventures group that then did well with it.

In fact, the new ventures group included those few original innovators who *did* have entrepreneurial talent. They were "spun off"—and they run the business today. That business is now a client of the new products center in that it receives what all the other clients get: early models of new products. That is (at last) as it should be.

Be True to Your Mission

The lesson: An innovation group performing within a certain innovation mode should stick to that mode. That pertains particularly to a new products center, which, in the course of its normal activities will, without meaning to, come up with occasional exciting new products that don't fit the available clients.

Licensing

Licensing is a legitimate "extracurricular" activity for a new products center to engage in. If the clients don't want "fallout" products, someone in the outside world might. Exercise care, however, when that someone is your client's competitor. In fact, if it looks good to a competitor, your client might want to reconsider.

The way to look at licensing-out for a new products center is that the licensee must be supported with technical aid if it is to make a success of the licensed product. The new products center should look upon the licensee as though it were just another company client, offering it additional candidates for licensing as they emerge as "accidental" additional fallouts from its company client programs. (I balk at purposely investing effort to create products for strangers. Stick to "accidental" fallouts, because the center's primary goal, service to its company clients, should dominate its actions.)

The results of licensing can often be very gratifying, supplying substantial income for minimal effort. (Chapter 19 explores licensing in more detail.)

Deep Identification with Each Client's Business

A new products center will succeed in proportion to how well it incorporates itself into the identities of each of its clients. Stanislavski, the great Russian trainer of actors, believed that the only way to perform was to "become" the person—or thing—being represented. Thus, fledgling actors are often given an assignment such as, "for the next half hour, be a tree." For that period they stand, feeling tree-ish, with arms waving in the breeze. The same holds for a new products center. Those who will inject new products into a business must feel that they are part of that business. In fact, they are not, so they must at least "act" as though they were—by becoming team members with the client's staff. Teamwork becomes the key to winning.

The Client's Plant and Technology

If a new product will one day be manufactured by the client's factory, the new products center should understand that factory, its processes and machines. At the same time, the NPC must be up to date with the literature—even the rumors—about what the processes and machines of the competition are like. But there is no substitute for prowling the client's plant and getting to know the members of its manufacturing department staff. The ones best fitted to perform this prowling are those in the NPC staff who will one day handle product transfer from lab to factory, but it does no harm for the inventors to participate as well.

The Marketplace and the Client's Position in It

The new product will be exploited in the marketplace, so the NPC must become market-wise for each client. Indeed, it must be as creative in market-driven innovation programs as in technology-driven ones. It must sensitize itself to what sells today, what new thing is likely to sell tomorrow, and what the trends may be. At the same time, it must understand the practices and strengths of each client in the marketplace. Such wisdom comes only from years of attending trade shows (even volunteering to do booth duty), reading the trade journals, and using similar products as though one were the customer. Indeed, nothing is as good as meeting customers and getting their ideas.

The Client's Key People

Teamwork comes down to team members. NPC staff must know their opposite numbers in every field in which they must interact. They must cultivate them, learn from them, exploit their strengths, and compensate for their weaknesses.

I have found it means a lot to team up with at least two kinds of client staff: the technical specialists and the market specialists (often called product managers). Dealing with one and not the other means having only half of the required understanding. It is natural for technical people to confine their relationships to other technical people, but that tendency must be combated. In fact, this extends to the turf of the client. It is often the outsiders, like employees of a new products center, who bring together the client's engineers and product planners, people who might otherwise rarely talk to each other.

But no one has a more vital role than the client's management people. As we have discussed in earlier chapters, innovation will not proceed without support from the CEO. Just as an innovation center needs a sponsor, so does the innovation activity of the client. If no sponsor has appeared, the center should help its client teammates find one.

Getting into the Planning Process

A good new product with good prospects, based on good teamwork with a client sponsor, has the ingredients for persuading client management to commit to it. In other words, to invest in it. The center and the client, if they believe in the new product, will push for this commitment and will reckon themselves successful only if they get it.

A new products center recognizes the forces that motivate client management and will strive to come up with models of new products that are consistent with those motivations. Thus, they can become welcome participants in the long-term planning process of each client—a desirable arrangement for all concerned.

New Products Centers Are Not Common

I encountered few instances of separately constituted new products organizations as I looked around the country, perhaps because many groups perform new product development for company clients without benefit of a separate identity. I have seen instances where *de facto* "new products centers" are subgroups within technical centers and research centers. For instance, Corning Glass Works carries out new product development for its many business entities through its technical center, and there is a similar arrangement at Westinghouse's technical center and at many other companies.

But there is good reason in some companies to establish a new products center. If no central innovation organization exists or if an existing one does not address the needs of certain business entities that would otherwise not engage in significant levels of innovation, much benefit can be derived from the establishment of such an organization. My own company, Raytheon, is an example of this set of circumstances.

A New Products Center: Raytheon Company

The Raytheon Company engages in highly technical, electronics-based government businesses, such as missile systems, countermeasures, radar, and underwater surveillance. These account for about 60 percent of its revenues. The remainder of its enterprises are in domestic, commercial, industrial, and service marketplaces. Yearly sales exceed $7 billion.

The large, complex government divisions and the larger subsidiaries are superbly staffed and facilitated. Each has its own captive R&D organization, some with several thousand engineers and scientists. Thus, these require no product development services from the New Products Center. Rather, they are resources of expertise, often serving as test beds and as consultants to the NPC, and thus to its clients.

On the other hand, the clients consist of a selection of those commercial businesses that, while staffed with competent engineers and facilitated with good laboratories easily the match of their competitors', are not in a position to engage in long-term or in-depth new product development programs. Here is where the NPC steps in. It undertakes to fill that gap.

These clients account for about a sixth of the company's sales revenues, which means that five-sixths of the company are not NPC clients. There is nothing wrong with that. The center carries out its mission where it is needed, and not every part of the company needs it.

Functional Relationships

Figure 14–1 shows how these organizations interact function-ally. The solid lines from NPC show client relationships in which early versions of new products (through Step 5 of the seven steps to innovation described in Chapter 4) are provided to the pertinent business entities. The heavy black arrows indicate technical aid from those groups flush with technical expertise.

Note that several of the businesses served are in effect made up of separate sub-businesses marketing separate lines of products. They operate with separate engineering and marketing staffs as well as separate bottom-line accounting, and each is a separate client.

Thus the subsidiary, Caloric Corporation, a major American supplier of cooking equipment for the home, is made up of three major businesses: Modern Maid, which addresses affluent customers with expensive, multi-featured, built-in products for new construc-tion and for remodeling; Glenwood Stove, which competes in the low-priced, high volume gas and electric range market; and a middle-market activity, also called "Caloric," which sells freestand-ing self-cleaning ovens for either gas or electric systems. The New Products Center serves a total of 13 clients in industries as different as x-ray radiology equipment and coin-operated laundry equipment. That means that the group never lacks for diversity, nor for

Figure 14-1. Functional relationships between Raytheon's New Products Center and other sectors of the company.

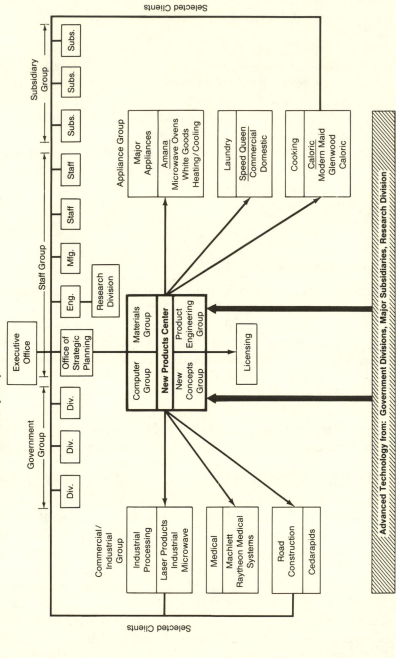

Courtesy of Raytheon Company

opportunities to apply synergy. In the New Products Center, cross-disciplines are the most frequently encountered disciplines.

Note also that one additional "client" is labeled "licensing." The Center has negotiated 12 active license agreements, and royalty income now amounts to one-fourth of the NPC's operating costs. The NPC does not retain these revenues, however. They are turned over to the businesses for which the work that resulted in the licensed products was originally intended, but that did not use the product. (There is no better way to make friends in a company than to let margins—without corresponding costs—appear on the prospective friend's P&L statement. And it is important for the NPC to have friends, because the more friends it has, the more effectively it can form productive relationships—teams—with its clients.)

Staff

The heart of the center consists of technical generalists and specialists. Figure 14–1 shows that the NPC is made up of four groups. Generalists make up the New Concepts Group; specialists are in two fields—computers and materials; and people who are combination generalists/specialists make up the Product Engineering Group. They perform the all-important task of product transfer to clients.

The center is staffed by 15 engineers and scientists trained in many disciplines with similar number of support personnel, many of whom are highly specialized technicians. This adds up to less than three dozen people. For such a large company, and for its breadth and number of clients, the center is small. But it is big enough to fulfill its mission, and in smallness there is strength, for the financial commitment to support it is not a strain.

Facility

The center is housed in a leased building in an industrial park in a Boston suburb. (See Figure 3–1, Chapter 3.) It has 28,000 square feet and is outfitted suitably with many different kinds of labs and shops, as well as a number of conference rooms. The shops and the technicians who staff them are capable of producing operating models for all its clients in a spectrum ranging from home appliances to x-ray tubes. When special capabilities for fabrication or testing are lacking, they are easily contracted for with the company's government divisions or with local firms.

Funding

The center proposes its entire budget yearly to the CEO through the office of strategic planning, to which it reports. Funds come from the corporate office and are not assessed in any visible form to the center's clients. The center thus has no need to solicit funds for individual projects from its clients, who therefore receive their services "free."

The advantage of this procedure is that NPC operates in a relatively stress-free and stable condition as long as a new product or two is introduced to a marketplace by its clients each year (1985 was a banner year with five new product announcements). The disadvantage is that the clients would feel greater involvement if they were assessed even a token amount.

A Centralized Function in a Decentralized Company

The New Products Center is a center, but the clients it serves are highly decentralized and have the choice of availing themselves of it or not as they see fit. And they might well not see the need to involve themselves with corporate shenanigans, because each has its own captive R&D staff. The only way a business entity will utilize the service provided by the NPC is to be convinced of its value; that means that the center must always be selling itself and raising the level of clients' perceptions. It helps for the center to have accumulated a track record of products taken up by its clients and translated by them into meaningful new business.

Track Record

The New Products Center can point to some 40 products introduced to the marketplace by its clients over an 18-year period, an average of two per year. Figure 14–2 is a montage of several of these. Most of these products, sometimes in forms little resembling the original models but still conforming to the original concepts, are still in production and account for significant fractions

Figure 14-2. Raytheon's NPC: some representative success stories.

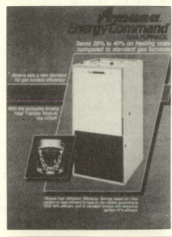

All these products originated in Raytheon's New Products Center. Clockwise from top left: home heating system, self-cleaning microwave, microwave pizza oven, x-ray system, conveyor-belt microwave, computerized dryer.

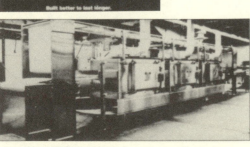

Courtesy of *Management Review,* December 1986

of the business revenues of most of the clients. Many of the products were art-leading when introduced and many are based on proprietary know-how and patents (over 100 issued in the lifetime of the center).

Sponsorship

In the early days, before a track record had been accumulated, the center did not have the credibility it has today. Thus it was confronted with the classic chicken/egg dilemma. It was born and survived its rocky infancy only because it had a company backer who had faith in the idea of a new products center. This was Palmer Derby, a vice president and then assistant general manager of one of the company's divisions. He was the only one—no other company executive had either the inclination or the clout to support the center through its lean years. But that is par, as they say, for the course. There usually is only one executive in a company who reacts with positive emotion about innovation.

Even with his support, the center was, at first, a tentative effort. In fact, the first New Products Center was set up in two rented trailers (why commit valuable floor space to such a nutty idea?), and as the first day of each month passed and the trailers were not dragged away, we knew that the rent had been paid and we were assured of survival for one more 30-day period.

Presently, the center is still sponsored by a company officer, the vice president for strategic planning, Robert Seaman. His sponsorship is indeed welcome—no innovation center ever truly outlives its need for sponsorship from the executive office.

15

Captive R&D

An innovation organization that addresses the needs of only a single business entity within a company is captive to that entity and has little interest in other businesses elsewhere in the firm. It will commit itself to a single mission, or sometimes to a combination of several of these, and will take on one of a variety of forms determined by the missions and by particular company circumstances.

Captive R&D organizations include innovation groups resident in a single division or subsidiary of a large company, similar organizations that fill all innovation needs of a small company, and skunk works.

Captive R&D in Large Companies

In most large companies, the approach to innovation is characterized by the presence of centers for technology, research and/or new product development as described in the preceding chapters. Where these centers exist, their relationship to their clients could fall anywhere within a spectrum from healthy and productive to hostile and nonproductive. But one organizational fact prevails in almost all cases: Regardless of how, how many, and how well corporate innovation centers function, almost every one of the separate business entities they serve will nevertheless also set up its own captive R&D group.

Then a kind of competition ensues, and duplication of effort occurs, for the missions of the captive groups often resemble those of the centers. They can include basic and applied research, new technology, development of new features or refinement for existing products, new product development, or even to new ventures. Is this a way to achieve efficiency?

Often it is, if only because it means that if two parallel approaches to innovation are taken, chances improve that one will work. Admittedly, that sounds like rationalization. More meaningful, however, is the fact that central R&D innovators and captive R&D innovators have each other to talk to—and few others—because often few others understand the language they speak. This is especially important when the time for transfer of a new technology or a new product approaches. However, the most operative reason for the existence of a captive R&D organization is that the division manager or subsidiary president to which it reports never feels he can entrust his fate to outsiders, which, being human, is how he tends to think of the central organizations.

So the division or the subsidiary establishes its own innovation group. It is more parochial than the elegant center located 1,000 miles away on the landscaped grounds of the executive office, but that is the way the boss wants it.

What does it do? The answer to that question is another question. What are the needs of its business entity? Is the challenge of the moment that manufacturing costs are too high? The captive innovators react by becoming investigators of improved technology. They often can find time to do this only by canceling other projects in other kinds of innovation. They do so without regret, because captives are comfortable philosophically with the idea of shifting priorities, as long as they know that the new priority is the one that is uppermost in the mind of the division manager or the subsidiary president. In like fashion, they will become new product developers, because management has committed itself to filling a requirement for a particular product in a near-term strategy. The group might even have one or two people who will undertake a research project, if that is what is needed.

The most telling quality of a captive R&D organization is its captiveness. It serves the boss; it offers little flak; it leaps flexibly from one kind of challenge to another; and, because its staff may be as creative as the central innovation group's, it produces. Indeed, it tends to produce more per staff member, per year, per invested dollar, because it is more motivated. Such increased motivation derives from being part of the group—an on-site team member. It is hard to think of such a group as being an example of inefficiency.

Adding to efficiency is the fact that some of the organizational structure required in central groups becomes less of an issue for captives. In the first place, there is little need for transfer specialists. The receivers of the innovation sit just across the corridor. They are in on the progress of the innovation from day one. As for generalists and specialists, they are needed and they are present, but the lines are less firmly drawn. They're like a catcher for a sandlot baseball team: If you ask them to play first base, the next question is, where can I borrow a first baseman's mitt?

But the central innovation organization is still very much needed because it is, by its nature, *not* parochial, *not* captive, more able to commit to long-term projects. This leads to a challenge. It is that captives and centers must work together. They must be mutually supportive and they must respect and trust each other.

It sounds like an unattainable ideal. But it can be done—at least, done well enough to be effective. Companies must make sincere efforts to attain it. Then innovation proceeds best—and with maximum efficiency.

The distinctions between captives and centers tend to blur for companies of the size and sophistication of General Electric, Du Pont, Eastman Kodak, and Xerox. The 100 biggest R&D spenders listed in Table 11–4, Chapter 11, include many of these. Innovation organizations reporting to individual sectors in such firms—and thus captives—contain hundreds of professionals of the most advanced capabilities, and even though their eyes are focused on the needs of that sector, they are so broad that both the term parochialism and the emphasis on short-term goals no longer apply. In fact, in some ways, they are centers too, because the sectors for which they work are made up of subsectors—most of which have their own subcaptive R&D organizations. Yet, it is significant that in all these instances, there are still corporate centers for technology and research.

General Electric is a good example. Its Appliance Park in Louisville, Kentucky, is a vast factory complex. Every kind of large home appliance is manufactured there—from dishwashers to washing machines and dryers, electric ranges, microwave ovens, and refrigerators. It also houses a technology center, a research center, and new product development activity. Taken by itself, it is the nation's largest maker of major appliances for the home. Still, it is but one sector of General Electric. Other sectors, equally well served by captive R&D organizations, include aerospace products, plastics, and others. Yet the company maintains a central research facility in Schenectady, New York, that supplements these R&D groups and serves them all.

Captive R&D in Small Companies

All that has been said about captive innovation organizations for large companies pertains to what we find in smaller firms, with the exception that the captive can turn to no central group when it requires people with new or different skills and long-term attitudes. The absence of a center also means no "outsider" will suggest "surprises," new ideas and new developments that will jar present products and processes out of long-established grooves. Thus, the captive has to function—as best it can—as a center, too.

Every company responds in accordance with its nature. Repligen Corporation (mentioned in Chapter 12), a small biotechnology firm, sees its destiny in the development of new technologies for the production of engineered proteins. It does no basic research and gives smaller priority to product development.

Other small companies may maintain an R&D group just to tickle and refine existing products, making each year's version incrementally more novel by the addition of some small feature. To some, R&D may mean no more than defensive actions such as investigations to meet changes in national codes or other "crises."

One kind of R&D group's whole mission is to improve design. Its staff rarely includes technically trained persons. Rather, everyone is some sort of artist to whom the challenge is to change a color, a texture, a shape so that the product will be more pleasing to the eye and easier to handle. That is innovation of a very valid sort, because it can incrementally increase revenues and profits just as much as can innovations based on state-of-the-art technology. However, in some companies it is the only type of innovation engaged in. It generally serves a single business entity, and is thus captive.

The most exciting kind of captive organization is that which engages in new product development in the environment known as the skunk works. Such environments may be set up in small companies or in large ones. In either case, they always look alike and function in the same way and with the same sorts of people.

Skunk Works

The classic skunk works is a single-mission innovation organization put together to innovate a single product or product line and to carry that innovation all the way to production and deployment to the marketplace. It is off in a corner, as though the work had an unpleasant odor (hence the word "skunk"), where a company has organized a group of employees to work on a specific innovation project. Peters and Waterman have described them as ". . . 8 or 10 zealots, often outproducing product development groups numbering in the hundreds."[1]

Distinctive Qualities of a Skunk Works

A skunk works is marked by intense dedication to this single goal and is generally led by a "driven" leader. Its activity is in the development category—it has no time for research.

It tends not to survive its project, regardless of whether that project is a success or a failure. But after innovation is completed, certain of its personnel may stay with the new program in a number of roles.

However, there are occasional cases when management recognizes it has a "good thing going" and decides to keep the same team together to skunk another work. When this occurs, it results in the subclasses of semi-permanent or permanent skunk works, of which the case of Xerox, described later in this chapter, is an example.

Those who successfully lead skunk works often end up as business managers with new titles such as division manager, vice president, or even president. In effect, their roles evolve from that of innovator to that of intrapreneur—and later, manager.

A skunk works thinks of itself as having no client but itself. However, in the end, it is most common for its successes to be incorporated into an existing company business entity, not so much as an extension of an existing product line but as the basis for a wholly new one (but one still "linked" to the parent business by function or market). That business entity might have provided the funds for the skunk works project in the first place. It is for this reason, and the fact that what has been achieved may one day be "taken back," that it is included here as a captive operation.

On the other hand, what a skunk works creates is often so different from existing company businesses that it becomes the basis of an entirely new business. Or an infant innovation that was initially sponsored by a company business unit and is thus captive to it inspires negative reactions, even revulsion in the sponsoring organization, and, in the end, is rejected. As a result, it has no place to go other than to try to make it on its own. Then the innovation becomes an internal venture, which will be discussed in Chapter 17.

Skunk Works: A History

The first identifiable skunk works was set up at Lockheed Corporation on the West Coast during World War II. The company needed a wholly new aircraft based on revolutionary new concepts, and they needed it fast. Kelly Johnson, a highly creative and purposeful engineer who later rose to become a Lockheed vice president, conceived the idea of an off-site product development laboratory in an unused hangar, and it was he who coined the expression. It was taken from the name of the major industry in Dogpatch, the locale of a popular cartoon strip of the day, "L'il Abner," whose creator was Al Capp. Johnson was assigned to lead the world's first skunk works, and he succeeded. (You can read all about it in his book.[2])

Another book, Tracy Kidder's *The Soul of a New Machine*, also describes innovation achieved through the skunk works route—although the author never mentions the word.[3] This classic skunk works created a significant art-leading new product in the computer field, leading in turn to significant business growth and increased market share for its firm, the Massachusetts-based Data General Corporation.

There have been some special enterprises that significantly affect our lives today that started as skunk works—in "a lab in the woods." Harking back to Kelly Johnson's time, World War II, there was the Manhattan Project, born in a gymnasium basement at the University of Chicago, that blossomed into Oak Ridge and Los Alamos and the whole nuclear field—bringing us the blessings of atomic weaponry and atomic power. There was the Radiation Lab, first set up in an MIT chemistry laboratory. (Mine, in fact. I well remember how in 1940, as sophomores, my classmates and I were kicked out of it in mid-experiment because of a "government project" taking over). That project gave us everything under the heading of "microwave," including radar, satellites, television, and those funny little ovens.

In 1949, I was wrenched from a routine job at Raytheon by the vice president of the vacuum tube division, Norm Krim, who said to me, "You are going to develop a new product I heard about at Bell Labs called 'the transistor.' " Within a year, we had two dozen people skunking it in a location one level below the basement. Little did we know that we were a skunk works and that Krim was that rarest of executives, simultaneously sponsor and champion. As a result of our efforts, Raytheon was the first company in the nation to sell high volumes of semiconductor products to the public (in 1953).

An example of a skunk works in the 1980s can be found at Xerox.

A Skunk Works: Xerox

Xerox's skunk works is located six miles away from its central operation in Rochester, New York, in East Rochester, a blue-collar suburb. It occupies 15,000 square feet, the third floor of the former B. J. Fryatt Department Store, now many decades defunct. The bottom floor was once occupied by a drug store, a coffee shop, and a diving-equipment outlet. The building dates from the turn of the century (see Figure 3–3 in Chapter 3). The group is known to all in the company as "the skunk works"—a designation "awarded" by its current board chairman, David T. Kearns—but its formal name is East Rochester Operations, ERO to its friends (who point out that if you add an "X" to each end of that acronym, you get "Xerox").

ERO is one of five R&D centers at Xerox that in 1986 invested $650 million in this category of activity out of total revenues of $9,355 million. At 6.9 percent, that is a very large proportion of sales and exceeds the national average by a factor of about two and a half. ERO is by far the smallest of the five, having a total personnel count of only 26 (half professionals, half technicians or model-makers).

No one knew they were giving birth to a skunk works in 1971 when ERO started. It began as a technical-support field operation in one Xerox division. It was engaged in "fire fighting," making fast fixes for new products developed by others, and developing improved diagnostic devices for the Field Service organization. It first hit its stride as a new product developer in 1978, when it turned out a cost-reduced, defeatured, different-appearing model of an existing copier in five weeks, in the process astounding its grander peers who might have consumed a year or more to attain the same end.

Track Record

In the period 1978 through 1986, four major products, all copiers, have gone to market; several others are currently under development and, in all likelihood, will make it. Elements of other projects have either been incorporated into products or have formed the basis for development effort. Resulting sales and profits impacts have been very significant.

All of the projects were marked by the same swift goal-achievement quality. The 2600 copier was less than a two-month effort for ERO and took only an additional five months to pass through final engineering and into manufacturing and the marketplace. The 8200 copier has had a similar history, and has been a Xerox product for seven years. The newest achievement is the 2510 copier (see Figure 15–1), unique in that it is a xerographic version of a blueprint machine and thus makes unnecessary all that blueness and ammonia-based chemicals and odor. One feeds it sheets of yard-wide paper. The 2510 is a very recent introduction, but it has already received enthusiastic response from the marketplace.

The major advance represented by the 2510 copier is not so much the inventiveness of its basic design—even though inven-

Figure 15-1.   The Xerox 2510 copier.

Courtesy of Xerox Corporation

tiveness is certainly there—as the fact that the design is manufac-
turing-oriented, making possible a price far lower than was ever
considered possible. At $4,495 each, it can be afforded by many
of us.

Reporting

The head of ERO reports directly to the group vice president
for corporate research, which makes it a center by our definition.
Although initially dedicated to (that is, captive to) the copier/

duplicator segment of the business, the unit no longer considers itself limited to that sector. This broader base of activity results in a higher level of sympathy for ERO's way of operating when viewed by a corporate sponsor than when seen by the more focused business sectors, which are already well staffed with researchers and developers.

Some of the new products have resulted in offshoot ventures still under the aegis of ERO; when that occurs, reporting is generally through a different company officer, such as a group VP or president of the Diversified Business Group. Note that this differs from the pattern of operation of new products centers described in the previous chapter, which see merit in giving up their new products when they reach the venture stage. (The Diversified Business Group, which administers other ventures with similar histories, conforms to an internal ventures center as described in Chapter 17.)

While these more recent business options will probably not be picked up initially by the existing copier/duplicator sector, which is their natural home, in several cases this will eventually occur, bringing the majority of ERO's activity full circle—back to the captive situation.

Sponsors

It is interesting that both of the corporate officers to whom ERO and its spinoffs report are more than just "bosses." By virtue of their status in the company and their philosophical interest in promoting innovation, both are, in addition, sponsors—an important distinction.

Manner of Operation

There is no formal, layered organization. Each employee's business card has only that person's name and the fact that he or she is part of East Rochester Operations. Bill Volkers is the leader, assisted by Ken Stahl and several individual project leaders/champions, who guide their respective teams.

Volkers pointed out to me that his goal is the creation of an environment that fosters creative thinking and facilitates the implementation of that thinking. Part of that is informal organization, part is informal dress, and part is an informal building. It all comes together in a culture and mind-set far different in all these regards from that to be found six miles up the street.

The corridors, with missing wall sections and ceiling panels, a paint job dating from the first Eisenhower Administration, and coffee cans strategically located to catch rain water as it seeped through from above nevertheless led to several elegant labs and superbly fitted-out shops.

Stahl is proud that in the former setting of the B. J. Fryatt Department Store, an environment for innovation has incontrovertibly been achieved. More than that, the environment is that of the commando unit. "Do one thing well," he says, "and do it fast."

He has a few more messages for us. To innovate effectively and fast, you must, in addition to providing the right environment, select the right people. They are usually employed someplace in your company, waiting to be plucked for this assignment. Look internally for the leaders, creative generalists, specialists, manufacturing people, and outstanding technicians and shop people, he says.

Also, be sure you get corporate support—sponsors—and use your company's resources. Network and borrow shamelessly.

No manufacturing takes place in the Xerox skunk works. Nevertheless, one of its offshoots does direct a manufacturing activity, Xerox Technigraphic Products (XTP), distributor of the 2510 copier (see page 265). It does this in a unique way: by contracting with outside firms for the fabrication of subassemblies. (It has brought so much business to small companies in the Rochester area that it is viewed as "Rochester Hero No. 1." A local newspaper headline announces, "Local Firms Supply Major Copier Parts,"[4] and the article lists five firms that have had significant incremental multi-million-dollar revenues from the 2510.) Then the modules have to be assembled and made to conform to Xerox standards of quality and reliability. Here XTP succeeded in contracting for quality approval services with one operation of the mother company itself.

Finally, XTP had to initiate promotion activity and set up sales channels. Indeed, it did everything new venturers have to do. Since 1978, the contribution to revenues and profits has been considerable—particularly for such a small group.

A Permanent Skunk Works

ERO is a skunk works and typifies such organizations in most respects. But it is different from most in that, with the birth of a venture, it does not disband. It has attained permanent status. I use it as my example because it is so good at what it does, and with the recognition that no real-world example is ever cleanly what it "ought" to be. There is always deviation in some kind of overlap of procedure or function.

References

1. T. J. Peters and R. H. Waterman Jr., *In Search of Excellence* (New York: Warner Books, 1982), p. 201.
2. K. Johnson, *Kelly, More Than My Share of It* (Washington, D.C.: Smithsonian Institution Press, 1985).
3. T. Kidder, *The Soul of a New Machine* (Boston/Toronto: Atlantic–Little, Brown, 1981).
4. *Rochester* (N.Y.) *Sunday Democrat and Chronicle,* May 11, 1986, p. 1F.

16

External Teams

There are organizations, even individuals, that are in the innovation business. They will take a contract to go through the first step or two of innovation and are set up, sometimes very elaborately, as self-supporting research or new product development groups. They can be found in universities or in consulting firms. Clients use such groups in order to take advantage of their particular expertise or to sidestep making an in-house investment in their own similar organization.

Scientists in university settings have recently become more businesslike, more organized, and more purposeful than they used to be. In effect, the word has got out to the academics, "You have more of a place in the industrial world than ever before." As a result, the cloisters have become somewhat uncloistered.

The Graduate-Student Task Force

It is still possible to look up some noted professor and get him or her to assign a graduate student or two to carrying out a specific task. There has always been a role for that kind of project. Sometimes they have all the organization and scale that is needed. Whirlpool Corporation testifies to the value of using grad students and notes that it is a way to "gain access to outstandingly creative people—and we get to hire some of them—notably, top-quality students with experience and ambition in one or more areas of technology in which we have interest."[1]

But that is only one mode Whirlpool engages in when it underwrites university research. It also invests in university work as one of many investors, giving it an opportunity to "share costs with others of similar interest." An organizational format that many institutions offer in this regard is the multi-client consortium, which will be discussed later in this chapter.

269

But first let us examine a case of the use by an industrial firm of a small external team in a university. You will see that it is full of surprises in that little turned out as originally intended, but perhaps in that regard it is "typical."

An External Team: Contex Graphics and the Faculty Team at Carnegie-Mellon University

The actors in this saga are Continental Can Company, of Pinebrook, New Jersey; Scitex, an Israeli company; and two faculty members of the School of Fine Arts at Carnegie-Mellon University* in Pittsburgh, Pennsylvania. Their interactions, dating from 1984, resulted in a joint venture with a name based on the "Con-" from Continental and the "-tex" from Scitex: Contex Graphics Systems, Inc., born September 1985.

Continental Can Company is the nation's largest maker of packaging materials and systems, with yearly sales exceeding $7 billion. Scitex is the world's leading maker of printing machinery that is focused on the printing text and decorative illustrations on packages; it has sales in the order of $150 million a year and operates through subsidiaries worldwide; its American arm is Scitex America Corporation of Bedford, Massachusetts.

Warren Wake and Alan Green are two driven yet flexible, energetic, market-conscious, technically first-rate, imaginative men. They put together (when they were Carnegie-Mellon faculty members and before they ever met people from Continental Can or Scitex), in the most exemplary cross-disciplinary way, elements of architectural and aesthetic design, graphic arts, and computer technology to come up with an art-leading concept and an operative first model of that concept. It marries computer-derived image creation with the interface to the machine that prints those images

---

* The role of the university is often minor or almost nonexistent in such external teams. Colleges have various policies in matters of this sort. Sometimes they involve themselves deeply in the consulting projects of their faculty members, to the point of requiring that the institution acquire partial ownership of proprietary knowledge that results from the work. However, it is more common for them to recognize that their staffs enrich themselves professionally (as well as financially) by participating in real-world programs; thus, after assessing such programs with overhead fees to cover use of facilities and services, they maintain a hands-off posture. Such was the case in this instance; the "participating partner" was the faculty team itself and not Carnegie-Mellon University.

on a mass-production scale, a combination never achieved before they did it in 1983-1984.

Here, a description of the industry segment being addressed is in order. It is "packaging." If you have visited many Third World countries, you may have noticed that when you buy something, what you get is what you bought—no more. There is no bag, there is no box, there is not even a wrapper. But as you ascend the economic and sophistication scale in this world, everything comes inside of something else—The Package.

But packages are more than containers. They are conveyers of seductive messages that murmur, "Buy me, because I am soft and pink all over." At the same time, they instruct the buyer on what is inside, how much it weighs, how to prepare and consume it, what the price is, and, sometimes, a statement to the effect that the contents may be hazardous to your health.

The innovative challenge turns out to derive from the fact that it is more of a problem to imprint the container than to fabricate it, especially at a factory where tens of thousands are being spewed out every hour or so. There are problems of exact dimensional registration (you can't have it say "Wheatie" on one side and "s" around the corner). The color must be true, and the package must have eye appeal.

The design process of a package imprint, involving layout sketches, artwork, film color separations, and a dozen other steps, normally consumes six to eight months and hundreds of man-hours. The Wake/Green process, which digitizes the image and allows for artwork to be done on a computer terminal, cuts this time in half and pays back on capital investment in less than two years. It is clearly a process that the packaging industry could use.

But Wake and Green were not in industry when they worked out the fundamentals of their process. Wake was a professor at Carnegie-Mellon and Green later joined him as research associate while pursuing a graduate degree. Furthermore, they knew that what would result from their work would be a machine that could link the computer with the printer. They would call it a design work station, and it would probably sell in the $100,000 range. It was clear that they needed an industry partner.

At the same time, Continental Can was looking for any type of technical advances in the field of packaging that would increase revenues and margins. Specifically, it wanted to improve its technology and not necessarily devise new products. Although established in-house organizations were already performing R&D in related fields of technology, that did not blind Continental Can's management to what the outside world had to offer in that area. Indeed, John Andreas of that firm had the assignment: "Look around. See what new techniques are evolving outside of our company. If you find something good that fits, we'll consider investing in it."

In effect, Andreas fits into our master chart (see Figure 1–2, Chapter 1) in the "External Ventures Center" block. He was seeking to acquire companies or take minority positions so as to aid existing business, and in the course of events he accomplished that; but in the end that led unexpectedly to the creation of a new venture of the "joint" sort. In this case, the path to that new venture was not the customary one of an immediate alliance with another established firm, even though that eventually occurred. Rather, as a result of sponsoring this innovation program with the external faculty team at Carnegie-Mellon, Continental Can was able to set the stage for the final joint venture by first building a capability that it otherwise would not have had.

Wake took the initiative (Green had actually joined him after some industry contacts had already been made). He knocked on the doors of several companies in the packaging field before coming in contact with Andreas, who offered Wake a one-year contract for his consulting services on a half-time basis. Wake then recruited Green and the services of several graduate students, and, in 1984, the program was launched.

By the end of that year, it was evident that feasibility had been well demonstrated and the scale of the contract was increased by about 20 percent and continued for another year with the goal of creating a prototype. When the second year had passed, the participants had gone passed the research phase, and a university was no longer the correct environment. The next phase required developing iterative, successively more refined engineering models leading to pilot production and field evaluation (Steps 4 through 7 of our seven steps to efficient innovation).

Another major issue next became apparent. To exploit the concept most efficiently, the innovation had to include the printing machine. It was evident that the venture would require not one, but two, fathers. Who better than Scitex, the leading maker of printing machinery for this industry?

The difficulty with bringing in a printer manufacturer was that such an action had no relation to Continental Can's original intention, which was simply to improve the efficiency of its own internal processing procedures. It was clear that if a printing firm were involved, it would want to sell any resulting product not only to Continental Can but to every company in the packaging industry.

Wake and Green persuaded Andreas of the wisdom of this course, and he in turn persuaded his management. What followed was the creation of a joint venture wherein Continental Can and Scitex were equal stockholders and Wake and Green held minority positions. With that, the world lost two academics and Contex Graphics was created.

It was located in Bedford, Massachusetts, the same town as Scitex's American subsidiary, Scitex America, so that technical interchange in the printing field could better be accomplished.

In its first year, 1986, Contex Graphics has had in excess of $4 million in sales. Continental Can has benefited from installation of the first machine in its own production line, where it performs admirably. Scitex now can offer the Contex Design System (Figure 16–1) as an option with its printer. (It offers significant enhancements, including an exclusive PC-based professional typesetting capability with access to hundreds of fonts and proprietary software for producing high-quality color proofs used to create exceptionally realistic mock-ups.) And the state of the art of packaging in the world has experienced an advance.

Figure 16–1 also presents an example of Contex artwork (the cookie package) created by a designer using a keyboard and a terminal instead of brushes, paints, and paper.

The Multi-Client Consortium

Multi-client consortia are based on a new concept called the "center of expertise." Such entities are usually separate organizations loosely associated with universities, but formats of this sort also exist in consulting firms or in separate organizations often partially funded

Figure 16-1. Contex Graphics System's work station and mock-up of one of its packaging products.

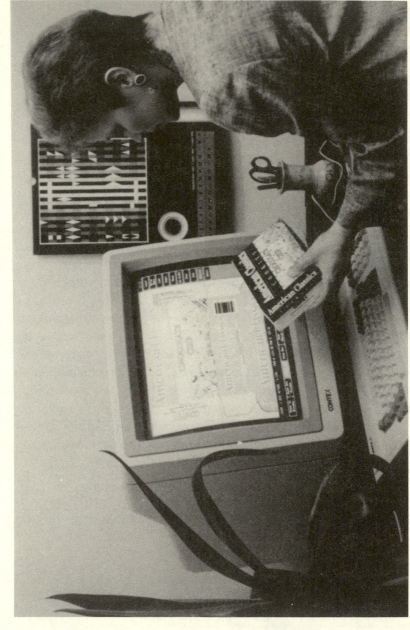

Courtesy of Contex Graphics Systems, Inc.

by federal or state funds. The best way to understand how a consortium works is by taking a look at a real-life example.

A Multi-Client Consortium: The MIT Ceramics Processing Research Laboratory

It turns out that for the last ten millennia, we have been doing pottery all wrong. (Because we are now in the 20th century, let's call it ceramics.) You may have noticed that if you drop a ceramic article on a concrete floor, it tends to shatter. Professor Kent Bowen of the Department of Materials at the Massachusetts Institute of Technology recognized, on the basis of years of research by himself and others, that this brittle quality of such materials is in large part due to included microscopic voids. These result from attempting to sinter (bond without melting by a heat treatment in a kiln) particles of different sizes. When the particles are pres-creened to fall into a single narrow size range and then sintered, the incidence of voids diminishes, and so does brittleness, by as much as a factor of ten.

The significance of this new perception is enormous. We can hope for a ceramic engine block for automobiles and dispose of cast iron and aluminum forever. Consider what high-density sintering means for machine tools that can cut at red-hot temperatures and for such diverse products as missile nose cones and the dishware in our homes. Figure 16–2 illustrates the qualities of this new generation of ceramic materials. (Ceramics Process Systems, Inc., the source of Figure 16-2, is a new company born out of the technology developed at MIT.)

Bowen has organized a consortium—the MIT Ceramics Processing Research Laboratory—directed at enlisting industry sponsorship for the research and development that will lead to new technology and then produce innovative ceramic bodies based on the idea of equal-size particles.

Those who join the consortium receive quarterly written updates of the status of the research and can periodically visit the laboratory sites and meet with those staff members conducting the research.

An interesting fallout of the consortium format is that, even without planning to do so, those who sign up meet each other. Somehow, the cause of common technological interchange to ad-

Figure 16-2. Comparison of traditional and new ceramic micro-
structures: a and b are traditional structures with
a wide range of particle sizes; c and d illustrate
the high-tech utilization of uniform particles.

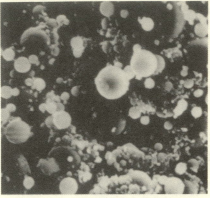

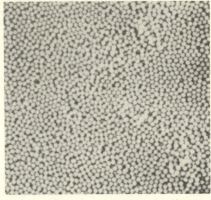

3000x magnification

a. Submicron ceramic particles tend to agglomerate in uncontrolled clusters. As shown in this photomicrograph, the particles in an unfired ceramic piece manufactured using traditional processes do not pack together tightly.

1100x magnification

b. This photomicrograph of a commercially available ceramic substrate shows that poor packing and agglomeration of particles in the unfired piece result in a porous microstructure in the fired, finished piece.

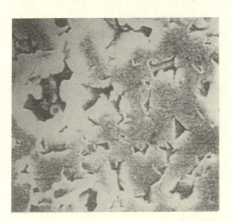

4000x magnification

c. Submicron ceramic particles that are nearly uniform in size and shape pack tightly in a uniform matrix.

900x magnification

d. This photomicrograph of a fired CPS ceramic substrate shows that dense, consistent particle packing in unfired pieces leads to a microstructure that is dense and comparatively free from defects.

Photos courtesy of Ceramics Process Systems, Inc., Cambridge, Massachusetts vance the level of understanding of ceramics technology outstrips the cause of dog-eat-dog competition (during the day of the visit, at least).

When last I checked, the MIT Ceramics Consortium had about 30 members from many major ceramics firms in the country and from the most important users of ceramics, in industries extending from electronics to automotive. The fee was $40,000 per year per firm, and each had to pledge support for a minimum of two years.

Consortia fees tend to be small. When one compares the individual $40,000 investment to the cost of an R&D engineer or scientist for a year, which in 1987 averaged about $175,000 in the United States, one realizes that one has bought participation for only the cost of one-fourth of a home-based professional. (The fees add up quickly, however, for the consortium organizer. The MIT group operates on a single program with a yearly budget in the order of $2 million—enough for no less than a dozen teams of scientists and graduate students.)

Such university consortia, addressing specific technical areas, are growing apace. There are dozens in many institutions of learning today; a decade ago, the idea was virtually unknown. I recommend their use.

Government-Supported Centers for Applied Research

While activities like the MIT Ceramics Consortium are entirely industry supported, there are many similar programs emerging with government support, with funding sometimes shared with industry. The National Science Foundation has embraced a new philosophy under its new head, Dr. Erich Bloch, of emphasizing applied research. This contrasts with previous NSF policy, which concentrated on basic research. The way a recent *New York Times* article put it, the world always saw the Foundation as "an ivory tower of esoteric research, nice to have but not very useful in terms of dollars and cents."[2] But usefulness and payback are the watchwords today—as emphasized throughout this book.

Without taking sides on what kind of research the government should sponsor for the long term, the point is that those companies choosing to ally themselves with and co-sponsor such programs stand to derive much immediate value.

Dr. Bloch is asking corporations to put up matching seed money for the formation of specialized technical centers. His plan is:

> to dot the nation's college campuses with special centers. . . . Some of the centers are already off the ground. . . . About $30 million will be spent on 11 centers this year [1987]—for example, a center for communication networks at Columbia University; for robotics at the University of California, Santa Barbara; and for organic/inorganic composites at the University of Delaware. . . . Four of five more will be added in 1987 and . . . there should be 25 engineering centers by 1990.[3]

There seems to be a bandwagon; perhaps you should get on it.

Consulting Firms

Of course, there are always the traditional consulting houses. Some are massive, with literally thousands of specialists of both the technical and nontechnical sorts. Can they innovate? Indeed they can. If you have a gap they can fill, go to them and you will get results—at the going rate of so much per engineering hour, plus a fee.

Recently, a number of "upstart" consulting houses—operating with a style far different from that of the major firms—have appeared. A *Newsweek* article describes them as "wizards" and "futuristic hired guns," and points out that their hallmark is delivering new products at breakneck speed.[4] With all deference to the traditional consulting firms, speed has not been their hallmark. What do these new companies want as payment? More than a fee—they want part of the action, in the form of royalties and stock.

Arrangements with Separate Companies

When large companies require innovation in unfamiliar areas, they often perceive that other companies have special, superior expertise in those areas. The companies with special expertise are usually relatively small and have good reputations as innovators. What can follow is an arrangement in which the larger company contracts to have the smaller firm perform the innovation task.

This is not the same as having a consulting firm or a university team do the job. The innovating company is not in the consulting business and views the arrangement as deviation from normal practice and therefore as a one-time unique event. Another difference is that the arrangement often blossoms into more than a mere contractual commitment in that the larger company often sees the wisdom of offering to buy into the smaller company as a minority stockholder.

An example of such an occurrence is that of a development program that the Gillette Company of Boston contracted for with a small biotech firm, Repligen Corporation of Cambridge, Massachusetts (mentioned earlier with regard to its technology orientation). The goal, as stated in a Repligen brochure, was "to identify materials [specifically a 'target protein'] for incorporation into certain Gillette personal-care products [such as antiperspirants, hair dye, hair waving agents, and anti-plaque dental agents] and to provide processes for the manufacture of those ingredients." Gillette was sufficiently impressed with the results of this work that it purchased a 7 percent equity in Repligen.

This kind of event happens frequently enough for it to receive detailed treatment in Chapter 18.

References

1. S. E. Upton, "The Outer Space of Industry-University Research," *Appliance Engineer*, August 1985, p. 51.
2. J. W. Anderson, "Pushing Ivory-Tower Scientists into the High-Tech Race," *The New York Times*, February 15, 1987, p. 6.
3. Ibid.
4. "Silicon Valley's Newest Wizards," *Newsweek*, January 5, 1987, p. 30.

17

Internal Ventures Center

There are many names for it: from the functional and dignified "holding company" and "diversified businesses," to the bravely dubbed and hopefully intimidating "Advanced Technologies, Inc." Some call it a "strategic business unit," or SBU. But there are less formal designations: the "reservation," the bucolic but glassed-in "greenhouse," the pediatric "incubator" or "nursery," and the heartstring-tugging "orphanage." Whatever we call it, it is the home of a collection of new ventures, born of or consisting of skunk works—which, for the moment, have no place to go.

Such situations are common. For most companies that engage in innovation, particularly large ones, it is like a law of nature; such waifs just seem to appear on their doorsteps—and several of them, not just one. The question, then, is what to do with them? A number of enlightened managements have accumulated these activities in one place, or at least under one director, and thereby create an internal ventures center.

The Need for a Corporate Haven for New Ventures

There really is no problem if the innovation being worked on in the lab or the skunk works is a poor one. Poor innovation usually just goes down the drain and nothing is lost but money, and somehow that seems to be tolerable. After all, there was an R&D budget and the R&D organization met its budget. (It almost sounds like good management.) The problem appears only if the innovation is good. Managers are often surprised—as though a trick had been played on them. "What do I do now?" they seem to be asking. There is a need to provide a mechanism that will grease the skids for a successful innovation about to launch itself into the outside world as a venture, hoping to extend its success to that process too.

It is easy to fall into the trap of doing only part of the job. The company, one way or another, may have performed well in discovering and supporting a handful of brilliant innovators and a number of blockbuster venture candidates every year, but it often falls short when it comes to following up. There may be a lack of people or organization to aid the progression into maturity of those fragile organisms that they have just coaxed into life.

However it may have been spawned, a freshly hatched venture now exists. "Don't make any special arrangements for it," you might say. "Let it make its way up the venture road on its own. If it and its leaders are of high quality, they'll make it." That's true sometimes, but not always. And ventures that do make it often proceed very inefficiently. There are two forces that stand in the way of achieving success with efficiency:

1. *Destructive interference.* The new venture may be structured to be part of an existing business entity, such as a division or a subsidiary, that is not ready to let any of its sub-organizations handle their own fates. The parent organization interferes and could do harm, either because of its unfamiliarity with the new business area or because it may have its own problems that it then imposes on the new venture.

2. *Lack of constructive intervention.* On the other side of the ledger, the new venture may need help from the parent corporation in any of a spectrum of specialties, from labor relations to tax law, from special test equipment to the kind of technical aid available from good networking. Smart intrapreneurial leaders will network and exploit the resources of their parent companies. But not all employed venturers think of doing this. Or, worse, they may be so pigheadedly self-centered that they disdain the potential aid their company can provide, thus losing the major advantage of being a company-sponsored, rather than independent, venture.

Without the help it needs, the new venture might be in deep trouble. It is the responsibility of the parent to give help when asked and to offer it when it is not asked for. Sadly, many parents are too involved with their own concerns to meet that parental responsibility, and they do harm by omission—by not encouraging or offering that kind of assistance, even when it is easily available.

By its nature, the new venture is always prone to another kind of trouble: running out of money. Then the corporation can provide that other fundamental kind of aid—funds—and bail out the destitute child. But when the chips are down, petitions for financial succor by the spur venture may fall between the cracks, for in the minds of line managers of mature "more important" businesses, themselves probably in need of fiscal bolstering, there are better ways to spend scarce money than on some problematical new project.

Suppose a skunk works has evolved to the point at which it has already attained venture status. It has announced its highly innovative new products, has promoted them, and has sold the first year's production. In fact, it has received favorable press. The terms "art-leading" and "revolutionary" are frequently tossed off.

Another year goes by. Birth pangs are over, but prospects for steady growth and stable position in the marketplace are still shaky. Yet the venture (now known as a business unit of the division from which it was born) has achieved significant revenues and profits, as evidenced by the fact that sales have hit $4 million a year, there are 97 employees, and profits net 18 percent before taxes. Initial success and the promise of long-term viability have been demonstrated. But there is an uneasiness, because the venture does not operate for itself alone.

It happens that the parent division, which makes products only remotely connected with those of the new venture and has sales of $200 million a year, is going through bad times. Not all are its own fault; the whole industry is in trouble. The division is in a condition far worse than that of its little tacked-on business unit. It doesn't make any profit at all that year. In fact, it just breaks even.

What is the division manager tempted to do when only profits on the consolidated P&L sheet for the division are contributed by the new venture? He or she is tempted to maximize that profit by milking the venture, draining it dry. If someone retires or dies in the venture group, the manager doesn't replace that person. If there is need for further investment in capital equipment for the new operation, he or she doesn't approve it. "They can do with the old equipment," management reasons. And why not? It's only a fringe business compared with the division's primary one.

Now let's take the opposite scenario. The same second year has passed, but birth pangs for the new venture are not over. Sales have hit only $1.2 million per year—produced at a cost of $1.9

million; the consolidated P&L sheet shows profit erosion; and the parent division's business is poor this year. What curative action to take? It's obvious: Kill the new venture.

If your company slips too easily into the "milk" or "kill" patterns, there is, without question, a need for a haven to protect the fledglings—at least through the early years. In fact, more than protection is needed: The company must provide encouragement bolstered with guidance.

Let us now examine an actual case of a venture haven: an internal ventures center in a large company, Eastman Kodak Company.

An Internal Ventures Center: Eastman Kodak

The Building

When you come upon New Opportunity Development operations (NOD), which also houses Eastman Technology, Inc. (ETI) at 64 Commercial Street in Rochester, N.Y., what you spot is a plain six-story brick building (it appears in the foreground of Figure 3–5 in Chapter 3) in a factory neighborhood on the edge of downtown Rochester. The neighborhood, more than a century old and now randomly spotted with similar structures rising from seas of parking lots, was originally the setting for many small and varied industries, clustered there because the Genesee River flows through the area.

The building that now houses NOD and ETI was once a foundry and most recently a small parts-manufacturing firm; it was being refurbished as I walked through. It is as old as Xerox's department-store-turned-skunk works a few miles to the east, and with about the same floor space (30,000 square feet) and number of bodies; but the atmosphere is different. For one thing, in this building every man wears a necktie and every woman is in business attire. Yet, there is still an informal ambiance that is not typical of the rest of the company.

The administration and NOD staff occupy one floor and the other five are enough to house a number of "late seed" and other new venture groups. Occupancy for about 12 to 18 months is typical for these, after which they are launched into more permanent quarters elsewhere. For example, Fastek is in Syracuse, New York, and KRS Remote Sensing is in Washington, D.C.

The Tenants

The number of ETI ventures is always fluctuating, but the most recent projects (excluding several still in the seed stage) are listed in Table 17–1. To illustrate how dynamic that list is, consider Ultra Technologies, a battery-manufacturing company that occupies a building in Newark, New York, about 30 miles east of Rochester. It has been "acquired" by Kodak's Photographic Products Group and now operates as a strategic business unit within that group. It has in effect, graduated, because in 1986 it attained its first acceptance in the marketplaces it serves (see the new product and two of the people responsible for it in Figure 17–1) and had generated real sales. Indeed, so have several other ventures listed in Table 17–1, and those that have not done so yet aspire to that goal.

Table 17–1 presents a strikingly diverse list. Yet all these business units of Eastman Technology, Inc., share common citizenship in the same major institution and a set of common values based on courageously winning in a highly competitive marketplace. The mere fact that they are thrown together in a single building is stimulating to all and has a synergistic effect.

The Company

Like Ford, GE, IBM, or Du Pont, Eastman Kodak is a household name. "Kodak" is a famous trademark. Kodak's sales in 1986 exceeded $11 billion, and it spent over 9 percent of its yearly revenues on R&D.

A schematic version of Kodak's organization chart is shown in Figure 17–2. The business is divided into five major sectors. Three (Photographic Products, Commercial and Information Systems, and Eastman Chemicals) are multi-billion-dollar businesses, and a fourth (Diversified Technologies) exceeds the billion-dollar level. Life Sciences is the fifth. Diversified Technologies is the subject of this example.

Table 17-1.
The business units that comprise Eastman Technology, Inc.

Company	Type of Business
Ultra Technologies	High performance batteries
Videk	Machine vision products
Beta Physics	Ultra thin films
Eastman Communications	Telecommunications software
Fastek	Membranes and filters
Estek	IC wafer cleaning and inspection equipment
Edicon	Computerized photo imaging systems
Discus Electronic Training	Electronic training products
Anastar	Plastic disposables and packaging
Sayett Technology	LCD overhead projector products
LVT	Digital color image writer
KRS Remote Sensing	Remote sensing
Pathtek	Selectively conductive molded devices
K-Technologies	Injection molding process control

How Kodak Organizes R&D

As is the case with most large companies, all of Eastman Kodak's established innovation organizations are either centers or captives performing R&D in the fields of manufacturing, research, and new product development. What is different organizationally from other companies is the existence of a staff network that has the express purpose of generating successful new ventures. As will be seen, many of these new ventures pursue their destinies in the incubator organization, reporting to Eastman Technology, Inc., a subsidiary of Eastman Kodak Company and a member unit of the Diversified Technologies group.

Strategy of the Diversified Technologies Business Group

It is one objective of Diversified Technologies to provide the vehicle for growth into new areas that lie outside the well-defined

Figure 17-1. Wilbur J. Prezzano (left) Kodak group vice president and general manager, Photographic Products, and James E. Moxley, president of the Ultra Technologies unit, pose with new, longer-lasting alkaline batteries.

Reprinted courtesy of Eastman Kodak Company

Figure 17-2. Organization chart of Eastman Kodak.

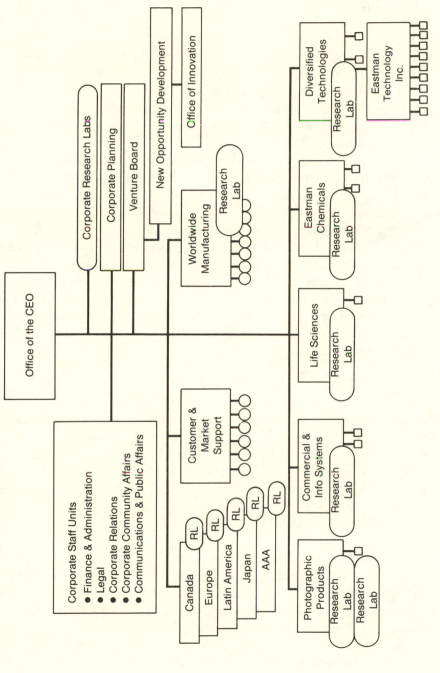

charters of the other four groups. Thus, this involves launching new businesses that only loosely fit general company strategies or that stray beyond the limits of these strategies while still preserving a connection with them. But in both cases they will take advantage of Kodak's exceptionally broad and deep technological base.

The Diversified Technologies group will probably not be the permanent home of most of the new businesses that achieve viability, because its primary purpose is to provide growth opportunities for the corporation. That implies that most of the stable and steadily maturing businesses that appear will somehow eventually find a home in one of Kodak's well-defined existing sectors or in one yet to be formed. ETI's venture business, while viewed as providing an opportunity to exploit future strategic options, fits into this charter. It provides a temporary home for start-ups until a permanent home can be found or created.

Dr. Robert Tuite, who directs New Opportunity Development, refers to 64 Commercial Street as an organizational home for carefully selected new business opportunities for Kodak, opportunities selected on the basis that they conform to a pair of defined constraints. These relate to (1) timing and (2) the extent to which they deviate from existing business areas within the established and well-defined sectors.

When the Time Is Right

The constraint on timing is an acknowledgment of the fact that every new venture has a life cycle. Thus, there is a crucial moment when it has outgrown (or has been cast out of) its birthplace and needs a more permanent home. While ETI is meant to be only a temporary home that the inmates will leave for the best of reasons, namely, that they have outgrown it, it is hoped that they will some day be attractive and mature enough to be brought back into the main Kodak organization.

Corporate and Internal Ventures

The constraint regarding a proper fit refers to the differentiation the company makes between a corporate venture and an internal venture. A corporate venture is defined as one having a good and obvious strategic fit with an existing business sector, so good and so attractive that from the moment of its first beginning it is embraced by and incorporated into that business sector. ("Captive

R&D" is its category.) On the other hand, what Kodak calls an internal venture is not—at least at the time it is spawned—considered to have an immediate or short-term fit with any existing sector of the company. Thus, if it is to achieve viability one day, it must be set up external to any existing sector (while still internal to the company).

An Exemplary Internal Venture

There is one internal venture, born decades ago at Eastman Kodak Company, that exemplifies all the hopes and desires of the firm for this category of venturing. It succeeded before there even was an Eastman Technology, Inc. It became Eastman Chemicals Division (ECD), now one of the company's four major sectors, and is today a leading manufacturer of certain kinds of plastics and organic chemicals in America.

ECD was born out of the Photographic Products (PP) sector. Some intrapreneurial innovators in PP recognized that the chemicals and processes used in the manufacture of camera film could, with some innovating, constitute the basis of a wholly new class of plastics. And, as internal innovators often do, they performed the required innovation tasks successfully and launched the new venture, in the process departing from Photographic Products while still remaining within and under the aegis of Eastman Kodak Company.

Kodak would like to repeat this experience with other new internal ventures. That is why Kodak has set up the unique staff organization structure, shown in Figure 17–2, which consists of the Venture Board (VB), the New Opportunity Development (NOD) group, the Diversified Technologies (DT) group, and Eastman Technology, Inc. (ETI) as a holding company for new ventures (represented by the row of small squares shown reporting to it) with good prospects for success. It is worth noting that the chairman of the Venture Board is also the general manager of the Diversified Technologies business group and the president of ETI. The manner in which these function and interrelate follows.

Kodak's Internal Innovation/Venture Process: Staff Functions

Kodak sees innovation and the creation of internal ventures as best promoted by an imaginative set of staff functions. Most of these reside within or report to the New Opportunity Development Organization. NOD's task is to develop venture start-ups from internally generated ideas and with internal entrepreneurs "discovered" and then facilitated and encouraged by a group that reports to NOD, the Office of Innovation. The Venture Board promotes the overall process, sets policy and guidelines, and approves new venture status and internal venture capital. Once new ventures are launched, ETI takes on the responsibility for providing management, oversight, and guidance and for monitoring the staged infusion of capital into the venture.

The Office of Innovation Unearths
the Venture Candidates

The encourager/facilitator technique pursued by NOD's Office of Innovation network is one that Kodak has pioneered (see Chapter 8). It invites innovation suggestions from Kodak employees in all job categories and receives them at a rate approaching 1,000 per year. These differ from what is derived from a "suggestion box" in that they are aimed at producing new products, new processes, or new business rather than just more efficient operating procedures.

The Office of Innovation facilitates the early development and evaluation of these and aids in finding sponsors to develop more serious business concepts and technical development. Innovators are coached in proposal development and in the elements of a preliminary business plan.

Most of the sponsorship comes from existing business units. However, this process also results in the selection of a very few, but at the same time very promising, venture candidates that existing businesses choose not to fund, but that nevertheless are expected to justify significant company investment.

New Opportunity Development Seeds Early Innovation

Once venture candidates are selected, NOD provides them with internal seed funding. This is allocated to the project champion (usually, but not always, the one who had been "unearthed" by the Office of Innovation) and negotiates some relief for that person from his or her present job assignment so that he or she might be free to generate a stand-alone business proposal.

NOD has a more participatory role in that it also provides guidance and discipline. Its ultimate goal is to aid in structuring the business and putting together the entrepreneurial team to fit the business plan. Dr. Robert Tuite is director of NOD and has a staff of nine technical, business, and market-oriented professionals who engage in all aspects of these tasks.

NOD reports to the Venture Board.

The Venture Board: An Internal Venture Capital Firm

The Venture Board functions much like a venture capital firm, but an internal or captive one. It performs venture appraisals with the help of NOD and the Venture Advisory Panel and also makes sure that any ventures approved are consistent with long-term Kodak strategy.

The Venture Board acts as liaison between senior management, that is, the office of the CEO (providing information about the creation of out-of-the-mainstream internal ventures) and the managements of the five business groups (providing information about the progress of start-ups that may ultimately be viewed as attractive acquisitions by existing sectors).

The Venture Board has a yearly fund to invest in new ventures amounting to roughly 1 percent of Kodak's capital investment for that year.

Line Functions: Eastman Technology, Inc.

Large companies are very skilled at running existing businesses, but they tend to be less effective with start-up businesses. For intrapreneurs, no less than for entrepreneurs, the opposite is usually the case, especially once the venture exceeds a certain critical size. Thus, the challenge for ETI has been to balance and reconcile these opposing qualities of large companies and ventures by providing an environment salubrious to both. According to Dr. Robert Bacon, NOD's director of special products, "ETI encourages creativity, innovation, and entrepreneurism while focusing on the pursuit of opportunistic or even serendipitous ideas."[1]

The Environment

The ETI environment allows both types of management to coexist. It facilitates the launching of new businesses consistent with long-term company strategy "in a relatively low-risk way by establishing the venture as a stand-alone unit under small-start-up-company guidelines. . . . It optimizes the opportunity for success, both by allowing the entrepreneur free access to corporate resources on an arm's-length negotiated basis, and by giving the venture loose identification with a large stable company in being labeled 'a Kodak company.' "[2]

The Board of Directors
Because every venture division in ETI is considered to be a stand-alone business in its own right, it requires a board of directors. NOD and the Venture Board fill this function as the initial board until a permanent one is formed.

The Time Scale
ETI will harbor successful start-ups for a "reasonable" period, expected to fall into the range of four to seven years, at which point an exit process takes place.

The "Fate" of Ventures
When a venture departs from ETI, several courses are open to it depending on its strategic fit and commercial viability. The most desirable outcome is that one of the existing sectors sees the venture as a healthy business that fits well with its own and acquires it to function as one of its divisions. If the venture does not fit anywhere within Kodak, the new enterprise may be divested by private or public sale or by employee buy-out. Finally, at the opposite end of the spectrum, should the venture fail to meet commercial objectives, funding may be discontinued and the project abandoned.

References

1. From a personal interview with Robert Bacon, November 1986.
2. Ibid.

18

External Ventures Center

Chapter 16 dealt with innovating by using external teams that drew on someone else's employees working at someone else's premises who worked for an agreed-upon fee. It is classic purchased service. After the job is done, the two participants usually part company and interact again either rarely or never.

In this chapter, we go one step further. We will buy not a service, but a thing. That is another way to innovate: Purchase another company's inventory of already achieved innovations, in whatever state they may be at the moment of the transaction. There are commonly accepted terms that designate such purchases. "Acquisition" for the purchase of a whole company and "establishment of a minority position" for the purchase of a small fraction of such a company. People and corporations establish minority positions in or acquire other firms all the time. We are interested in those cases when they perform such actions primarily as mechanisms to achieve newer and better innovations faster.

A variation on purchasing all or part of a company is the "joint venture." In a joint venture, one company forms an intimate relationship with another in order that they may take advantage of each other's unique expertise. (A company's expertise is based on its innovation history and on the state of its ongoing innovations.)

The Contex Graphics/Carnegie-Mellon example (see Chapter 16), which started out as a contract for R&D between one company and a university team, evolved into a joint venture between two companies. At Repligen Corporation, a small biotechnology firm, an inter-company arrangement evolved in another manner. Even though the company was not in the primary business of performing innovation for a fee, it did accept a contract from the Gillette Company to investigate a way to make a family of proteins that could advance Gillette's personal-care products. Gillette was so pleased with the results that it offered to buy a minority position (7 percent) of Repligen, an offer that was accepted.

Acquisitions

One company determines to buy a second company because such a move fits the buyer's strategy, which is based on many complex requirements and desires. Here are some cases in which the strategy included a desire for increased R&D capability:

- It is accepted wisdom that General Electric purchased RCA for the billions of dollars worth of annual sales represented by its electronics products and for the profits and power of its NBC subsidiary. But the biggest sweetener was RCA's Princeton Labs.
- General Motors bought Hughes Aircraft and Ross Perot's Electronic Data Systems Corporation, not because it needed another $7 billion in annual business, but rather because it hopes its auto business will profit from the efforts of the acquired companies' electronics and computer software R&D groups.
- Raytheon Company acquired Amana Refrigeration in the mid-1960s because it had a sword from World War II that it wanted to beat into a plowshare: the ability to subject foodstuffs to microwave energy, thereby causing them to experience an increase of temperature not dissimilar to what they undergo when subjected to a cooking process. Amana knew how to sell appliances to domestic customers, which Raytheon did not know how to do; that was one reason it made the acquisition. In addition, Amana had a team of innovators that could join in with the acquirer's Boston-based radar engineers to create a product that would sit on a kitchen counter, plug into an ordinary electric socket, pose no hazard, look attractive, and heat a cup of coffee in one minute and fifty seconds without recourse to gas flames or red-hot electric heaters.

The Need to Integrate

What the purchaser should understand when acquiring another entity—one that's often as big as the parent and that has another set of skills and leads another way of life—is that the two are entering into an arranged marriage. The acquirer is getting a respectable mate whom he will not be ashamed to bring home. If he is marrying in order to bring new blood (innovation skills) into the family, he will want his new spouse to interact pleasantly and forever with all his previous kids from previous marriages.

If the new acquisition is to perform as required by company strategy, it must be integrated into the existing organization. That is the challenge. As far as innovation goes, integration means that the acquired company's innovation centers and innovation captives, which perform in different modes, like research and technology and new product development, must develop healthy relationships with similar organizations in the acquiring company. Redundancies must be dealt with and, at the same time, the incremental new capabilities must be added to existing networks in order to upgrade the previous level of networking.

The Need to Integrate Wisely

If you acquire a new firm for the purpose of adding its innovation skills to yours, take steps to meet this challenge: "Adding" must include integrating. Each case is unique, involving ingrained practices and established facilities and personal prides, but if you are sympathetic and sensitive you will succeed.

Minority Positions

One buys minority positions in other companies for the same reasons that one buys whole companies: Such actions fit long-term strategies. Buying only part of a company is a strategic maneuver of the hedging variety. The buyer may have no strategic reason to want to be in the acquired company's business, but it does desire something that company has, and putting one's foot in the door with a minority-interest investment ensures first dibs on that something. There are additional advantages.

The Advantages of Taking Minority Positions

It costs less to buy only a minority interest than to buy the whole company, and is thus less risky. Also, you can buy ten minority positions in ten wildly disparate (and exciting) innovative small companies for the same money that might have been needed to acquire just one large established company—with all its large established problems. For a large acquirer, buying minority positions in small companies brings small problems. If you have to choose between large problems and small ones, small ones win by a mile.

There may be many aspects of the subject company that will motivate the larger firm to invest in it. Not the least of these is that it may be judged to be poised for a leap to the head of its industry and that in the next two or three years its sales will increase tenfold and its stock will become a Wall Street high flyer. The minority-position investor will always be on the lookout for such a firm to buy into, just to improve the balance sheet.

Also, owning part of another company means the new stockholder also owns a proportionate share of the new profits. This can become the most delightful of R&D investments, a self-supporting one. In the happiest of cases, it could even turn investment in innovation into a negative cost. Mark Radtke, a principal of Venture Economics, Inc., of Wellesley, Massachusetts, which publishes *Corporate Venturing News,* points out that this happens often enough to be a significant consideration. His designation for such investments is "self-funding."

But for our purposes, one reason for the investing outweighs all the others: The buyer becomes privy to a scientific or technological advance that it would otherwise not produce in so timely a fashion using its own innovation resources. That is what qualifies this procedure as one of our innovation implementation modes. When I met with them, Radtke and his associate, John Papp, had more advantages to offer that they had distilled out of their experiences in dealing with hundreds of minority acquisitions in the last half-dozen years. Let me summarize them.

First, buying into a small innovative firm is a way to supplement and strengthen the innovation capability that you already have, not a way to supplant it. Internal and external innovation should be considered as the same with regard to the dynamics of utilizing creative people in order to develop new products and new business. Thus, there is no need to resort to going outside unless your own innovation organizations will not achieve what is required within desired times and investment constraints. But—and this an important but—if you perceive that a new approach is going to be too upsetting to an existing innovation organization, indeed, if it is mired in an old technology, then you may need to funnel some of your resources into the parallel path of an outside enterprise rather than attempt to remake the existing people and their ingrained practices. The word "parallel" implies that the old way still has value and that it's better not to erode it.

Second, the new way can be risky. Its prospect for success may be one in three. It is better to take a minority position in a company that has already stuck its neck out. If you make three deals, on average you should end up with at least one winner, and compared with setting up just one approach from scratch in your own labs, all three put together will probably cost less and take less time. In the process, your chance of having a stake in the one that is "the way of the future" has increased, and that is probably a way that your own CEO would have been too cautious to commit to in-house.

Third, the people you get to work on the project are often "pure class." Radtke and Papp say that the nation's reservoir of outstanding innovators—people combining creativity with dedication—who still work for large companies has been massively depleted by today's venture capital culture. Although the message of this book is that if you organize well for in-house innovation you can make a success of it (in the process employing and retaining your own first-class innovators), I must admit that, in practice, there is no denying that there is much truth in what Radtke and Papp tell us.

A company should go down both paths. When its employed innovators perform poorly, the company should strive to improve its own ways of selecting, supporting, and motivating creative people until they rival the innovators in small entrepreneurial firms. But if circumstances warrant, a company should not hesitate to benefit from what the small firms have to offer. That means you should become a venture capitalist; that's what you are when you take a minority position in a new art-leading company.

Making Use of a Minority Position

Having purchased an interest in a company with an outstanding innovation portfolio, how does the purchaser take advantage of that portfolio? By becoming a member of the smaller company's board of directors; the purchase agreement must include provision for board membership. As a board member, the new person sitting at that mahogany table has access to all relevant information as well as a voice in the discussion. Thus, he or she can influence future strategies, particularly as they pertain to his or her own firm's strategies regarding a particular innovation.

But more important, the doors are open. The acquirer can send a team of specialists to visit the innovation lab that created the desirable new product or new technology. Another team of specialists can visit the production floor and see how that innovation is manufactured or otherwise utilized. It doesn't stop there. The new part-owner can learn about the marketplace and can find out who among the competition is buying the product and how they are using it.

All this leads to increased sales of the "internal" sort. The larger firm was probably already a customer, but now it is motivated to buy more—and those purchases will include some items that had not yet been announced to the public. If the essence of competition among innovative companies means being first with the newest and most advances, here is a way to achieve that.

What's in It for the Seller?

It is important to note that this is not a one-way street. The firm that has sold off a minority portion of itself has much to gain. First, the mere sale itself has infused a significant sum of needed dollars. It is typical of small high-tech firms that ideas flow like mighty rivers, but cash flows like a rivulet.

In addition, the large firm has much non-monetary aid to offer. It can be in mundane areas, such as helping to set up good purchasing or accounting procedures. Or there may be a need for the advice of specialists whom the large company employs in spades: tax lawyers, labor lawyers, international trade specialists, patent attorneys, licensing specialists, liability specialists, and so on.

Is there a requirement to test the new module for performance to a military specification? "No problem," says the new board member, "You just call Kevin Toomey at extension 2317 in building K. He'll set up the test for you in his environmental lab." This extends to advanced technical aid. What if there is a magnet in that module that changes characteristics unacceptably with increased temperature? "It so happens that magnets is one of our skills," continues the same board member. "Get in touch with Dr. Heinrich Apfelfeld in the Central Research Lab. He ought to be able to help you out." And so it goes (or should, if all are doing their job right).

If this is reminiscent of the benefits that accrue to fledgling new ventures in the internal ventures centers of Chapter 17, that is as it should be, and everyone will benefit because the minority-position company is now considered part of the family.

The Scale of Minority-Position Venturing in the United States

Figure 18–1 indicates the number of companies that have set up formal external ventures centers reporting to senior management, and graphically illustrates how steady their growth has been. (The number for 1986 has reached 76 companies. While that is not a large number of companies, it takes on added significance when note is made of the fact that most of them are on the *Fortune* 500 list.)

Such external ventures organizations are always relatively small in financial terms. They usually are provided with a yearly budgeted fund of between $10 million and $50 million, which, although not massive, is large enough. (You can buy a lot of minority with a few million dollars.)

In most situations, the manager of such a group is a company officer reporting to the CEO or a high-level manager. Like funding levels, the number of people making up a group engaged in this kind of activity for a sizable firm is not large: from one to six people.

Figure 18–2 shows the number of investments in minority positions taken by all firms in recent years (those from Figure 18–1 plus companies that have not set up formal external ventures offices).

How large a portion of venture capital investment emanates from industrial firms? Venture Economics, Inc., states that for the year 1985, 9 percent of all such investments (nearly $2 billion out

Figure 18-1.   The growing number American companies that have
set up external venture capital programs.

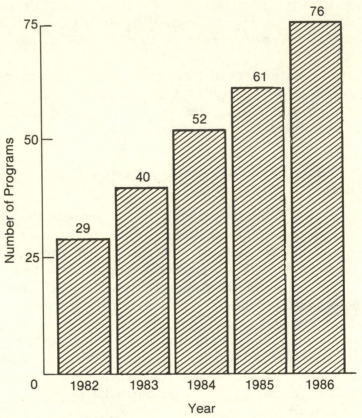

Courtesy of Venture Economics, Inc., Wellesley Hills, Massachusetts

of $19.6 billion) was committed by industrial firms and not by
enterprises wholly engaged in the venture capital business.

Not all of these firms are motivated to find companies with
advanced innovation capability; many pursue this avenue simply as
a way to make good investments of available funds. But a significant
fraction, including Eastman Kodak, Analog Devices, Grumman,
Warner-Lambert, American Cyanamid, and Raytheon Company,
concentrate primarily on acquiring advanced innovations and advanced innovation capability. Let us consider Raytheon as an example.

Figure 18-2. Number of corporate strategic investments in ven-
              ture-capital-backed firms, 1982–1986.

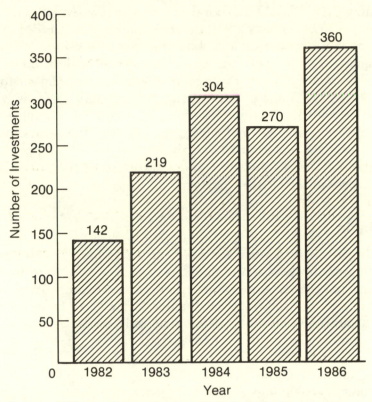

Courtesy of Venture Economics, Inc., Wellesley Hills, Massachusetts

An External Ventures Center: Raytheon Company

"This is a situation where every time you come up, you get at
least three at bats," says David Dwelley, president of Raytheon
Ventures (RV). "Yes, an operating element of our company, the
division or subsidiary that pointed us to the new venture in the
first place ['This one's going to be a star, Dave,' they said], gets
a handle on some art-leading technology. At the same time the
venture has an opportunity to learn market implications of their
advanced products to Raytheon and similar large companies that
may never have been apparent to it. But more than that—there

is a collateral business relationship resulting in enhanced sales volumes which benefit both buyer and seller simultaneously." Dwelley's predecessor as president of Raytheon Ventures, David Steadman, now CEO of GCA Corporation, expresses essentially the same message in another way: "Raytheon is looking at businesses that either have a product or are about to have a product. After our investment, the company continues as an independent enterprise, operating under its own management and serving the customers in its industry. But we want them to feel that there is a real association with Raytheon. This kind of investment has augmented Raytheon's existing technologies over the past two years, and in return, these entrepreneurs not only receive financial support, they also gain Raytheon's guidance and assessment of the potential for the markets in which they participate."

The Investments

Now in its third year, RV has been recognized by the venture capital community as a prominent player. To date, nine minority positions have been consummated, none exceeding 15 percent. These are in the following companies located in almost as many states around the country. (Note that only eight are listed. The ninth didn't make it. Not a bad average.)

Digital Techniques
Bipolar Technology
Millitech
Mosaic Systems
Sciteq
Sepracore
Speech Systems
Steinbrecher Corporation

The industries served by these small firms include video communications systems, millimeter wave components, advanced frequency synthesis, biogenetic separations and catalysis, advanced radar communications, programmable silicon substrates, customized integrated circuitry, and speech-to-text technology. Dwelley or one of his professional staff members, Clyde Rettig, serves on the boards of each.

Figure 18–3 shows Dwelley in action on the occasion of a regular visit to one of the ventures, Digital Techniques.

Raytheon Ventures (RV) has the mission of serving Raytheon's existing businesses by providing art-leading innovation tailored to defined needs. Thus, the process starts with them. RV makes it its business to communicate with the technical and business managers of all the business entities that comprise the company (no small matter, because they number in the many dozens) to ascertain what technical advances are needed and which are not being adequately addressed within existing innovation organizations in the company. This networking also uncovers many leads, often consisting of lists of innovative firms already serving particular business organizations as vendors. From these starting points, Dwelly and Rettig begin to look at the outside world.

To date, more than 600 candidates have been examined—resulting in the above-listed eight, as well as a number that are now "in process." The yield is between 1 percent and 2 percent.

How Has It Worked Out?

All the Raytheon business centers that have participated feel that they have derived very positive benefits that they otherwise would not have had. These include Raytheon's subsidiaries, Badger Company and United Engineers, which are both constructors of large-scale chemicals and energy plants that now have access to advanced process-control techniques from one of their new "associates," as well as the Semiconductor and Equipment Divisions (the latter manufactures radar equipment), which are already employing unique software and electronics innovations made available as a consequence of other new relationships.

Start-Ups

Having forcefully made the point that internal venturing addresses only more or less established small high-tech companies, I must now waffle by saying, "not all the time." "We are venture capitalists," says Dwelley, "thus we are interested in start-ups too." This represents an evolution from the original philosophy of Raytheon Ventures. Steadman had said, "We are not looking at start-ups." But Dwelley counters that "we have learned our business

Figure 18-3. High-tech housecall—David Dwelley (left), President of Raytheon Ventures, Inc., tours the demonstration facility of Digital Techniques, Inc. Peter J. Dikeman, chief technical officer (seated), and Vincent J. McGugan, CEO, demonstrate their TOUCHCOM system with which customers, by touching the screen, can call up and analyze every item in a company's product catalogue.

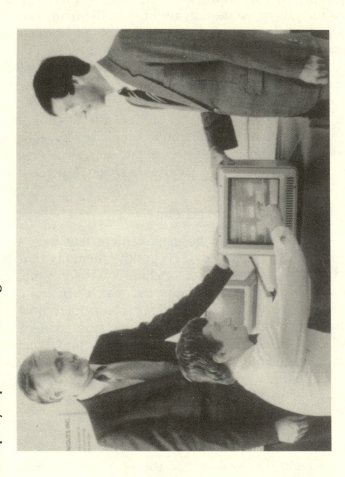

Courtesy of Raytheon Company

well enough now to know that we can handle taking minority positions in selected completely new entrepreneurial ventures as well. So even though most of our ventures will continue to be in young companies that have already created a creditable history over several years, we are aiming for a balanced portfolio of ventures that will include a scattering of newborn companies as well."

Joint Ventures

CEOs play a more active role in joint ventures than in any other type of external venture. They do more than merely support innovation, they cause it.

In putting together a new jointly owned company, two different companies meet and agree to work together, merging and utilizing the unique, and, until now, disparate, strengths of each for the benefit of both. A good reference in this field is K. R. Harrigan's *Managing for Joint Venture Success* (Lexington, MA: Lexington Books, 1986).

An outstanding American joint venturer—with most of its relationships arranged with the aim of building its business by implementing innovation—is the Corning Glass Works. Let us make it our example.

A Joint Venture: Corning Glass Works

At last count, Corning had 21 joint involvements worldwide. Its ownership portion in these ranges from 33 percent to 50 percent, with most at the 50 percent level.

Dr. Thomas MacAvoy is vice chairman of the board and vice president, technology, and heads up Corning's Research and Development Facility (the Sullivan Park Technical Center, shown in Chapter 3). It houses most of the company's research and innovation in technology and new products. He informed me when I visited that his firm aims to establish all future joint ventures on a 50-50 basis. "The only way to have a partner, when each partner is a leader in its own industry," he said, "is to have an equal partner."

Then crucial decisions relating to technology and strategy are made, presumably, only as a result of rational discussions based on factual data.

In 1985, sales for Corning itself and its subsidiaries were $1.7 billion. But sales calculated on the basis of its equity in its joint ventures exceed this. They were *an additional $1.8 billion.*

Many of the joint companies are well known as leaders in their respective fields: Siecor, Ciba Corning Diagnostics, Pittsburgh Corning, Genencor, Owens/Corning Fiberglass (now divested), Dow Corning, and others. In each case, an alliance was made between Corning and another large company, a leader in another very different kind of product area from Corning's. (Fragments of their original names—Siemans, Genentech, Ciba, Dow Chemical—are incorporated in the joint names.)

The arrangements that have resulted in the birth of 21 new companies have put this producer of glass and ceramic preformed materials and dishware for the kitchen into many new fields that it would otherwise never had been in, or, had it entered these fields, never in such big-league fashion. These business areas include fiber-optic cables, enzymes for the food processing and chemicals industries (processed in special glass containers), and laboratory diagnostic products such as instruments and reagents, foamed-glass insulation, and plastics, among others.

Dow Corning, the joint venture that put Corning into the plastics business, is an interesting example. Two decades ago, the world moved toward making use of the fact that organic chemicals, which are the basis of plastics, are compounds of carbon in which the molecular arrangement is characterized by the four atomic bonds of carbon that can make arrangements like the benzene ring, and that silicon could be substituted for carbon in the same arrangements. The silicon atom also has four atomic bonds and also can form such molecular relationships.

This was a revolution in chemistry, because silicon-based "semi-organic" polymer materials would have superior high-temperature qualities compared with those based on carbon, as well as many other improved properties, such as high lubricity, extreme resistance to wetting, and physiochemical resistance.

Corning reasoned that there was no better way to facilitate the innovation process of developing specific silicon formulations and technologies for their manufacture than to combine the skills of a leading company in carbon-based organics with a leading company in the field of silicon. Dow Chemical was the right firm in organic chemistry, and for the silicon specialist, who better than Corning? Silicon, as silicon dioxide (silica), is the primary material out of which glass is made.

The rest is, as they say, history. The joint venture, Dow Corning, pioneered this important class of material, and dubbed it "silicone."

Silicone with an "e" (don't confuse silicon with silicone) is now a word you can find in any dictionary. You can also find it as an essential gasket material in high-temperature valves and engines as a means to hold heat-absorbing tiles onto space vehicles, as cosmetic implants used by plastic surgeons, and in squeeze tubes for caulking anything around the house.

And, although other companies now also make silicone materials, Dow Corning, Inc., remains a world leader in the field.

19

Licensing Arrangements

Almost no one innovates for the prime purpose of licensing. Companies engage in R&D so that they themselves may exploit the fruits of that effort, not so that someone else might pick those fruits. Yet many companies license-in and license-out. In fact, so many companies engage in licensing that it qualifies as a valid innovation mode, a pathway to new products and new technologies leading to increased revenues and profits. It usually comes about because the opportunity presents itself as a fallout of another activity, and it turns out to be wiser to grasp that opportunity than to let it pass by.

Why License?

Done wisely, licensing is another technique available to businesses to help them flourish. What's special about licensing is that significant benefits can accrue for two parties: for both the licensee (who licenses-in) and the licensor (who licenses-out). Here are some of them.

To Fill Gaps and to Shorten Time to the Market

We have already discussed procedures companies use to have innovation performed for them by people who are not their employees. Chapter 16 describes contracts with consulting firms and universities; Chapter 18 discusses acquisitions, purchases of minority positions in innovative firms, and joint ventures. Licensing is another strategy to add to this list. If it is correctly handled, it can achieve the same purposes: filling gaps in your own capability and within your own organization and telescoping the time scale for exploiting innovation.

To Maintain Technical Dynamism of an Industry

D. W. McDonald and H. S. Leahey, in a summary article on the subject, cite references that point out that high-technology companies flush with the fruits of innovation, those that spend more than 3 percent of revenues on R&D, are more likely to license-out than others. Having extra know-how to sell is only one motivation. Such firms often license-in and license-out simultaneously (cross-license) for a more subtle reason: "to maintain the technical dynamism of the industry . . . and not primarily to gain royalty income."[1] But such altruism is probably founded on pragmatism.

In technology-intensive industries, your competitors will instantly pirate your great new innovation the minute they become aware of it. They can't resist. So it's better to license than to engage in lawsuits—as long as your competitors let you license their great new innovations too.

Global Impact of Licensing

It is not commonly recognized how widespread the effects of licensing can be. The Japanese built their new industrial base after World War II using technology licensed mostly from us, and licensing is still their major source of the early steps of the innovation process.[2] In the 1960s, RCA freely licensed-out electronics know-how to Japanese companies, and that has had much to do with that Japan's present dominating position in consumer electronics. It may also have something to do with the fact that today RCA is but a division of General Electric. (But let's not finger RCA—the practice was and is widespread.)

Yet, licensing to foreign companies can have very constructive consequences for the small number of American firms that build such a practice into their strategies, rather than letting it happen as an accidental fallout. (IBM is such a firm.)

Advantages and Disadvantages

McDonald and Leahey identify nine advantages and nine disadvantages for both licensing-in and licensing-out. The most important of them have been selected for discussion below.[3]

The most compelling reasons to license-in are that it buys time and it buys expertise, both of which are otherwise not so expeditiously available. The disadvantages to being a licensee can, for the most part, be satisfactorily dealt by wise management practices. For example, the licensee may be confronted with the significant erosion of profits caused by the drain of paying license fees. But excessive fees should not be agreed to in the first place. A company should negotiate low—and fair—royalty percentages. A fair fee should not be considered a drain; the same money would have had to be amortized if it had been expended internally to fund an innovation program.

The most important reasons to license-out are, first, because an opportunity is provided to profit from inactive innovations that will otherwise not be used. Such profit can be considerable; keep in mind that net royalties go right to the before-tax profit line. If you normally make 10 percent profit before taxes, $1 million of licensing royalties is equivalent to profits from a $10 million business, with virtually none of the problems a business brings. (The licensee deals with all those problems.)

The second advantage of licensing-out is that it is a way to create a second supplier—a competitor, if you will—of your own choosing. It is not usually good business practice to be the *only* source of a new proprietary product; it makes the buying public uncomfortable. By licensing-out, you do not "lose" the customers who go to that competitor; for every item sold, a share of the profits goes to you.

The most serious disadvantage to licensing-out is that the licensor must secure and maintain worldwide patent protection, which could result in costly legal entanglements.

Organize for Licensing

McDonald and Leahey have a message for us: Don't settle for random fallouts of R&D programs as the only basis for licensing-in or licensing-out. Build a strategy for integrating such actions into overall company planning.

Whether license opportunities emerge by chance or are formalized in company strategies, one thing should be planned: Certain individuals should be delegated to work together as a team with the responsibility and skills to *perform* licensing.

A well-managed company accepts that licensing will inevitably occur, establishes a department skilled in the legalities of licensing (sometimes called Directorate of Licensing), and identifies one technical person as the champion of licensing. When a licensing director is combined with a champion, even if one or both are part-time, that team can be unbeatable. If you have such a team and your competitors do not, you'll have a decided advantage; for the small investment it costs to maintain them, much incremental revenue can accrue. Indeed, it can provide the best ROI you have.

The Director of Licensing

If you work for a large company, it is likely that there is a group in the legal staff, usually an organizational entity within the patent department, that specializes in licensing and is run by a director of licensing. If there is no such director, you can request that a patent attorney handle licensing deals. All patent attorneys include licensing in their resumes. But be cautious: Some patent attorneys who are brilliant in drawing up and pursuing a patent will fall flat when it comes to negotiating royalty fees and down payments. If you need to, you can engage a license specialist on a contract basis as the occasion arises.

The point is, if you are going to engage in licensing, don't proceed without expert help. Treat licensing as a professional specialty (it does have its own society, journal, and yearly conferences). Throughout this chapter, the director of licensing is referred to as the DL, whether the company formally names such a director or not.

The DL knows all the laws, all the rules, and all the practices of licensing, for this country and for many foreign countries as well. That knowledge is one important reason you are paying that person's salary or fee. But that knowledge is only the baseline; it is necessary but not sufficient.

As is the case with many lawyers in other specialties, the DL's real value—primary reason you are paying—comes from his or her recognition of the value of what is being bought or sold and the ability to negotiate effectively for the best fair deal.

Like good patent attorneys, good DLs understand these values because they have a technical background. If a qualified patent attorney is an engineer gone astray, then a qualified DL is a patent attorney gone the same way. The value of a technical background is especially important because the DL functions best when working as one part of a two-part team, of which the other part is the technical champion of licensing.

The Technical Champion of Licensing

A champion is someone in a company who attempts to prevail—using every kind of skill, including political—against commonly accepted company practices in the interest of a concept he or she believes in with passion. Such a person can be a top-level manager or someone in middle management. We have encountered different types of champions throughout this book.

A technical champion for licensing (TCL) is an engineer or scientist with a broad understanding of the company's technology, products, markets, industry, and strategies. The TCL also has inherent respect for the DL's expertise, and is able to judge whether what is to be licensed is patentable or is to be considered as know-how (discussed in Chapter 6). In addition, TLCs must have well-honed entrepreneurial qualities: They should be able to feel in their guts that something is going to sell and make money for the company.

The TCL knows that there is unmined gold buried in the company's basement or in a competitor's product line. So, in league with the other team member, the DL, the TCL begins the mining process. For licensing, that usually amounts to generating a program of action and then implementing it.

Generating License Business

Of course, if someone comes to you asking, "Please, may I license the following items?" the required actions for potential licensors are easy. The DL/TCL team should be assigned to interact with such supplicants; only that team has the skills and experience to derive the best benefits from any license contract.

The greater challenge, however, lies with generating license arrangements from scratch, when no one comes eagerly knocking at the door. Then the thing to be licensed must be actively marketed and sold, and the DL/TCL team members become salespeople.

It's nice to have something so marvelous that people flock to your doors asking to buy, but in the real world (RW), that happens infrequently. In the RW, salespeople take the initiative. They identify the potential customers and go knocking on people's doors. Then, having gained ingress, they open their satchels and display their goodies. Thus the licensing team needs a budget—most of it for travel.

It is best for the team to travel as a team, and the potential customer should be warned. The unspoken message is, "I am coming to tell you of an attractive license opportunity, and I am bringing my lawyer, so you might want yours present as well."

The item must be shown to its best advantage, and the best performances are live ones. At some point, the licensing team should invite the potential licensee to have a tour of the innovation organization, meet the innovators, and see a demonstration of the product or process. Who can resist? It is at this point that salespeople proceed to make the sale.

Universities as Licensing Sources

So far, all discussion has focused on company-to-company licensing relationships. But it would be wrong to omit one other category of interactions that has been and will increasingly be another important source of such agreements: company-to-university relationships. The faculty, staff, and students of a college or university often generate intellectual property that has potential commercial value.

This should be expected in view of the fact that fully 15 percent of all our country's R&D funds are expended by people affiliated with universities. You might not be surprised to find that nearly $7 billion of the $13.3 billion spent in this country in 1985 in basic research went to colleges and universities; but of the $71.6 billion invested in the development category, $6.5 billion—or a hefty 9 percent—went to educational institutions, and that might be a surprising number.[4]

In a discussion with Ronald Scharlack, one of six technology licensing officers of the Technology and Licensing Office (TLO) at the Massachusetts Institute of Technology, I was made aware of how MIT goes about licensing-out. It employs a set of procedures pioneered at Stanford and increasingly being adopted in other educational institutions with high levels of scientific and technical expertise.

The first principle of such institutions is to never forget its prime purpose. The one expressed by MIT is typical: "to benefit society through providing education and performing research." Then, should technical advances be generated that may benefit society, MIT will take suitable actions to expedite the transfer of such advances into society. (That would seem to qualify as their second principle.)

It wasn't always so. Legal staffs in colleges used to be merely "helpful," acting as legal agents to obtain patents or as gatekeepers; but as exemplified by MIT's TLO, a number of them now identify which of their institutions' ideas have the greatest potential, secure patents where warranted, and then actively seek out and negotiate with targeted companies.

MIT's TLO was organized in a variety of incarnations going back many decades, but it was reorganized into its present larger and more active format in 1986. At this writing, it is up to a rate of 250 potential patent disclosures submitted yearly from within; 16 license agreements with industry were consummated in 1985, 32 in 1986, and 64 are expected in 1987.

This one institution can point to some license deals it made in the past that were no less than blockbusters. These include the synthesis of penicillin, patented by Professor John Sheehan in 1957 and now the basis of a $500-million-a-year industry. Add to that the LOGO and LISP computer languages, synthetic skin, and a heat-reflecting coating that triples the life of conventional light bulbs, and advances in fiber-optic transmitter and receiver components.

If your company wants to explore new developments in its field with the possibility of licensing some of them, drop in at the local college campus. If you are in the medical products business, look in at the nearest large teaching hospital, which handles matters of this nature as though it were a university. For example, Brigham and Women's Hospital in Boston, affiliated with the Harvard Medical School, maintains a staff position with the title of vice president for new ventures. The woman who holds that position called me recently to say, "Let me tell you about a new development by one of our senior research people that will not only do untold good for society, but will be a good revenue-producing item for your company's medical division." She went on to suggest, "Perhaps you would like to consider a license. . . ."

Optimizing the Terms of the License Agreement

This is not the place to explore the many possible business arrangements that will constitute license agreement between companies and between companies and universities. But let it be understood that being a skilled practitioner in the art of licensing pays off.

Fair Value

There are several kinds of value to be kept in mind when negotiating a license. There is the historical value, consisting of the investment that was made by the seller to create the item being bought and sold. There is the (sometimes negative) value to the seller of sharing this creation with an outsider. There is the value to the buyer in incremental revenue and profit. There is even an intrinsic value to the public, if not to mankind itself. Put a price or a rate on these values. Down payments and royalties to be negotiated between both parties should be based on that price.

The arrangement should be fair. In a good license agreement, no one is cheated. What is good for the licensee is good for the licensor, and vice versa. Not only is it fair, it is good business, because disproportionate benefits do not last.

Down Payment

There should always be a down payment, if only to show good faith. A down payment generally serves to pay the licensor for the expense of transferring the elements of knowledge that underlie the item being licensed. As stated above, it should be for a fair sum.

Royalty Rate

Negotiate a royalty rate that will not put the licensee at a disadvantage with the competition by causing prices to be so high as to undermine sales. Some experts have worked out formulas for calculating "fair" rates. Scaglione has related royalty rates to expected returns and has generated an easily read graphical representation of these variables—a nomograph—that can be valuable in negotiations, at least as a starting point.[5]

Exclusivity/Nonexclusivity

There should be an exclusivity provision in every license agreement. It either is or it isn't exclusive. If you are selling, you want more than just one customer, so you desire nonexclusivity. If you are buying, you want no one else to be able to buy in; you want exclusivity. The results you get are the consequence of your DL/TCL team's negotiating skills.

Time Limits

There have to be time limits. Values don't stay at the same level year after year; they generally decline or disappear, which should be taken into account with corresponding declines in royalties. Again, this is to be negotiated.

Support

The biggest mistake a licensor can make is failing to support the licensee. I refer primarily to technical support, but often there are other kinds of support as well. For example, the licensor can steer the licensee to market opportunities that otherwise would not be known to him. The better the licensee's sales, the bigger the royalty income. In case the licensor is at first not disposed to provide support, the licensee must negotiate, insisting on contract provisions that ensure it, including a tutorial. The licensee is buying so as to increase capability, and thus must learn. The DL/TCL team sets up whatever may be required for this, including allowing licensee personnel to "dwell" in the licensor's premises for a few weeks.

However, "free" transitional support can't be limitless. After a reasonable amount of free workdays, it is common to settle for a consultant agreement at so much per day.

Support mostly involves smooth transfer of information in the beginning and hand-holding later. Elsewhere in this book, we discussed the transfer process within a company and the internal client relationships, which, in their way, are also "support." Consider license arrangements in the same way: If you license-out to someone, he is a client—and clients, within rational limits, must be served.

All this serving and supporting takes money. It should come from the down payment and from the ongoing royalties, leaving some as profit. It sounds simple, but it is not. Avaricious executives quickly allocate those checks, as they come in the mail every quarter, to whatever bottom line in their organization needs money—unless the licensing team makes arrangements beforehand to prevent such actions.

Reciprocal Arrangements for New Innovation

As time goes on, the neophyte licensee will become expert in the technology of the innovation. In fact, it is not unusual for a licensee to become more expert and achieve greater sales than the licensor. By the same token, the licensor may be increasing his store of expertise, which can be crucial to improving the market position of the licensee.

The way to deal with this circumstance to the advantage of all is to negotiate a reciprocity provision into the original license agreement. After defining what is being licensed, it is advisable to commit both parties to sharing future innovative advances made by either one, within the subject matter of that definition.

It is common for such reciprocity agreements to require no payment by the licensee back to the licensor for these contributions. As for the licensor, technical advances by the licensee are also not paid for; they are "gravy," and often very valuable. In both cases, these conditions prevail so long as they are confined to the overall definition of what has been licensed in the first place.

What is being bought and what is being sold? It is property, and as such, it is quite buyable and sellable. (Guidelines on how to carry out the process of defining this property are given in Chapter 6.)

References

1. D. W. McDonald and H. S. Leahey, "Licensing Has a Role in Technology Strategic Planning," *Research Planning,* January-February 1986, pp. 35–40.

2. M. J. Peck and A. Goto, "Technology and Economic Growth: The Case of Japan," *Research Policy:* Vol. 10, 1981.

3. McDonald and Leahey, op. cit. pp. 35–36.

4. *Statistical Abstract of the United States, 1986,* 106th ed. (U.S. Department of Commerce, Bureau of the Census).

5. P. Scaglione, "Licensor View of Royalty Rates," *Les Nouvelles,* September 1981, pp. 231–232.

Afterword

Innovation Is an Act of Will

The best way to make something happen is to "will" it. Having all the tools—the autonomous innovation organizations, the skilled staff, the facilities and funds, and all of these supported by high-status encouragers and facilitators and even by an enlightened CEO—is not enough. Those doing the innovation, as well as those supporting it, must *want* it to happen—very much.

They must express that desire by doggedly persisting in doing it and doing it right, against all odds. Those odds may include others in the company who just as doggedly want it *not* to happen, for "will" works for nay-sayers just as effectively.

Note that those who participate in the "willing" of a new product, a new system, or a new technology are not just the innovators. Their bosses and other company staff who want it to happen, too, and who convert this desire into positive actions, are just as essential to achieving fruition. In this regard, it is not important if you are forced to say, "Oh, I'm not creative like those people in the lab who came up with the concepts and the inventions," because even "uncreative" people can be essential to the success of an innovation. Indeed, certain nonconceivers and noninventors in a company can compensate for their lack of creative qualities by their super-abundance of will—and that can make all the difference.

The creation of something that never existed before and that people will some day buy, use, even delight in, while the user and the maker both profit from it, is one of the most remarkable processes human beings can engage in. Activities not involving creation of newness are usually done at the level of a person's capability. Somehow, those engaged in innovation programs, whatever their role, seem to exceed their abilities. The word for this process is "over-achievement," and it can only occur as an act of will.

Appendix 1:

Example of an Innovation Concept Report

```
                                    ICR 87-91
                                       Rev. 2
                               July 29, 1987




         INNOVATION CONCEPT REPORT: METAL GLUE




                    Marlene Mason
```

This is a replica of the title page of the report.

STATEMENT OF THE IDEA

a. The Problem

Much industrial assembly of metal structural elements today is achieved at room temperature with adhesives and glues. These are almost exclusively formulated out of organic chemicals. That means that, should the finished product later be exposed to elevated temperatures, such assemblies will fail, because the adhesive or glue will melt, char, or burn. This is taken care of in normal practice by resorting to other joining techniques, such as brazing, welding, or soldering—none of which require organics. But they introduce another problem: All require temperatures at the moment of assembly high enough to melt metal, and there are products that cannot tolerate the temperatures of these all-metal joining techniques, even for the short time required to effect the joint.

In summary, the problem is that the process of making metal joints is always temperature-related. In the case of organic glues and adhesives, the joining technique is done without resort to high-temperature exposure, but the resulting joint can't stand being heated up later. In the case of joints made with melting metal-bonding materials, there is little problem of deterioration with subsequent heating; but the joining process can be destructive.

b. The Solution

Develop an all-metal joining material that works like an organic glue. This will be achieved if a metal alloy is identified that is liquid at room temperature, that wets the surfaces of the metal parts to be joined, and that—like glue—hardens

— 1 —

or solidifies at room temperature and is then able to maintain the bond between those parts at reasonably elevated temperatures without remelting.

CONSTRAINTS

The metal-adhesive alloy, now designated as "metal glue," must satisfy the following requirements:

1. Remelting point to exceed the charing temperature of organic glues (above 450°F).
2. Easy to apply (as in merely "painting it on").
3. Not costly. Cost per joint not to exceed cost for welding, brazing, or soldering. Less than $0.15 per joint, or more depending on its complexity, will be acceptable.
4. Safe. No ingredient is to be toxic or irritating to human skin, nor may it evolve toxic or irritating vapors.
5. Reasonable storage life.
6. No unconventional manufacturing techniques required.

STATEMENT OF THE CONCEPT

a. Metallurgical Theory

There is a class of metal alloys that will, in theory, satisfy the goal and listed constraints. Such alloys are liquid at room temperature but harden with time into a new crystal phase with a far higher melting point. These are the amalgams. They are usually binary alloys consisting of a very-low-melting metal compounded with a very-high-melting one.

— 2 —

An example is the formulation used by dentists for filling cavities in teeth. In that case, mercury, melting point -38°F, is mixed with silver, melting point 1762°F. When first mixed, the resulting liquid slurry has a viscosity similar to that of the mercury alone, but after a few minutes the two alloy ingredients progressively combine to form an intermetallic compound with a new melting point that exceeds mouth temperature (conveniently thermostated by nature at 98.6°F). Indeed, that temperature is 261°F, which is higher than that of the hottest soup or any hot food, so it will stay solid for as long as the tooth remains in the patient's mouth.

This concept is based on amalgam theory and it is to employ amalgam metallurgy and techniques in nondental applications.

b. Alloy Candidate

Making this concept practical requires an alloy system that wets surface alloys to metals that must be joined to each other. It should be conveniently packaged for the user so that there is no alloying during shipment and storage. As in the dental system, alloying must be made to take place only at the moment of use.

Mercury is rejected as the low-melting ingredient because it can be toxic when used in industrial environments. A non-toxic metal that can serve in its place is gallium, melting point 85°F.

This is a very convenient liquification temperature because the metal is solid in a normal air-conditioned room (temperature 75°F.)

Amalgamation does not occur when the gallium is solid. Unless the gallium atoms have the mobility of the liquid state, they will not interact with the high-melting metal. This should

— 3 —

mean that storage can be indefinite and convenient so long as the glue is kept below 85°F.

Gallium is not cheap, having a market price of about $200 per pound. Yet any joint will require very little of this material—probably no more than 0.1 gram—at a cost of about $0.05 each, which is a tolerable cost. Gallium is a by-product of aluminum manufacture, and large amounts are stored in warehouses because there is today no volume use for this metal. If this idea works, and "tonnage" quantities are needed, the present (artificially high) price should come down significantly.

Silver in powder form may be used for the high-melting ingredient, as it is in dental amalgams, but it is too expensive. Copper powder has similar properties and melting point, and is reasonable in price.

Gallium and copper form two intermetallic compounds with elevated melting points. $CuGa_2$ melts at 489°F and Cu_9Ga_4 at 1537°F, and both meet our temperature requirements.

c. Application Procedure

To use, merely heat the glue and the elements to be joined to about 90°F on a warm heating plate or in a stream of warm air. The gallium then melts and begins to amalgamate (form the new intermetallic compound with the copper). At this moment, the operator places all parts into suitable juxtaposition, often with the aid of a jig, and applies the metal glue to the region to be bonded. This can be done with a simple tool, like a paintbrush or small spatula.

Another way to apply the glue is in previously stamped-out preforms that exactly fit the geometries being joined. Preforms are in common use in assembly of solid-state electronics components and circuits.

— 4 —

MANUFACTURING PROCEDURES

The copper must be in particle form in the size of about 100 mesh. It can be purchased in that size particle from copper metal suppliers.

The gallium is easily available in pure form from aluminum companies.

The "manufacture" consists of little more than preparing separate "premix" portions in required proportions in clean conditions (to minimize oxidation). Premixes are then packaged in commercially available capsules made of plastic or glass, similar to what is today provided to dentists.

Preforms can be stamped out from already mixed sheet stock and shipped to customers in temperature-controlled conditions (to arrest the alloy process) similar to those used by food suppliers. The only limitation this imposes on manufacturing is that it be conducted in an air-conditioned room with a temperature below the melting point of gallium.

No expensive tooling seems to be needed. Only conventional processes will be utilized. However, it is recommended that early in the experimental work, the advice of a packaging engineer be obtained.

MARKET PROSPECTS

When one surveys conventional adhesive applications, one confronts a multi-billion-dollar industry. 3M, Eastman Kodak, Borden, and most large chemicals companies sell vast quantities of glues and adhesives in a wide spectrum of forms, such as liquids, pastes, sprays, and tapes. Adhesives have replaced riveting and welding in many subassemblies in the auto industry, and it is interesting that aircraft today are essentially held together almost exclusively by glues rather than by rivets.

— 5 —

While organic glues and adhesives are satisfactory for those cases, consider spacecraft. Glues will not do there, as evidenced by the lack of adhesion of heat-shield slabs on satellite skins when exposed to the heat of re-entry. This is a low-volume but high-priced market that should provide high margins to a small business.

High-power semiconductor components and other electronic devices are usually soldered into place onto chassis boards. But such soldering often damages the sensitive materials out of which these devices are made. This practice has always imposed limitations in this field—a problem that has never been solved. Metal glue, however, promises to solve this problem. The magnitude of this application is very large. Millions of such assemblies are made daily at a joint cost of several pennies each. The possibility of using preforms provides substantial value-added and will increase acceptable selling prices. The 1987 edition of the *Solid State Processing and Production Worldwide Buyers Guide and Directory* lists 27 makers of solders for semiconductor products alone. Projected sales for this niche market should be no less than $100 million yearly.

Another less exotic but still important market possibility is that of on-site repair of plumbing and home appliances. Usually, this is done with a welding torch and brazing alloy-bonding filler. This practice introduces a fire hazard, and every year one hears of fires and explosions resulting from the flames from welding torches touching off gas or oil.

Surely other applications that do not occur to the writer will appear to take advantage of the metal-glue principle.

EXPERIMENTAL PROGRAM

The most uncertain factor in this product-development program is that of whether the gallium and copper will indeed

— 6 —

interact above 85°F to form stable, high-melting, intermetallic compounds. This must be investigated as a first step.

If this indeed works, optimum alloy proportions must be ascertained that minimize the amount of gallium required, because that is the most costly material in the system.

Gallium is known to be an excellent "wetter." Experiments must be conducted to find out whether this means that fluxes (required in all other inorganic metal-joining systems) can be done away with.

All intermetallic compounds are brittle. This is the case in dental amalgams and is the reason that fillings are prone to cracking unless the cavity is drilled in a way to minimize tension forces (compressive forces give no trouble). For the metal-glue application, this means that attention must be given to establishing principles of optimum joint design.

Physical test methods and criteria must be established so that every step of this investigation can be quantified with force-to-failure data.

Techniques for package and storage must be established.

Appendix 2:

The Spencer Patent

Jan. 24, 1950   P.L. SPENCER   2,495,429

METHOD OF TREATING FOODSTUFFS

Filed Oct. 8, 1945

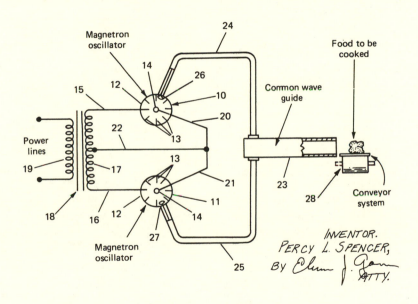

329

UNITED STATES PATENT OFFICE

2,495,429

METHOD OF TREATING FOODSTUFFS

Percy L. Spencer, West Newton, Mass., assignor
to Raytheon Manufacturing Company, Newton,
Mass., a corporation of Delaware

Application October 8, 1945, Serial No. 620,919

6 Claims. (Cl. 99—217)

1

My present invention relates to the treatment of foodstuffs, and more particularly to the cooking thereof through the use of electromagnetic energy.

Such energy has been used before for this purpose, but the frequencies employed have been relatively low, for example, not over 50 megacycles. I have found that at frequencies of this order of magnitude, the energy necessarily expended in order to generate sufficient heat to satisfactorily cook the foodstuff is much too high to permit the practical use of the process. I have further found, however, that this disadvantage may be eliminated by employing wave lengths falling in the microwave region of the electromagnetic spectrum, for example, wave lengths of the order of 10 centimeters or less. By so doing, the wave length of the energy becomes comparable to the average dimension of the foodstuff to be cooked, and as a result, the heat generated in the foodstuff becomes intense, the energy expended becomes a minimum, and the entire process becomes efficient and commercially feasible.

It is, therefore, one of the objects of my present invention to provide an efficient method of employing electromagnetic energy for the cooking of foodstuffs.

In the accompanying specification I shall describe, and in the annexed drawing show, an illustrative embodiment of the method and means for treating foodstuff of my present invention. It is, however, to be clearly understood that I do not wish to be limited to the details herein shown and described for purposes of illustration only, inasmuch as changes therein may be made without the exercise of invention and within the true spirit and scope of the claims hereto appended.

In said drawing, the single figure is a schematic arrangement of apparatus which may be utilized to carry out the method of my present invention.

Referring now more in detail to the aforesaid illustrative embodiment of my present invention, with particular reference to the drawing illustrating the same, the numerals 10 and 11 generally designate electron-discharge devices of the magnetron type, each including, for example, an evacuated envelope 12, made of highly conductive material, such as copper, and provided with a plurality of inwardly-directed, radially-disposed anode vanes 13. The arrangement is such that each pair of adjacent anode vanes 13 forms, together with that portion of the envelope 12

2

lying therebetween, a cavity resonator whose natural resonant frequency is, as is well known to those skilled in the art, a function of the geometry of the physical elements making up the same. For the purposes of my present invention it is desirable that the dimensions of each such cavity resonator be such that the wave length of the electrical oscillations adapted to be generated therein is comparable to the average dimension of the foodstuff to be cooked, for example, of the order of 10 centimeters or less.

Centrally located in each envelope 12 is a highly electron-emissive cathode member 14, for example, of the well-known alkaline-earth metal oxide type, said cathode member being provided with conventional means (not shown) for raising the temperature thereof to a level sufficient for thermionic emission.

Each electron-discharge device 10 is completed by magnetic means (not shown) for establishing a magnetic field in a direction transversely of the electron path between the cathode and anode members thereof.

The conductive envelopes 12 of the electron-discharge devices 10 and 11 are connected, respectively, by conductors 15 and 16, to the opposite terminals of the secondary winding 17 of a transformer 18, the primary winding 19 of said transformer being connected to a source of raw A.-C., for example, the conventional 60-cycle power lines. The cathodes 14 of said electron-discharge devices 10 and 11 are tied together by conductors 20 and 21, which are, in turn, connected, by a conductor 22, to a center tap on the secondary winding 17 of the transformer 18.

Thus, the electron-discharge devices 10 and 11 are connected for push-pull operation, whereby said devices alternately deliver hyper-frequency energy to a common, hollow wave guide 23 through coaxial transmission lines 24 and 25 which are coupled to their respective oscillators, for example, by loops 26 and 27.

Adjacent the outlet end of the wave guide 23 I provide an appropriate, transversely-moving conveyor system 28 for carrying the foodstuff to be cooked into a region where it will be exposed to the energy emanating from said wave guide, the speed at which said conveyor system is operated being determined by the nature of the particular foodstuff to be cooked, and the time required for cooking the same.

With the system described, I have found that an egg may be rendered hardboiled with the expenditure of 2 kw.-sec. This compares with an

3

expenditure of 36 kw.-sec. to conventionally cook the same. I have also found that with my system a potato requires the expenditure of about 240 kw.-sec., which compares with 72,000 kw.-sec. necessary to bake the same in an electric oven. These examples are, it is to be clearly understood, merely illustrative. I have observed similar results with other foodstuffs. In each instance, where the wave length of the energy is of the order of the average dimension of the foodstuff to be cooked, the process is very efficient, requiring the expenditure of a minimum amount of energy for a minimum amount of time.

This completes the description of the aforesaid illustrative embodiment of my present invention. It will be noted from all of the foregoing that my process is simple and easily practiced; it is economical; and it requires relatively simple and inexpensive equipment.

Other objects and advantages of my present invention will readily occur to those skilled in the art to which the same relates.

What is claimed is:

1. In the method of treating foodstuffs, those steps which include: generating electromagnetic wave energy of a wavelength falling in the microwave region of the electromagnetic spectrum; concentrating and guiding said wave energy within a restricted region of space and exposing the foodstuff to be treated to the energy so generated for a period of time sufficient to cook the same to a predetermined degree.

2. In the method of treating foodstuffs, those steps which include: generating electromagnetic wave energy of a wavelength falling in the microwave region of the electromagnetic spectrum; concentrating and guiding said energy within a restricted region of space; and conveying the foodstuff to be treated through said region of space at such a rate of speed as to expose the same to said energy for an interval of time sufficient to cook the same to a predetermined degree.

3. In the method of treating foodstuffs, those steps which include: generating electromagnetic wave energy of a wavelength falling in the microwave region of the electromagnetic spectrum; concentrating and guiding said energy within a restricted region of space to establish an electromagnetic field therein; exposing the foodstuff to

4

be treated to said field for a period of time sufficient to cook the same to a predetermined degree; and moving said foodstuff relative to said field while said foodstuff is so exposed.

4. In the method of treating foodstuffs, those steps which include: generating electromagnetic wave energy of a wave length of substantially ten centimeters; concentrating and guiding said wave energy within a restricted region of space and exposing the foodstuff to be treated to the energy so generated for a period of time sufficient to cook the same to a predetermined degree.

5. In the method of treating foodstuffs, those steps which include: generating electromagnetic wave energy of a wave length of substantially ten centimeters; concentrating and guiding said energy within a restricted region of space; and conveying the foodstuff to be treated through said region of space at such a rate of speed as to expose the same to said energy for an interval of time sufficient to cook the same to a predetermined degree.

6. In the method of treating foodstuffs, those steps which include: generating electromagnetic wave energy of a wave length of substantially ten centimeters; concentrating and guiding said energy within a restricted region of space to establish an electromagnetic field therein; exposing the foodstuff to be treated to said field for a period of time sufficient to cook the same to a predetermined degree; and moving said foodstuff relative to said field while said foodstuff is so exposed.

PERCY L. SPENCER.

REFERENCES CITED

The following references are of record in the file of this patent:

UNITED STATES PATENTS

Number	Name	Date
1,181,219	Goucher	May 2, 1916
1,863,222	Hoermann	June 14, 1932
1,900,573	McArthur	Mar. 7, 1933
1,945,867	Rawls	Feb. 6, 1934
1,981,583	Craig	Nov. 20, 1934
1,992,515	Uhlmann	Feb. 26, 1935
2,052,919	Brogdon	Sept. 1, 1936
2,094,602	Kassner	Oct. 5, 1937
2,382,033	Supplee et al.	Aug. 14, 1945

Index